SHADOW VIGILANTES

SHADOW VIGILANTES

HOW DISTRUST IN THE JUSTICE SYSTEM BREEDS A NEW KIND OF LAWLESSNESS

PAUL H. ROBINSON AND SARAH M. ROBINSON

Prometheus Books
59 John Glenn Drive
Amherst, New York 14228

Published 2018 by Prometheus Books

Gavel image © AVN Photo Lab/Shutterstock
Shadows image © Alex Linch/Shutterstock
Cover design by Liz Mills
Cover design © Prometheus Books

Inquiries should be addressed to
Prometheus Books
59 John Glenn Drive
Amherst, New York 14228
VOICE: 716–691–0133 • FAX: 716–691–0137
WWW.PROMETHEUSBOOKS.COM

22 21 20 19 18 5 4 3 2 1

Library of Congress Cataloging-in-Publication Data

Names: Robinson, Paul H., 1948- author. | Robinson, Sarah M., author.
Title: Shadow vigilantes : how failures of justice inspire lawlessness / By Paul H. Robinson and Sarah M. Robinson
Description: Amherst, New York : Prometheus Books, 2018. | Includes bibliographical references and index.
Identifiers: LCCN 2017049226 (print) | LCCN 2017051108 (ebook) | ISBN 9781633884328 (ebook) | ISBN 9781633884311 (hardcover)
Subjects: LCSH: Criminal justice, Administration of—United States. | Law enforcement—United States. | Crime prevention—Citizen participation—United States. | Vigilantes—United States.
Classification: LCC KF9223 (ebook) | LCC KF9223 .R637 2018 (print) | DDC 364.1/34—dc23
LC record available at https://lccn.loc.gov/2017049226

Printed in the United States of America

To Edward Raymond Robinson (1901–1979)
and Nancy Bray

CONTENTS

IV. THE VIGILANTE ECHO

LIST OF ILLUSTRATIONS

ACKNOWLEDGMENTS

We are very much indebted to many people for their help with this book, especially Mitchell Heyland, Brandon Kenney, and Daniel Atlas of the University of Pennsylvania Law School and Todd Costa and Taryn McKinney of the University of Pennsylvania classes of 2016 and 2017, respectively, for their exceptional research assistance; Silvana Burgese, Kelly Farraday, and Jennifer Evans of Penn Law's Faculty Support Services for their endless help in the preparation of the manuscript; Edwin Greenlee, Merle J. Slyhoff, and Joseph Parsio of the Penn Law Library for their monumental efforts to find us all manner of materials, old and new, common and rare; and Penn Law deans Michael Fitts, Wendell Pritchett, and Ted Ruger for their unstinting support for this work. We thank them all.

For permissions to reprint photographs, we thank Deanna's Voice (DeannasVoice.org), which continues to fight to bring awareness to the problem of domestic violence; the family of Brenda Schaefer, who have been so generous in sharing pictures of their lost sister; Helen Zia, who maintains the website Remembering Vincent Chin on behalf of the estates of Vincent and Lily Chin; and Harry Maclean, author of *The Story Behind* In Broad Daylight, for his contribution of the Ken McElroy photograph. We would also like to provide attribution to the artists who painted the mural in memory of Herman Wrice—David McShane and Eurhi Jones.

In the effort to bring an accessible version of these issues to press we thank our many friends who took the time to read early drafts, especially George Sevier, Nancy Bray, Catherine McAlpine, and Reinhild Muenke. To Steven L. Mitchell, editor in chief of Prometheus Books, we are indebted for his careful reading and useful comments.

PREFACE

In modern societies, citizens give up most of their natural right to defend themselves or to respond to wrongdoing, in return for a promise of protection and justice from the government. But what happens when the government breaches that social contract and persistently fails in its promise? There are difficulties with citizens taking matters into their own hands, but it is hard not to empathize with people in desperate situations where law enforcement seems indifferent. And there are some persuasive moral arguments that people can make in support of some forms of constrained vigilantism.

Vigilantes have long been vilified, often with good reason, as with the racist lynchings by the Ku Klux Klan. But the original American "vigilantes" in 1850s San Francisco were models of democratic action who were saving their community from an ineffective and corrupt government. And there has been a long line of vigilante groups that could fairly claim their conduct to be morally justified, albeit technically illegal.

One might hope that serious failures of justice and protection are rare and that the government takes seriously its obligation under the social contract. However, rightly or wrongly, ordinary people sometimes believe they have reason to doubt the criminal justice system's devotion to doing justice. In a wide range of rules and practices—what might be called the *doctrines of disillusionment*—the criminal justice system seems to many to advertise an indifference to the importance of doing justice: courts feast on technicalities, treating criminal justice as if it were a game; judicial rules suppress reliable evidence and thereby let serious offenders go free; decision makers use their discretion to avoid deserved punishment for serious offenses; and criminal law defenses shield clearly guilty and blameworthy offenders from liability.

Ultimately, the doctrines of disillusionment tend to undermine the criminal justice system's moral credibility, and that loss in turn undermines the criminal justice system's ability to harness the powerful forces of social influence and internalized norms. In other words, there are not only strong deontological reasons to be sympathetic to moral vigilantes. There are also compelling instrumentalist crime-control reasons to pay attention to ordinary people's disillusionment with a system they see as failing to give serious offenders the punishment they deserve.

While vigilantism is something considerably more nuanced than the evil incarnate that its Ku Klux Klan paradigm might suggest, it is not so easy to clearly mark out the importantly different categories of moral versus immoral vigilantism. An attempt to set out a code for the moral vigilante, as chapter 5 does, illustrates the complexity of the problem and the fuzzy lines that inevitably remain.

And even if one could construct a clear and detailed code of conduct, once the red line of official criminal prohibition has been crossed, it is easy—too easy—for even the well-meaning vigilante to lose track of the boundaries of moral justification. Perhaps even more troublesome, even if the vigilante is successful in staying within the boundaries of moral justification, it is commonly the case that even moral vigilantism can be problematic for the larger society. The bottom line is that official action is always to be preferred over vigilante action.

But it does not follow that the moral vigilante must simply suffer in silence. First, this may not be possible. Strong feelings of disillusionment may spark action no matter what the law threatens. Further, asking moral vigilantes to suffer in silence is not only a poor crime-control strategy but, more importantly, ought not to be asked. The government has obligations to its citizens under its social contract and is not free to simply choose not to perform them. The criminal justice system ought to take seriously its obligation to assure that justice is done and crime avoided so that people are never put in the position of having to consider moral vigilantism.

But the real danger is not of hordes of citizens, frustrated by the system's doctrines of disillusionment, rising up to take the law into their own hands. Frustration can spark a vigilante impulse, but such classic aggressive vigilantism is not the typical response. More common is the expression of disillusionment in less brazen ways by a more surreptitious undermining and distortion of the operation of the criminal justice system.

Shadow vigilantes, as they might be called, can affect the operation of the system in a host of important ways. For example, when people act as classic vigilantes or when people exceed the legal rules in their use of defensive force against apparent criminals, or when law enforcement officials exceed their authority in dealing with offenders, shadow vigilante citizens can refuse to report the crime or to help investigators, or they can refuse to indict as grand jurors or refuse to convict as trial jurors. Further, frustration with doctrines of disillusionment can lead politicians to urge legal reforms that seem to avoid failures of justice, but that also overreach and produce regular injustices.

Shadow vigilantism can also be seen in the conduct of officials within the system who feel morally justified in subverting the system because they see it as regularly and indifferently producing failures of justice. Such subversion is apparent, for example, in officials refusing to prosecute vigilantes, police, or crime victims who stray beyond legal limitations when using force against aggressors. It's also apparent in police "testilying" to subvert search and seizure technicalities (and judicial toleration of it) and in prosecutorial overcharging to compensate for past perceived justice failures.

The danger of shadow vigilantism is not only in the systemic distortions that it provokes. These distortions, in turn, have their own effect in further undermining the system's credibility and its crime-control effectiveness. For example, lenient sentencing provokes mandatory minimums, and search and seizure technicalities provoke testilying, but the excessiveness of mandatory minimums and the lost credibility from institutionalized testilying in turn provoke "stop snitching" campaigns, which guarantee greater witness intimidation, greater criminality, and less justice.

We would all be better off if this dirty war had never started. Systemic failures of justice, shadow vigilantes' distorting response, and blowback from those distortions end up producing more crime and more failures of justice—ending in a downward spiral.

The only way to effectively stop this tragic cycle is for the criminal justice system to publicly commit itself to the importance of doing justice and avoiding injustice at all costs. That means avoiding the application of the doctrines of disillusionment where there is no compelling societal interest in doing so, or where the interest could be as effectively promoted through a less justice-frustrating means.

The only way to prevent the downward spiral of lost credibility is to acknowledge the importance of doing justice both as an essential ideal and as a practical necessity.

Part I

THE WHO AND WHY OF VIGILANTISM

How should we think of vigilantes? Are they vicious and arrogant attackers of the democratically shaped social order, to be despised by all who value the rule of law, justice, and stability? Some vigilantes clearly see themselves quite differently, as the true defenders of democracy, justice, and the social order. Which of these conflicting views represents the truth about vigilantes?

As it turns out, both views are flawed because vigilantes come in a wide range of flavors, some acting in the most despicable of ways and some in the most admirable of ways. Yet even vigilantes with the best of motivations, even when performing conduct that is entirely moral from their perspective, can cause harm to a society. We would be better off if such moral vigilantes never felt compelled to act.

What a more careful examination of vigilantism reveals is that a society that does not take seriously enough the importance of doing justice (and avoiding injustice)—giving the offenders the punishment they deserve, no more, no less—can condemn itself to a downward spiral of resistance and subversion from which it will have difficulty recovering.

1

FEAR, MEET INDIFFERENCE: BREACHING THE SOCIAL CONTRACT

People may have a natural right to defend themselves against wrongdoing and to respond to wrongdoing against them, but in modern societies we give up those rights in a general social contract under which the government takes a near monopoly on providing protection and doing justice.

Obviously the government can't be perfect in its duty. There will always be crime, and not every offender can be caught and punished. We can only expect that the government will appreciate the importance of these ends and devote itself seriously to them.

But what if the government doesn't? What if it binds us to our obligations under the social contract to defer to it but then simply fails to take seriously its own obligations? What is a person to do?

THE STALKING OF DEANNA COOK

Deanna Cook lives in Balch Springs, Texas, with her husband, Delvecchio Patrick, who has become increasingly violent during their marriage. In January 2009 Patrick kicks open the bedroom door, shoves Cook against the wall, and chokes her to unconsciousness. When she revives and calls 911, Patrick threatens her with a knife, screaming that he is going to "do it." He is arrested by the Balch Springs police but released a month later.[1]

Cook moves out and files for divorce. Upon his release from prison, Patrick begins calling her hundreds of times, threatening to kill her, and he repeats the threats in personal confrontations, sometimes in front of her two daughters. He also threatens the girls and arranges to have some of his friends sexually harass and assault them. In August he chokes her and calls her mother, threatening to kill her; he is arrested and required to wear an electronic monitoring device. But this changes little. In November Patrick confronts Cook in an East Oak Cliff store, screaming at her and repeatedly punching her in the face; he is arrested again.

Fig. 1.1. Deanna Cook was killed by her ex-husband, Delvecchio Patrick, in Dallas, 2012. (Courtesy of DeannasVoice.org)

From March 2010 to April 2011, Cook experiences a welcome period of safety while Patrick is in jail. Her divorce becomes final in May, but upon his release from jail, Patrick again begins threatening, harassing, and stalking Cook. In May alone, records show he calls her 107 times and tells her repeatedly that he is going to kill her.[2] She is often afraid to leave for work because Patrick has threatened to break into her house.

Throughout this period, Cook makes regular calls to 911 complaining of Patrick's threats, his stalking, his violation of the terms of his release, and his physical confrontations. The police do nothing. Cook begs the 911 operators for help. One tells her to keep track of her calls to the police.[3] On another occasion, Cook tells a different operator that Patrick is outside, watching her house, and that "he's already tried to kill me three times. I'm really just fed up with this. I can't keep moving and changing my life because of this [expletive]."[4] During this call, she explains that a previous operator had advised her not to open her door. On another 911 call she is heard pleading, "I don't want him to know I even called [911]. You know what I'm saying? That's the thing. That triggers him when he knows I called. He tears the stuff up in my house."[5] In yet another call her despair is clear: "I've been going through this for five years with him. It's still the same thing. I have complaints. If you look up my name, you'll see there are a hundred thousand complaints, but ain't nobody doing nothing."[6] Among the catalogue of 911 calls, there is one in which she describes Patrick's addiction to PCP. Cook is tired of begging for help, and she figures the operators are equally tired of hearing her frantic voice. In yet another call she explains that she has called 911 so many times that "they're probably tired of me calling" but adds, "They just need to get him away from there. I don't know what else to do."[7]

BREACHING THE SOCIAL CONTRACT

What is she supposed to do? Clearly, the criminal justice system is failing Deanna Cook. The threats and continuing danger to her and her children are being willfully ignored by authorities. This young mother depends upon the government for protection and justice but gets neither. Her stalker is bigger and stronger—she can hardly overpower him. Maybe she should get a gun and go shoot him? Criminal law says no; she must wait until the moment when her stalker chooses to attack. If she is able to anticipate his attack and get the drop on him, the law says she still may not shoot but must let him run away to pick another, better time to attack her next. Given the government's failure to protect her, is she relieved of her moral obligation to abide by the government's rules?

A string of philosophers—Thomas Hobbes, John Locke, Jean-Jacques Rousseau, and others—have thought about this situation a citizen may face. They believed that people are born with certain unalienable rights, including the right to use force to protect themselves and to do justice, but people give up many of those natural rights to their government in exchange for the government's promise to do justice and provide protection.[8] In this case, the government has breached what the philosophers would call "the social contract." The government, having taken over the monopoly of power from its citizens, is now welching on its promises, despite Deanna Cook's repeated pleas.

The social contract is fundamental to our vision of government. Perhaps more than any other country in the world, the United States was created with the social contract at its core. As the US Declaration of Independence announces at its start, we are born with certain rights: "All men . . . are endowed by their Creator with certain unalienable Rights, that among these are Life, Liberty and the pursuit of Happiness," and it is "to secure these rights [that] Governments are instituted among Men."

But when the government breaches its promise under that social contract, what recourse does the private citizen have? How can Deanna Cook find safety? The Declaration of Independence might hint at an answer: "But when a long train of abuses and usurpations, pursuing invariably the same Object evinces a design to reduce them under absolute Despotism, it is their right, it is their duty, to throw off such Government, and to provide new Guards for their future security." That is, the violent creation of the United States was itself an act of vigilantism: people took the law into their own hands as a response to the British government's breach of the social contract.

If the point of the government is "to establish Justice [and] insure domestic Tranquility," as the preamble to the US Constitution proclaims, then the government's miserable failure at providing justice and protection to Deanna Cook must alter her moral obligation to that government. Deanna Cook is hardly in a position to "throw off such Government," but we may wonder what moral obligation she has to continue restraining herself in the exercise of her "unalienable rights" to life and liberty.

Before Deanna Cook could find a way to force the government to protect her unalienable rights, her life and liberty were taken.

THE KILLING OF DEANNA COOK

On August 12, 2012, Patrick breaks into Cook's house. She frantically calls 911. Operator Tonyita Hopkins answers, but Hopkins only hears her screams and pleadings. The phone connection remains open, and Operator Hopkins quickly ascertains the general location of Cook's cell phone but needs to do more work to uncover her exact address. Hopkins notifies the patrol dispatcher that the call is an emergency domestic violence situation and gives the dispatcher the street name.

Hopkins stays with the call. Cook begs for her life: "Why are you doing this to me? Please, Red [Patrick's nickname] I didn't do nothing! I am nice. I am nice. Please!"[9] Seven minutes into the call, Patrick is screaming, "I'll kill you. I'll kill you. I'll kill you."[10] The operator hears sounds of a struggle, and then the human sounds are gone and only the sound of a barking dog can be heard.

It takes police officers Julia Menchaca and Amy Wilburn an additional twenty-six minutes to start heading toward Deanna Cook's house. They stop at a 7-Eleven to buy water. At 11:45 a.m. they arrive at Cook's house and knock at her door. Five minutes later, when nobody answers, they leave.[11]

Two days after the call, Cook's family becomes worried when she does not arrive at church. Her mother and sister, with her children in tow, go to Cook's house to investigate.[12] Getting no response when they knock at the door, they kick it in. Cook is floating in her bathtub, where she has been drowned.

Patrick is arrested and charged with murder.[13]

A TERRORIZING BULLY RUNS LOOSE

The government's breach of the social contract can affect not just an individual but an entire neighborhood. And sometimes the system's failure will provoke a violent response.

Dictionary Hill is a quiet neighborhood of homes built on the side of a hill, with beautiful views of the San Diego Valley and the ocean beyond. It is a neighborhood favored by retired couples seeking to spend their later years enjoying the sun, the views, and their gardens.[14]

In 1992 John Harper Jr., the adult son of a neighborhood couple, moves in with his parents. Harper is an auto body mechanic devoted to muscle cars, methamphetamine, and his silver El Camino. The quiet neighborhood becomes his personal NASCAR track. In an early encounter, a resident is driving home when, at an S-curve on Helix Street, he sees Harper's El Camino approaching from the opposite direction. Harper steers into the other lane. The resident is unable to get out of Harper's way. When the two cars are within twenty feet of each other, Harper swerves back into his own lane.

A couple is returning from dinner in town when Harper drives up behind them, revving his engine. He tailgates them, swerves erratically, and uses his high beams, all of which scares them. The couple pulls to the shoulder to allow the El Camino to pass; Harper pulls up and begins yelling obscenities: "Don't fuck with me, I know where you live!"[15]

In another typical encounter, a neighbor has just turned down Highview Lane, headed home, when Harper's El Camino appears out of nowhere and races toward him, only to screech to a halt just inches from his bumper. This is repeated two more times, leaving the neighbor frightened and shaking.[16]

It is also common for Harper to attack neighbors who drive by his home. One driver has a rock thrown at her windshield. The police are called repeatedly, but Harper is always let off.

The encounters with Harper grow more frightening as he escalates the aggression. In another incident, Steve Hendrickson, who is just passing through town, gets Harper's treatment when he is run off the road into a telephone pole. Hendrickson relates what happened and gives a physical description of the car and Harper. The neighbors call the police, who arrive and take a statement from Hendrickson. When the police interview Harper, he denies being involved, and the police decline to do anything because, as they explain, it is just Hendrickson's word against Harper's.[17]

The neighborhood decides that the community will make a record of every past, present, and future incident involving Harper. As of that date, they record over 150 incidents against forty-two neighbors. When a neighbor tries to take a picture of Harper's El Camino for their report, Harper advances toward him, yelling, "I'm going to fuck you up!"[18]

When members of the neighborhood group try to present their plight to the police, they get the usual runaround: "We'd call the Sheriff's Department and they'd refer us to Highway Patrol. We'd call Highway Patrol and they'd say, 'Call the Sheriff's Department.' That's about all the help we got." After an incident in which Harper terrorizes a neighborhood child, a neighbor explains, "I called the sheriffs. They went down there and came back and said, 'Well, he wasn't home, and we will check in with him some other time.' And it just kind of dropped."[19]

The group drafts a nine-page letter threatening to sue Harper's father for harboring a public nuisance, but that tactic also fails. Efforts to get help from the California Department of Motor Vehicles and the federal Drug Enforcement Administration also produce no results.

When the wife of a San Diego police detective happens to be driving through Dictionary Hill with her nine-year-old daughter, Harper's El

Camino appears in their rearview mirror and accelerates as if to ram their car but swerves at the last moment. He continues to follow them, honking, swerving, accelerating, and ramming their rear bumper, almost forcing them off the road—in other words, doing what Harper has been regularly doing to the entire neighborhood for several years. Suddenly, the police are paying attention.

Harper is arrested but released on bail. A police detective overhears Harper saying, "I know the neighbors had this done to me. If they think it was bad before, just wait till they see me now."[20] Harper is scheduled for trial in November, four months away, on charges of felony assault with a deadly object. When the trial date finally arrives, very few neighbors are willing to testify against Harper in open court. Harper knows their children, and the law has done nothing to protect them in the past. Would it be wise to assume that suddenly they are going to get the protection they have been seeking? At the end of the trial, the jury is hung, eight to four, in favor of conviction. Rather than a retrial, Harper is offered a plea deal to a lesser offense and walks out of the courtroom with a sentence of probation and a five-hundred-dollar fine. Harper is allowed to get back into his weapon of choice and motor off to his hunting grounds. Even before he returns home, he gets high on meth and is again racing up and down the streets.[21]

A TOLERABLE FAILURE OF JUSTICE?

Given the government's repeated failures to provide protection and justice to this neighborhood, are the neighbors nonetheless still bound by the government's limitations on their use of defensive force? Having breached its promises under the social contract, can the government still demand that the citizens nonetheless keep their promise—to continue on as helpless victims waiting for the next violation? Or are they now morally entitled to take back their unalienable rights to justice and protection and to deal with the threat in whatever way they can to stop Harper's terrorizing ways?

The law sometimes allows a citizen to use force in protection of a person or property. Everyone knows about the right of self-defense. But even here, criminal law has a strong preference to have the state deal with a problem and to keep its near monopoly on the use of force. For example, as a private citizen, you may not use force that risks serious bodily injury to a thief in order to protect your property.[22] The law says that it is better to let the thief have your goods—in the hope that the police and courts can deal with the thief later—rather than inflict serious harm on another. Similarly, in many states, you may not use lethal force against an attacker intent on killing you, if you can retreat in safety.[23] You must give in to the unlawful attack and run away rather than use defensive force that risks serious injury to the attacker. Nor can you ever act in anticipation of an attack, even one that you are certain is coming. You, like Deanna Cook, must wait until your attacker elects to attack, even if doing so compromises your ability to defend yourself.[24] In other words, the law commonly obliges a victim to sacrifice her own interests to protect the interests of the lawbreaker.

Some victims will be unhappy with the sacrifices required of them, but the rules can be defended from a societal perspective that takes account of all parties' interests, even those of the lawbreaker, and reduces the overall risk of escalation even if it means sacrificing the victim's interests.[25] It is better to defer to the courts, it is argued.

But what if the system fails to uphold its end of the social contract in serious ways? What if these policies and practices allow crime to become a serious problem in the lives of citizens and the system does not respond to their requests for help? What if the system lets crime become a serious problem for some members of society but not others? What if, having gotten its near monopoly on the use of force, the system simply becomes indifferent to citizens' beliefs that dispensing justice and fighting crime are important? Obviously, doing anything beyond the strict rules of justification defenses will be illegal, but will it be so clearly immoral?

A NEIGHBOR TAKES ON THE BULLY

On the morning that Harper walks free with his government-issued plea deal, Danny Palm, a neighbor who had elected to testify, receives a phone call from another neighbor, warning him that Harper is driving toward Palm's house. Palm's wife then yells, "He's out front!"[26] Palm, a retired navy commander of twenty-nine years, is in his shorts and socks, but he grabs his .45-caliber pistol and ammunition and runs out the side door, hiding while trying to get a look at Harper in his driveway.

Harper then eases his car out of the driveway and slowly moves up the street. Palm sees Harper as escalating his aggression to a new level. Perhaps he is now headed off to intimidate the few others who dared to testify against him. The law has again shown itself to be useless in providing protection and justice. Palm feels that he must do something.

Still in his shorts and socks, Palm gets in his car and begins to follow Harper, but Harper immediately pulls over to the side of the road and waves Palm forward. Pulling up next to Harper, Palm shows him that he has a gun, hoping that this will be enough to scare him away from further attacks. Harper yells, "You and your family are as good as dead!"[27] Palm then shoots at Harper thirteen times; nine shots hit him. Palm returns to his house and awaits the police, who appear three hours later to arrest him and charge him with murder.

The neighborhood quickly raises $54,000 to help Palm post bail. The case gathers media attention. Eighty percent of a local radio show's callers say that Palm "should get a medal."[28] The neighbors describe Harper as "an unstoppable drug-crazed terrorist." Many people, while not necessarily supporting the killing, say that if they were on the jury, Palm would get off. Melody Hurt, a Harper victim who had been in court just the week before for the case that involved Harper ramming her car, claims that Palm is her savior and that he most likely has saved many lives by the sacrifice he made. The Spring Valley County supervisor states, "I think what Danny Palm did is exactly what you want somebody to step forward and do in the community that had . . . basically a terrorist running around threatening people."[29] Another community member explains, "Danny Palm did not abandon the legal system. It is clear that the problem was ignored by law enforcement and the neighborhood was ultimately abandoned by a twisted and polluted legal system."[30]

Fig. 1.2. John Harper drove a silver El Camino, which is towed after the killing, 1995.

On June 5, 1996, Palm is sentenced to eighteen to twenty years in prison after being convicted of second-degree murder.[31]

THE VIGILANTE ECHO

Clearly, what Palm did was illegal. On the other hand, we can understand his frustration and that of the entire neighborhood after apparently being abandoned by the criminal justice system. Did he do the right thing? Probably not. He acted in anger, fear, and frustration. But the fact that we can so easily understand the source of that frustration and to some extent sympathize with it suggests that it is an injustice to treat him like any other murderer. There are compelling mitigating factors at work that make him less blameworthy than a person who intentionally kills with no claim to self-defense or defense of others.

Part of the problem with failures of justice, then, is their tendency to provoke a vigilante response that not only breaks the law but also creates the potential for injustice in judging those who overreact when trapped under relentless lawlessness. But one may argue that this is a relatively easy problem to solve: the law can punish vigilantes but give them some mitigation, perhaps convicting a Danny Palm of the lesser offense of manslaughter.

The more serious problem, for which there is no easy fix, is the effect that justice failures have on the larger society and citizens' faith in the effectiveness and credibility of the system. The residents of Dictionary Hill will now think differently about the criminal justice system, and that may lead them to act differently toward it in a variety of often disturbing ways. Their eroded belief in the justness of the system may inevitably create distorting effects in their interactions with it and in how they help shape it through political reform.

Tragically, many of these distorting effects cause injustice. Will the people in the neighborhood be increasingly inclined to support Draconian legislation that does injustice in order to more effectively fight crime? Will these distortions create their own backlash as residents in other neighborhoods are hurt by the new distortions? More on this in part IV of the book.

This is the vigilante echo. Once the government's failures of justice are serious enough or regular enough to undermine the credibility of the criminal justice system in the community it governs, the citizens' cries for justice, sometimes in the form of angry and cynical reactions, can create further dysfunction, further aggravating the system's credibility problem in an endless downward spiral. This book illustrates and explores this tragic dynamic and examines what causes it and what can fix it.

2

THE MORAL VIGILANTE

Vigilantes have a bad name. As one prosecutor put it upon convicting a vigilante, "There is no room for vigilantism. There is no room for what he has done. And no one in authority will ever tolerate vigilantism."[1] Robert Kennedy condemned vigilantism in broader terms: "Whenever men take the law into their own hands, the loser is the law . . . and, when the law loses, freedom languishes."[2]

And much of vigilantism's bad reputation is well deserved. To many people, the paradigm case of evil vigilantism is the Ku Klux Klan. And the image of vigilantes that the Klan presents is appalling. Consider a few details.

THE KU KLUX KLAN AT WORK

On Christmas night, 1951, Harry Moore and his wife, Harriet, go to bed in their home in Brevard County, Florida.[3] The small wooden house is soon on fire when a bomb planted by the KKK detonates under their home. Harry dies on the way to the hospital. Harriet succumbs a week later. Having founded the first branch of the NAACP in Brevard County, Harry Moore has been a prominent civil rights figure.[4] Nobody is charged.[5]

Reverend George W. Lee is seated in his car in Belzoni, Mississippi, in May 1955 when he is shot in the face.[6] Reverend Lee, the first African American to register to vote in Humphreys County since Reconstruction, was actively urging other African Americans to register.[7] Nobody is ever charged with the murder.[8]

On August 13, 1955, in Brookhaven, Mississippi, Lamar Smith is shot in broad daylight at the Lincoln County Courthouse as he helps other black voters complete absentee ballots.[9] While there is a crowd of witnesses, no one is willing to talk about who murdered Smith. Nobody is ever charged with the crime.[10]

This is the immediate history of unchecked violence against blacks and civil rights activists when on August 24, 1955—eleven days after the murder of Lamar Smith in Brookhaven—Emmett Louis Till and a group of other teenagers go to a local general store to buy refreshments after a day of picking cotton in the fields.[11] While in the store, Till talks engagingly with Carolyn Bryant, a white woman married to Roy Bryant, the white proprietor of the store.[12]

Till was born near Chicago on July 25, 1941, to Mimi Till and Louis Till.[13] He grew up in a middle-class black neighborhood on Chicago's South Side.[14] In August 1955 Till's uncle Moses Wright takes him and his cousin to Money, Mississippi, to visit their southern relatives.[15] The day before Till leaves, his mother gives him his late father's signet ring, inscribed with his father's initials.

Four days after Till's visit to Bryant's store, Roy Bryant and his half brother J. W. Milam go to Moses Wright's house and physically take Till.[16] They toss him into their truck and take him to a barn near Milam's house, where the half brothers are joined by at least five other men. The group beats the teenager and pistol-whips him.

The men then force Till into Milam's truck, also loading a large metal cotton gin fan, and they drive to the nearby Tallahatchie River. A neighbor hears Till yelling. Because the men cannot get the truck all the way to the river's edge, they compel the beaten teenager to carry the seventy-four-pound fan to the riverbank. Then Bryant and Milam each shoot Till in the head. The pair then takes a length of barbed wire and attaches the heavy fan to the body. The corpse is a horror; Till's right eye is dislodged from its socket, his skull is visibly smashed, and several of his teeth are dislodged. They dump Till's weighted body in the river.[17]

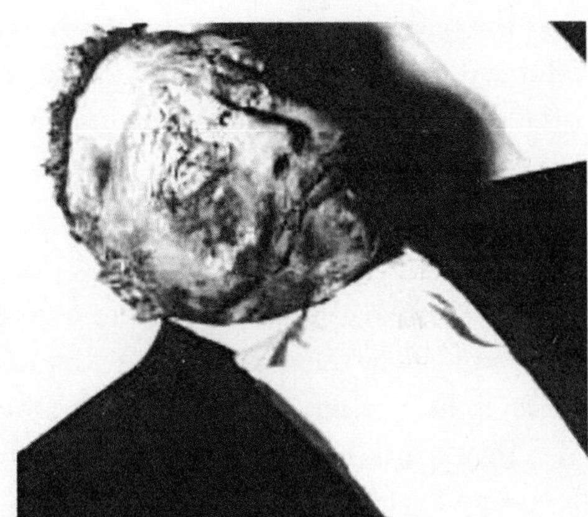

Fig. 2.1. Emmitt Till shortly before his death in 1955 and after his body was recovered. (Courtesy of Flickr.com, https://www.flickr.com/photos/11304375@N07/2534273097, CC BY 2.0)

Till's remains are eventually found, and on September 5, 1955, Bryant and Milam are charged with kidnapping and murder. At trial, Moses Wright identifies Bryant and Milam as the men who took Till, and that evidence is never disputed by the defense. Till's mother identifies the body. The signet ring that had belonged to Till's father is found on the finger of the corpse.[18]

The defense claims that the body found is not Till's.[19] During closing arguments, the defense urges the jurors that "every last Anglo-Saxon one of you has the courage to set these men free."[20]

As jury deliberations begin, the members quickly vote to acquit Bryant and Milam. Sheriff-Elect Harry Dogan sends word to the jury that they should wait awhile before returning a verdict in order to "make it look good."[21] After deliberating for an hour and seven minutes, the jury formally acquits Bryant and Milam. By most accounts, the jurors did not doubt that Milam and Bryant had murdered Till, but they saw the acquittals as necessary to preserve the white supremacy that they were still clinging to in the Deep South.[22]

Today, the Ku Klux Klan is viewed as the classic paradigm for vigilantism. And with the image of Emmett Till's murder in mind, it is not hard to see the disgust that many have for vigilantes. In his televised remarks to the nation on March 26, 1965, after the killing of civil rights worker Viola Liuzzo in Alabama, President Lyndon B. Johnson expressed the common view:

> Mrs. Liuzzo went to Alabama to serve the struggle for justice. She was murdered by the enemies of justice who for decades have used the rope and the gun and the tar and the feathers to terrorize their neighbors. They struck by night, as they generally do, for their purpose cannot stand the light of day. . . .
>
> I call on every law enforcement officer in America to insist on obedience to the law and to insist on respect for justice. No nation can long endure either in history's judgment or in its own national conscience if hoodlums or bigots can defy the law and can get away with it.[23]

Almost thirty years later, President Bill Clinton was still railing against vigilantes. On March 11, 1993, speaking of the killing of Dr. David Gunn, a provider of abortions, Clinton said, "I was saddened and angered by the fatal shooting in Pensacola yesterday of Dr. David Gunn. The violence against clinics must stop. As a nation committed to rule of law, we cannot allow violent vigilantes to restrict the rights of American women. No person seeking medical care and no physician providing that care should have to endure harassment, threats, or intimidation."[24]

A DIFFERENT PERSPECTIVE ON VIGILANTES: THE DEACONS FOR DEFENSE

From a larger perspective, however, the apparently abhorrent nature of vigilantism is not so clear. Consider again the plight of African Americans and civil rights activists in the Deep South in the 1960s. No doubt it is comforting to them that President Johnson condemns the Ku Klux Klan attacks. But there is also no doubt that even more comforting would be to have somebody stop the attacks or at the very least to punish the attackers as a tangible signal to other potential victimizers and victims that such conduct is condemned and will be seriously dealt with.

The existing criminal justice system has proven itself sometimes ineffective in providing either protection or justice, as vividly illustrated by Emmett Till's case. In that state of affairs, might the best course for the victimized be to take the law into their own hands?

It is 1964, and the Congress of Racial Equality (CORE) plans to stage a desegregation campaign in the heavily segregated city of Jonesboro, Louisiana. In an effort to prevent this, the local Ku Klux Klan organizes a motorcade through the city's black neighborhood, littering the streets with pamphlets that threaten violence against anyone who takes part in the desegregation demonstrations. To reinforce the message, Klan operatives, with the help of local police, cut electrical power to the black neighborhood.[25]

In response to the threats, Ernest "Chilly Willy" Thomas and Frederick Douglas Kirkpatrick recruit a group of twenty African American men to serve as an armed paramilitary group to defend against the Klan. Calling themselves the Deacons for Defense and Justice, most members are veterans of World War II or the Korean War. The group is the first of a new breed of civil rights organizations that uses force when needed to defend against racial oppression.[26] They meet weekly to plan upcoming actions, such as guarding activists, patrolling black neighborhoods, and protecting demonstrators not only from the Klan but also from the local police.[27]

In 1965 in nearby Bogalusa, a black paper mill manager named Robert Hicks hosts two CORE activists at his home. The night they arrive, Bogalusa police chief Claxton Knight comes to the Hicks home to escort the two CORE workers out of town. Knight explains that if Hicks does not comply, the Klan will pay Hicks a visit. The Klan follows up Knight's visit with a phone call threatening to firebomb Hicks's house if he fails to turn over the CORE workers.[28]

Fig. 2.2. The 1963 march in memory of church bombings organized by CORE, protected by Deacons for Defense. (Courtesy of Thomas O'Halloran, U.S. News & World Report Magazine Photograph Collection, Library of Congress)

Hicks, a leader of the local NAACP, calls friends to help guard the house. The Klan decides not to show. Three weeks later, under a continuing threat, Hicks meets with the leaders of the Jonesboro Deacons, with whose help he forms the first satellite branch of the group. In similar fashion, branches of the Deacons for Defense and Justice spread across the Deep South into Mississippi, Alabama, and Louisiana.[29]

Later in Jonesboro, African American students picket Jonesboro High School to protest its continued segregation. While the student protest is peaceful, police officers nonetheless prepare to turn fire hoses on the students. The Deacons arrive and begin loading their shotguns in full view of the officers. The authorities elect to send the fire trucks away.

Prominent African American civil rights groups denounce the

Deacons' acts as "aggressive violence,"[30] but as the civil rights movement comes under increasing physical attacks, the Deacons' proven defensive effectiveness becomes more attractive. Ultimately, Dr. Martin Luther King Jr. asks the group to accompany him as a security force during the March against Fear from Memphis to Jackson, Tennessee, in 1966. The Deacons go on to provide armed security for Charles Evers's desegregation campaign in Natchez, Mississippi, and for a number of other civil rights campaigns in the region.[31]

At their height, the Deacons expanded to twenty-one chapters. While their willingness to use armed force prompted an FBI investigation, the authorities' interest in the reactive organization soon evaporated when other far more aggressive organizations such as the Black Panthers began operations. Replaced by these more radical groups, the Deacons ceased operations in 1968 and faded into relative obscurity in the history of the civil rights movement.[32]

The Deacons for Defense and Justice are not an aberration. Many groups have, with moral justification, taken the law into their own hands. This is the essence of vigilantism. Indeed, the origin of the term "vigilante" suggests something very different from popular use, which brings to mind a Ku Klux Klan lynching or abortion doctor shooting. The original vigilantes were the epitome of responsible democratic action fighting an inept and often corrupt government.

SAN FRANCISCO VIGILANCE COMMITTEE, 1850S

The nineteenth century is a politically turbulent time for the California region.[33] It had been a Spanish colony but is now a state in the Mexican Republic. Seeing an opportunity to gain control of much of the North American continent, President James Polk in 1846 sends a small force to claim the West for the United States. Fearing British retaliation, Polk needs the action to seem to be the will of the locals. On June 14 his force arrives at the home of California's leading citizen, don Mariano Vallejo. Vallejo, a Mexican general currently out of favor with the Mexican government and in command of no troops, remains the nominal military authority in this frontier. The party informs the general that he is a prisoner. Vallejo, who had been asleep, "had difficulty understanding what war he [is] a prisoner of." The group drinks local brandy, chats, and writes a formal statement of terms, and "by its third paragraph, the product of good native liquor, the California Republic [is] born."[34]

While President Polk put the takeover in motion, the region cannot be admitted into the United States without congressional action, and this is a touchy issue. California is against slavery. An additional free state in the Union would numerically put the slaveholding states at a disadvantage. The result is an awkward limbo. Congress will not vote California into the Union, but the state is thought too vital to American interests to let another country control the area.

San Francisco became the base camp for the gold rush, which began in early 1848. More than 150,000 men pass through San Francisco on their way to the mountain mines. The dynamic, chaotic population is beyond the control of the officials in what a few years earlier was a small town of two hundred.[35] San Francisco has very little in the way of law and even less capacity to enforce the laws that do exist.

Understanding the city's vulnerable situation, a criminal gang calling themselves the Hounds begins raiding stores and restaurants, forcing them to supply the Hounds' demands and "charge it to the Hounds."[36] One Sunday in July 1849, the Hounds are especially violent in their activities, beating everyone they rob and shooting one of their victims. Several townspeople call for a meeting to deal with the violence. Within days, a self-formed committee of citizens forcibly takes most of the Hounds into custody. A second meeting is called to decide their fate. During the meeting, a court and a grand jury are formed, and the Hounds are "indicted, and charged with a conspiracy to commit murder, robbery, etc."[37] The court, consisting of a judge, a jury, and attorneys to prosecute and defend the Hounds, ultimately convicts the men, sentences them to exile, and threatens with execution any who return.

Fig. 2.3. San Francisco vigilante movement migrated from the gold fields, 1848. (Courtesy of "Judge Lynch" California Vigilantes, 1848, Library of Congress)

Mass meetings and popular tribunals become the accepted means of criminal justice in San Francisco. The citizens appoint an alcalde, a local magistrate, to organize the efforts, a practice first begun by the miners in their camps. Justice is swift. In a common burglary case in 1850, the burglary occurs at four o'clock in the morning. The alcalde issues warrants for the thieves. "They are pursued, arrested, indicted by a grand jury, convicted by a petit jury, sentenced, whipped, and turned out of town within twelve hours."[38]

On October 18, 1850, California is officially admitted to the United States. In consequence, a number of political offices are created. A commonality between those voting and those seeking office is that they do not view San Francisco as anything more than a means to an end. It is not their home. For most of them, securing a political position is "solely . . . a means of obtaining money for a speedy return to the East."[39]

The earlier "courts of the people" were rough justice but were difficult to manipulate on a large scale because judges and attorneys were appointed by the group and changed from case to case. The new courts, however, are staffed by men with dubious histories and operate without oversight and with little motivation to serve the community. They become "notorious for their failure to convict and punish criminals, especially those who [can] pay for skillful defense. . . . This immunity [is] almost universally attributed to flagrant corruption within professional circles."[40]

Before statehood, a trial would have been held by interested neighbors soon after the crime had occurred. The new system transfers the responsibility for doing justice to a physically and emotionally remote authority, usually long delayed from the offense. By 1851 the crime rate has skyrocketed. In response, citizens return to what they know: they form a Vigilance Committee, and every man in the city is invited to join. The group elects officers, keeps records, and places its own police on the streets and in patrol boats in the harbor. Members also act as detectives, jailers, lawyers, judges, and jurors.

The Vigilance Committee hears hundreds of cases. Committee members hang four men, all of whom are convicted of, at minimum, murder. Persons convicted of robbery and some lesser crimes are transported on ships to distant shores or simply banished from the city itself. The committee confronts innkeepers who are known to aid criminals and warns them to stop or they will be shut down. One man convicted of possession of stolen property is whipped.[41]

Samuel Whittaker and Robert McKenzie are career criminals who have long been protected by authorities as they steal, assault, rob, and burn their way to criminal profits, which they have used to help some current officials buy their way into public office. When the Vigilance

Committee finally gets them into custody on August 8, 1851, they boast of their influence with the local authorities, including the current city marshal, Malachi Fallon, whom they helped get into office.[42] After a public trial, during which their boasts are read back to them, the committee concludes that "both men [are] self-confessed robbers who [do] not hesitate at any violence, that they [are] a menace to the community, and that it would be unsafe to hand them over to authorities."[43] The men are sentenced to hang on August 18. Before the sentence can be carried out, however, public officials spirit them away. When the Vigilance Committee regains custody, it rings a signal bell, and a crowd gathers to watch the two men hang.

With the committee back in action, the crime rate again drops. New elections are held, and with the election of men who are more invested in the good of the community, the Vigilance Committee disbands itself.

Groups that can lay claim to being moral vigilantes have continued to exist. More than a century after the San Francisco Vigilance Committee, the same city was still provoking moral vigilantism. Where the government fails to protect and to do justice, victimized citizens are left with little option but to do these things for themselves.

SAN FRANCISCO LAVENDER PANTHERS, 1970S

It is San Francisco, 1973, and young gay men leaving the Helping Hands Gay Community Service Center are confronted by a rowdy group that has assembled, as it commonly does, to harass those visiting the center.[44] The rowdies scream derogatory remarks and shove the young men in hopes of provoking a pushback that will give the rowdies an excuse to start an all-out brawl.

Reverend Ray Broshears, a Pentecostal evangelical minister who runs the center, contacts the San Francisco police. He has seen this kind of harassment regularly and is concerned that it is getting out of hand. The police come, but when they arrive they do nothing to stop the brawlers' aggression. Instead, they inform the group that it was Broshears who called the police and that he plans to file a complaint against the group. As soon as the police leave, the group attacks Broshears and beats him severely.

Broshears has a history of helping the gay community in San Francisco. He organized San Francisco's first Gay Pride Parade and operates a local gay newspaper, the *Gay Crusader*. But as it becomes clear that the assaults will continue and that law enforcement will do nothing to stop them, he decides that his vocal advocacy approach is insufficient. Seeing the rise of the Black Panthers with their message of self-reliance in nearby Oakland, Broshears decides in July 1973 to form his own group to provide protection and deal out justice, a group he names the Lavender Panthers.

The Lavender Panthers train in various martial arts and often arm themselves. During one press conference, Broshears, holding his shotgun and flanked by two fellow Lavender Panthers who are lipsticked, rouged, and armed, urges "all homosexuals in San Francisco to arm themselves in their homes and places of business."[45] As the police refuse to provide protection, Broshears argues that the Lavender Panthers have no alternative. Even if the assailants are caught, he claims, the police often advise the offender to "say that [a] queer made an advance towards you."[46] The gay basher is then freed, and the victim is arrested.

Initially, the group numbers twenty-one members with two women included. Usually armed with chains, red spray paint (a substitute for the then outlawed Mace), billy clubs, pool cues, and whistles, the members hold training sessions in which they teach defensive skills to other members of the homosexual community.

The Lavender Panthers patrol areas known for a high incidence of violence against homosexuals. They also appear at trouble spots as they arise, such as outside gay bars where groups of gay bashers often gather to harass patrons. When the Lavender Panthers appear on the scene, however, the old pattern of intimidation and beatings changes.

In one typical incident, a group of gay bashers is shoving patrons as they leave the Naked Grape, a well-known gay bar. Lavender Panther members pull up in their trademark gray Volkswagen bus and confront the troublemakers with swinging pool cues. The bashers flee. In this particular incident, however, would-be bashers make a tactical error and leave their car keys behind. Needing their car to get home, the bashers are obliged to return later in the evening to negotiate for their return.[47]

Within a year, the right of gays to live openly in the Bay Area has progressed significantly. The incidents of harassment have been reduced to such an extent that the Lavender Panthers determine that they are no longer needed, and they voluntarily disband. The Panthers' success came not just from the protection and justice they provided but also from their ability to embarrass the San Francisco police into taking the ongoing threat to homosexuals more seriously.[48]

The Lavender Panthers had probably never heard of the original San Francisco Vigilance Committee, but the group was born of the same belief that such failures of justice simply could not be tolerated and that it was sometimes both necessary and moral for people to take the law into their own hands. If the government breached its social contract with its citizens, the 1973 Lavender Panthers, like the 1851 Vigilance Committee before them, had little choice but to take up their natural right to protect themselves and to do justice when the official system had forsaken them.

It is easy to think of moral vigilantism as a thing of the past. But the truth is it exists today and will continue to exist as long as the government breaches its social contract with its citizens. The unfortunate truth is that such breaches are a part of modern life.

INDIA'S PINK GANG

In 2006 Sampat Pal Devi, a forty-eight-year-old Indian woman, watches as her alcoholic brother-in-law beats her sister and drags her by the hair around a courtyard and finally out into the streets of Banda.[49] Unfortunately, this is not an unusual occurrence in Banda, which is in Uttar Pradesh, India's most populous and impoverished state. The region is well-known for its repressive treatment of women, including child marriage practices. Devi's family sold her into marriage when she was nine years old.[50] By age thirteen she was a mother.

The domestic and sexual abuse of women is an everyday occurrence in the region, especially for poor women. When spouses walk together on the street, the wife is expected to walk a few paces behind her husband in order to acknowledge his "superior, God-like status." The social acceptance of the oppression of women means that local authorities simply do not intervene when a violent man is beating a woman, especially a poor woman. As Devi puts it, "Nobody comes to our help in these parts. The officials and the police are corrupt and antipoor."[51]

But faced with the public beating of her sister, Devi concludes that she will no longer stand by and do nothing. She rounds up a group of neighborhood women, who arm themselves with whatever they can find—iron rods, sticks, and cricket bats—and chase the abusive brother-in-law into a sugarcane field, where they beat him. The realization among the women that they are not helpless against the abuse emboldens them to form a vigilante group that will stop attacks when possible and will punish oppressive men when justified. The Gulabi Gang, or Pink Gang, as the women call themselves, trains women and arms them with police batons, bamboo rods, and axes. As Devi explains, "None of the men here pay any attention to us. The only way to get them to listen is to scare them. I am not scared of any of them. But to make sure we have the upper hand, we always go with sticks and axes to deal with someone."[52]

Fig. 2.4. The Pink Gang has continued to grow, 2012. (Photo by McKay Savage, 2012)

The Pink Gang and its unorthodox methods bring much-needed attention to the mistreatment of women, and its membership expands. The organization quickly gains two hundred members in Banda and within a few years spreads to many other cities. Membership numbers are now reportedly over forty thousand women (and some men), with ten district commanders operating in a thirty-six-thousand-square-mile area. The small center that Devi opened in her hometown where women are able to come and seek help is replicated in towns throughout the organization's territory.[53]

As the group expands, so does its agenda, broadening to include not just the oppression of women generally but also the mistreatment of the poor. In one incident, Pink Gang members storm a police station, demanding that officials stop selectively enforcing laws according to the victim's caste. In another raid on a police station, the women chastise officials for stealing and reselling subsidized grain intended for the city's poor.[54]

The success and influence of the Pink Gang grows, and its agenda broadens such that by 2011 it has become an active political party with twenty-one Pink Gang members elected in municipality-level elections.[55] While the newfound political power enables the group to promote a more expansive array of projects, including repairing and constructing local roads, providing clean drinking water, and developing sustainable agricultural projects, the group's main focus remains the improvement of conditions for Indian women in a male-dominated, largely feudalistic society.

The lesson to be learned from these cases and many others in this book is that vigilantism is not itself an evil. Indeed, it may be a moral response to an otherwise impossible situation. Vigilantism is like war: while it is never desirable, it is sometimes just. However, as a closer examination in the chapters ahead will reveal, vigilantism in almost any form has societal costs that are not always immediately evident.

3

THE SHADOW VIGILANTES

We traditionally think of vigilantes as people frustrated by what they see as the criminal justice system's failures of justice, and who are thereby provoked to go into the streets—taking the law into their own hands. As the previous two chapters make clear, such classic vigilantism can be inspired in a wide variety of situations and some cases can be entirely morally justified.

What is generally not understood is that the same frustration with the system's failures of justice can inspire a reaction of lawlessness short of the physical confrontation of classic vigilante action. "Shadow vigilantism," as it might be called, occurs when ordinary people, instead of taking the law into their own hands by going into the street, seek to manipulate the operation of the criminal justice system in order to force from it the justice that it seems so reluctant to do on its own. While shadow vigilantism may be less confrontational, as will become apparent, it is ultimately more pervasive and more damaging.

Shadow vigilantes can be ordinary people who seek to influence the operation of the criminal justice system whenever they have contact with it, as witnesses, as jurors, or even as voters shaping the system. But shadow vigilantism is also common among the official participants in the system who essentially conspire to undermine those rules and practices that they see as regularly frustrating justice. Thus, shadow vigilantes can be police officers, prosecutors, judges, and others.

Here are two examples of the shadow vigilante dynamic in action, one by ordinary citizens and one by police officers.

JURY NULLIFICATION

New York City in the 1980s is far from the safest place in America. In fact, as depicted by films such as *Escape from New York* and *The Warriors*, New York may be one of the most dangerous cities in the world. Between 1966 and 1981 violent crime rates in the city had more than tripled, from 325 violent crimes per 100,000 to approximately 1,100 crimes per 100,000 people.[1] The crime rate reaches an all-time high in the early 1980s, especially for violent crimes such as murder, rape, and robbery.[2] In 1980, on average, nearly six New Yorkers are murdered each and every day. The city's *reported* crime statistics are more than 70 percent higher than the rest of the country.

The subway in particular is an incredibly dangerous place for any New Yorker. Subway cars are nearly unrecognizable, since almost every car is spray-painted with overlapping rainbows of gang graffiti. The train cars are heavily occupied by muggers, druggies, panhandlers, and the homeless. The sense of danger on the subway is more than just hysteria; the numbers tell the story. On average, thirty-eight felonies are committed on the subway every day.[3] Between the summers of 1979 and 1980, crime on the subway rises a staggering 70 percent.[4] In comparison, in Paris, where angry citizens have been asking the army to help quell the gangs working the subway, there is only one-eighth of New York's subway crime rate.[5]

By 1982 safety on the subway has deteriorated to the level that Metropolitan Transportation Authority chairman Richard Ravitch tells members of the Association for a Better New York that even he will not allow his teenage sons to ride the subway at night. As an adult with intimate knowledge of the system and with influence among the workers, he himself is quite nervous about riding the trains.[6] That October, New York sees the lowest ridership on its subways since 1917, largely because of crime fears.

In November 1982 a gang robs and pistol-whips five people in three subway stations within a half hour. That same year sees a 60 percent increase in transit crime.[7] In the decade from 1975 to 1985, forty-four million fewer people ride the New York subway, primarily because they are afraid to.[8]

On Saturday, December 22, 1984, four African American teenagers—Troy Canty, nineteen; Darrell Cabey, nineteen; James Ramseur, eighteen; and Barry Allen, nineteen—prepare to ride an Interborough Rapid Transit Company subway train from the Bronx toward Lower Manhattan.[9] Two of the men, Cabey and Ramseur, have screwdrivers hidden in their coat pockets.

Bernhard Goetz, a thirty-seven-year-old white man, joins the four young men on the train platform; there are approximately fifteen to twenty other passengers at the Fourteenth Street station stop. Three years prior, Goetz had been mugged during a robbery at the Canal Street subway station and sustained permanent physical damage to his chest and knee from the encounter. Although the perpetrators were apprehended, they spent less time at the police station than Goetz spent giving his statement. He now feels the need to carry his unlicensed .38-caliber pistol, loaded with five rounds of ammunition. (He had applied for a permit but was denied due to insufficient need.

Upon boarding the train, Goetz takes a seat on the long bench right by the entrance to the car. The young men approach him. Canty asks Goetz, "How are you?" to which Goetz responds, "Fine." The four men then exchange signals with one another and shift their bodies, positioning themselves so as to isolate Goetz from the rest of the passengers. Once the young men are in position, Canty steps closer to Goetz, with Allen at his side, and firmly says, "Give me five dollars." Goetz then sees one of the men reach into his coat pocket; the pocket appears to be "bulging out." Understanding that he is now facing a robbery attempt, Goetz asks, "What did you say?"[10]

Goetz then stands up and fires four bullets, moving from left to right, aiming for the center of each man's body. The men scatter. The first shot penetrates Canty's chest; the second enters Allen's back; the third bullet passes through Ramseur's arm and into the left side of his body; and the fourth barely misses Cabey. After missing Cabey, Goetz takes a few seconds, surveying the scene, and then walks over to Cabey, who is now sitting on a seat. According to Goetz's videotaped account, he says something like, "You seem to be all right, here's another."[11] The final bullet severs Cabey's spinal cord. Three of the men, although initially listed in critical condition, fully recover; Cabey, however, is paralyzed and has brain damage, leaving him with the mental capacity of a third grader as a result of the shooting.

Nine days after the shooting, Goetz voluntarily surrenders to the police in Concord, New Hampshire, making two lengthy tape-recorded statements. He tells police that he interpreted Canty's demand for five dollars to mean that the young men wanted to "play" with him and rob him. Based on his prior experiences in New York City, Goetz was fearful of being seriously "maimed." He also reports that he intended in that moment to "murder, to hurt them, to make them suffer as much as possible." In regard to his more controlled shooting of Cabey, Goetz adds, "If I was a little more under self-control . . . I would have put the barrel against his forehead and fired," and "if I had more [bullets], I would have shot them again, and again, and again."[12]

Americans across the nation from Hawaii to Chicago voice their support for Goetz's "heroic" actions. Out of their own frustration and anger about unchecked crime in their own cities, they are excited that someone has taken a stand against the criminals. "This case hit a real raw nerve," said Dave Walker, former cohost of CNN's *Take Two*. "There is a broad sense of frustration and anger over the state of the criminal justice system, and right now people don't seem to care about the facts or whether or not Goetz used appropriate force. They have found themselves a hero."[13] In Boston, radio listeners not only voice their support for Goetz but even pledge money to pay for his defense.

The state of New York seeks an indictment against Goetz in January 1985 for attempted murder, assault, reckless endangerment, and criminal possession of a weapon. But the first grand jury refuses to indict Goetz for anything except the gun possession charge. However, a few weeks later, armed with newly available evidence, including additional witness testimony from some of the victims and others, the prosecutors try again. This time, an indictment for the attempted murder charges is returned. However, in January 1986 Judge Stephen Crane grants the defense's motion to dismiss the new indictment because of errors in the prosecutor's jury instructions regarding Goetz's defense of justification for the use of deadly force.

Fig. 3.1. Bernhard Goetz turns himself in, 1984. (Photo by Mel Finkelstein)

Six months later, the New York Court of Appeals reverses Judge Crane's decision.[14] Judge Sol Wachtler affirms the prosecutor's original jury instructions, that a defendant's *subjective* belief that he is in imminent danger does not by itself justify deadly force. Instead, Wachtler holds that one's beliefs must be *objectively* reasonable. The court reinstates the dismissed counts of the indictment and sends the polarizing case to a jury.

The Goetz trial begins on December 12, 1986, and lasts more than seven weeks. A jury comprised of four women and eight men (six of whom had been mugging victims themselves) listens to ten thousand pages of testimony and both of the two-hour videotapes of Goetz's interviews.[15] After thirty-five separate votes over a four-day period, the jury concludes that Goetz, the man who intentionally fired a bullet into Cabey, severing his spinal cord, is cleared of twelve of the thirteen charges against him, including ten major felonies.[16] The jury convicts Goetz only of criminal possession of a weapon in the third degree (carrying a loaded unlicensed weapon in a public place).

Legal commentators argue that the Goetz jury partook in jury nullification—acquitting a defendant although the law would say he is guilty. Alan Dershowitz, professor of law at Harvard Law School, believes that the jury nullified the self-defense standards set by the law, even though by definition Goetz's actions clearly violated New York and almost every other state law. Burt Neuborne, a professor at NYU Law School, says, "The jurors had so little faith in the criminal justice system, both to protect us and to bring the guilty to justice, that they were willing to tolerate a degree of vigilante behavior that I think rationally cannot be justified."[17] New Yorkers, who, like members of the jury, are concerned about safety in the city, overwhelmingly supported the verdict. A Gallup poll taken shortly after the decision showed that 83 percent of non-Hispanic whites and 78 percent of Hispanics supported the verdict.[18]

While it seems difficult to see how a jury could conclude that Goetz "reasonably believed" his second shot at Cabey was necessary to protect himself, as the self-defense statute requires, the jury acquitted Goetz of all assault charges. The law has its rules, but shadow vigilantes, armed with the power of jury nullification, have their own.

Frustration with failures of justice and the shadow vigilante impulse that it provokes is found not only among civilians but also among criminal justice professionals. And police, prosecutors, judges, and others have an even greater opportunity than civilians to subvert or manipulate the criminal justice process in an effort to force justice from it.

For example, it is not unusual for some police officers to circumvent technical search and seizure requirements by lying in court about the circumstances of the search or seizure—what the police call "testilying." Shadow vigilantism by prosecutors is shown in a disinclination to charge civilians or police who make culpable mistakes in confrontations with wrongdoers. It is also shown in prosecutorial overcharging of an offender—charging a host of overlapping offences for a single criminal act—to compensate for past offenses that went unpunished. And it is clear that judges tolerate much of the above and might even add in a few manipulations of their own. These players take the system's repeated failures of justice as their moral justification for subverting and manipulating it to force from it the justice to which it often seems indifferent.

Consider an example of police as shadow vigilantes.

POLICE SUBVERSION OF THE EXCLUSIONARY RULE

Bill Bradford is a sexual psychopath.[19] His first sexual crime occurs in 1972 during his midtwenties. Bradford tries to force his penis into a seventeen-year-old girl's mouth and then masturbates onto her breasts. In response to the girl's cries, Bradford shouts that "he always wanted to do it so he did."[20]

Two years later, Bradford and a fifteen-year-old begin an intimate relationship. During the relationship, Bradford beats his girlfriend on a weekly basis, sometimes forcing her to have intercourse with him during the assaults. The girl becomes pregnant. Bradford tries to kill the baby by slamming his girlfriend's belly into a door, and once the baby is born he tries to kill it several more times, twice by throwing it against the wall and once by tying a windbreaker around its face. Over the years the pattern continues: Bradford treats a woman brutally, is arrested, is convicted, and is soon free again.

In the summer of 1984, while out on bail and awaiting trial for rape, Bradford assaults Shari Miller, a twenty-one-year-old struggling to make it on her own. She has held various jobs in the past, including being a bartender at the Meat Market, a popular bar in Los Angeles. Miller tells her mother that she is going to get a job as a model for a photographer and heads out at 3:00 p.m. one afternoon. Bradford goes with Miller into the desert, takes various nude photographs of her, and then strangles her to death. He then mutilates the body, removing her nipples and various other pieces of flesh.

More than a week later an office worker who has parked behind his workplace in an alley notices a foul smell. He spots a large bundle covered by a quilt, soaked in blood, from which a hand is protruding. Identified initially as Jane Doe No. 60, the body is that of Shari Miller.

Tracey Campbell is a fifteen-year-old girl who lives in the same complex as Bradford. On July 12, one of Bradford's roommates hears Bradford and Campbell talking and hears Bradford say he has a job for Campbell. Bradford takes her out to that same spot in the desert, photographs her, and then strangles her to death; he leaves the body to rot in the desert heat.

When the Campbell family starts to ask around regarding Tracy's whereabouts, they learn from Bradford's roommates that the two had been together. The next morning Campbell's mother files a missing person's report at the police station. One of the roommates tells a caller that Bradford has "taken the little girl next door the previous day and was not yet home."[21]

On July 14 and on July 16, the LAPD interviews Bradford in his apartment concerning Campbell. Bradford tells the officer that she had come to his apartment to use the phone and that he had then dropped her off to buy cigarettes and hitchhike to the beach. Two days later, Bradford consents to a search of his apartment and car, but nothing significant is found.

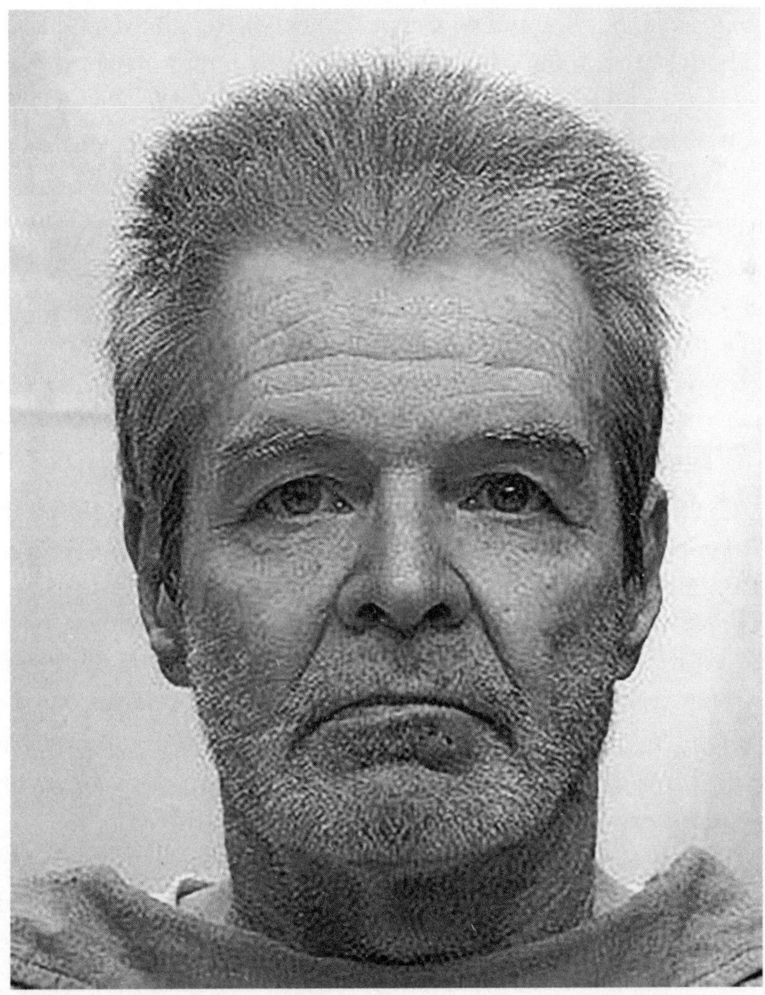

Fig. 3.2. Bill Bradford, while in prison, 2008.

Bradford remains the main suspect due to his connection to the girl and his long rap sheet of previous sexual and violent assaults. On July 31, pursuant to a warrant, LAPD officers arrest Bradford and execute a more thorough search of his apartment and vehicle. This time, they recover numerous Polaroids and negatives from which they recognize photos of

Jane Doe No. 60. The police match the girl in the photographs to the dead body they had found earlier in the month and soon determine that Jane Doe No. 60 is Shari Miller.

Over the course of the next two days, the police interrogate Bradford. They ask him about his connection to Miller, to which he responds that he had known her for years and that she had wanted to get into modeling. He admits to taking modeling shots on July 1 and says he has not seen her since. After being held for three nights, he is released from custody due to insufficient evidence.

On August 11 a body is found in the desert at the location Bradford is known to have previously visited for a camping trip. The location matches the background of some of the seized photos of Miller modeling. The body is determined to be Tracey Campbell. Because both murders are similar and the location of the remains matches Bradford's photos, the previous suspicions of the police seem to be confirmed.

The police have a problem, however. While it is more clear to them than ever that Bradford is their multiple murderer, they do not have sufficient new evidence that will allow them to obtain a warrant to search his apartment for the third time. Their warrant application must have a stronger showing of probable cause for yet another search than they have had in the past.

Understanding that the serial killer might escape their grasp, Detective Charles Worthen, who assisted with the July 31 search warrant, does what he believes he needs to do to get the warrant. In the warrant application, Worthen leaves out certain pieces of information. He leaves out information that Miller was seen alive after June 30, even though several of her friends reported this. He asks for authorization to search for a silver spoon ring, blue cutoff shorts, and any articles of clothing as seen in a series of attached photographs, even though some of these items are already in police inventory from the previous search of Miller's car. Finally, he mentions the two previous searches only in the appendix rather than in the main application itself. The tactics work, and the warrant is granted.[22]

On August 16 the LAPD again arrests Bradford. After being read his Miranda rights, he initially refuses to speak without a lawyer, but then Bradford waives that right and agrees to an interview. He sticks to his original stories. When asked how it could be possible that Campbell's body was found almost in the exact same location as the photo shoot for Miller, Bradford responds, "I can't explain it to you."[23]

Armed with the newly issued warrant, the police search his home and vehicle for the third time. In the hall closet they find a wristwatch flecked in paint similar to the one Miller is wearing in some of her photographs. In another closet they find a portion of white rope, numerous photographs and documents, and several items believed to be owned by Miller. The rope is found to make impressions identical to those in the ligature marks on both victims' necks. Police have found the murder weapon. In Bradford's automobile, the floor mat in the trunk tests positive for presence of human blood.

Now the collection of evidence against Bradford is very strong. He is charged with two counts of first-degree murder, goes on trial, and is found guilty of both counts. During Bradford's closing testimony in sentencing he says, "Think of how many you don't even know about."[24] The jury sentences him to death. Bradford appeals his conviction, citing the police misconduct in obtaining the final warrant. As a result of his appeal some evidence is excluded, but Bradford's conviction is affirmed.[25]

It seems likely that Detective Worthen wrote the application for the final warrant, which led to the conviction, in a way that was intentionally misleading. Yet in his own mind, the deception no doubt seemed justifiable, given the justice-frustrating nature of the search and seizure exclusionary rules and the real danger that this sadistic serial murderer and rapist might escape conviction and punishment.

Part III of this book gives many more examples of shadow vigilantism in different contexts by both ordinary people and criminal justice officials. The real threat that vigilantism presents to an ordered society lies not in its classic form but rather in these common acts of shadow vigilantism, which are essentially impossible to stop and which create unpredictability and distortion in the operation of the system. As part IV details, the damage comes not just from the acts of shadow vigilantism but perhaps even more from the dysfunctional reaction of others to these acts.

Yet, despite the chaos that shadow vigilantism inspires, the current criminal justice system, apparently oblivious to the dangers, continues to provoke it by adopting rules and practices that regularly produce what are seen as appalling failures of justice, as the next chapter illustrates.

4

SPARKING THE SHADOW VIGILANTE IMPULSE

We know that people can be outraged by the criminal justice system's avoidable failures of justice, as you may have been outraged when reading the cases of Deanna Cook and the Dictionary Hill bully in the first chapter. But perhaps these are isolated and unusual situations that, thankfully, are increasingly confined to the past. Do ordinary American citizens have any reason to feel outraged about the current criminal justice system's failures of justice? Could there be systemic problems with practices that predictably provoke outrage and thereby encourage the vigilante impulse?

Our studies suggest that the system has adopted a wide range of rules, policies, and practices that, in the view of ordinary people, seem to allow offenders who commit serious crimes to go unpunished, even when identified and caught by the police. To the offender, the escape from liability may be an unexpected gift. He has won the lottery! But to ordinary citizens, his release can suggest a criminal justice system shamefully indifferent to the importance of doing justice—to give offenders the punishment they deserve.

Some of the system's failures of justice may be unavoidable and may be easily forgiven by even a demanding public. The criminal justice system can only do so much to catch offenders and to reliably reconstruct what happened during some past event. Few people are likely to hold such failures against a system otherwise trying to do its best to dispense justice. The public would be appalled by wrongful convictions and the unjust punishment that might result from cutting corners on reliable adjudication of the facts. What is upsetting to many, however, is when serious offenders escape the liability and punishment they deserve even though their guilt is clear.

Set out below are some examples of the kinds of cases that we know, from our research, outrage people. These are the types of cases that make the news and thereby advertise the criminal justice system's apparent indifference to the importance of doing justice. These failures are not instances in which the system's rules and practices are being subverted by law-breaking rogue judges and officials. They are, rather, instances in which the law is observed and the perceived failure of justice is one that the law officially and publicly tolerates and even aggressively promotes.

These *doctrines of disillusionment*, as they might be called, come in a variety of forms. Some are practices by a judiciary that is seen as following a rigid, rule-obsessed view of criminal adjudication that too often sees the process as a game rather than a search for truth and justice. Others are rules, such as the suppression of reliable evidence, that undermine effective enforcement and investigation efforts and are seen as enabling criminals and creating avoidable crimes. Still others are seen as made possible by vast, unchecked discretion given to decision makers in the criminal justice process. Finally, some are formal liability rules that give defenses to clearly blameworthy offenders who have committed serious offenses.

But what about the old adage that "it is better that ten guilty men go free than one innocent man be convicted"? Don't many of these doctrines of disillusionment simply promote the values behind that adage? And doesn't any proposal to constrain these doctrines conflict with the values of the old adage? Absolutely not. The adage rightly emphasizes the importance of avoiding wrongful convictions. And everything in this book supports that view. One can't care about justice without also caring about avoiding injustice. If a rule or practice protects innocent defendants from conviction, then all bets are off; the rule ought to be enthusiastically supported. This perspective is consistent with the community view, which of course strongly objects to wrongful convictions. The focus here, and what provokes the vigilante impulse, are very different sets of cases: those rules and practices that let *clearly guilty offenders* escape the punishment they deserve.

An academic could offer an argument in support of many of the doctrines of disillusionment, and many of these rules and practices are the product of healthy debate over competing interests. (One of us has done a detailed analysis of the underlying justifications for such rules, in Robinson and Cahill's *Law without Justice: Why the Criminal Law Doesn't Give People What They Deserve.*) But the point of this chapter is to give a sense of how very plausible and understandable it is that many people are outraged by the current system's results. Whether people are right or wrong to feel outraged is beside the point. What is important here is to see how easy it is for people to feel upset about the system's results. Criminal justice should at least acknowledge the dissatisfaction that doctrines of disillusionment bring about.

Below are some examples of the kinds of cases that are likely to disillusion ordinary people. The appendix provides dozens more examples.

CRIMINAL JUSTICE, THE GAME

A common source of disillusionment are cases in which judges seem to be too caught up in applying technical rules rather than being guided by principles of fairness and justice.

Too Many Jurors Voting Guilty

In 2007 Charles Devol Mapps shoots his girlfriend of ten years, Roseann Siddell.[1] He tells police that he did it at her request as part of a suicide pact. She had never fully recovered from the emotional trauma of having been the victim of a sexual assault years earlier, he explains, so they decided to end their lives together. Police learn that Siddell went to school, worked two jobs, and gave every indication to family and friends of being well-adjusted, and they simply do not believe Mapps's story.

Mapps is charged with murder and use of a deadly weapon. His trial is held in Houston, Texas, in February 2009. "It doesn't take a long time for the state to put the case on. There really isn't any other evidence than [Mapps's] statements," defense attorney Skip Cornelius recounts.[2] Judge Mark Kent Ellis is on the bench, and under his watch the case goes smoothly.

At the conclusion of the evidence phase, Judge Ellis sends the jury out to deliberate. A mere forty-five minutes later, jurors return with a unanimous decision of guilty for the murder and for using a deadly weapon.

But now someone notices that there are thirteen jurors in the jury box. The alternate juror, who had sat through the entire trial next to the other jurors, had been officially dismissed by the judge as the jurors filed out to deliberate. But the usual bailiff had called in sick, and the substitute bailiff was confused about whether the alternate juror was to remain in the jury room during deliberations or be excluded.

Because of the presence of the thirteenth juror, the judge feels compelled to invalidate the jury's decision.

Freed for Stabbing Murder Because of Clerical Error

In 1978 Henry Lee Thomas is living with Dorothy Terrell in Chicago.[3] On the night of October 15, the couple gets into a fight about their relationship, after which Terrell goes to bed and falls asleep. Still angry, Thomas takes a knife from the kitchen and plunges the blade into Terrell's neck. She wakes up and gasps, "Why did you do this, I love you."[4] To silence her, Thomas punches her twice in the mouth and then stabs her multiple times in the chest. He then takes a pillow and holds it against Terrell's face, smothering her until she goes limp. For the next three days, Thomas keeps Terrell's body hidden in his apartment. He then wraps her nude body in a quilt, keeping the quilt in place with an electric cord, and hides the body hid in a nearby wooded area.

Terrell's body is discovered on October 21. Because Thomas was the last person seen with Terrell, he becomes a suspect and, after some investigation, is arrested and asked to take a polygraph test, which he fails. After being read his Miranda rights, Thomas confesses to the police. Based on the evidence, a jury convicts Thomas at trial of the murder of Terrell.

Thomas appeals the decision, and in 1984 the appellate court rules that Thomas must be given a new trial because certain incriminating testimony, as well as the polygraph results, should have been excluded from trial. Following its usual practice, the appellate court conveys its decision to the lower court through a letter, notifying the lower court that a retrial is required.

The clerk of the lower court receives the appellate court's letter on November 9, 1984, but fails to notify the lower court or the prosecutor of the reversal and the need for a retrial. The defense counsel knows of the reversal on appeal and watches the days pass, during which no new trial date is set, but the defense counsel never advises the court or the prosecutor of the clerk's error.

After 120 days pass, Thomas's lawyers argue that his right to a speedy trial has been violated and he must be freed without prosecution. Even though Thomas's lawyers, so concerned about a speedy trial, could have gotten one immediately if they'd asked, the judge nonetheless grants their motion, and Thomas walks free, despite his earlier conviction for murder. When he hears that his case is being dismissed, Thomas smiles and shakes his lawyers' hands.[5]

In some cases, it is not an obscure technical rule that a court allows to pervert justice but rather outright trickery by a defendant or defense counsel, which the court goes along with, seeming to take a this-is-a-game view of the criminal justice system.

Defense Agrees to Delays, Then Seeks Dismissal for Lack of a Speedy Trial

In August 1992, Kevin Healy picks up a hitchhiker, Laura Sage, while driving through Cicero, Illinois.[6] For forty dollars, Sage has sex with Healy. Three months later, Healy's wife goes to Minnesota for treatment at the Mayo Clinic, so Healy drives back to Cicero to visit Sage. At a hotel he again pays her for sex, and the arrangement continues throughout the following week. Sage uses the money to purchase various narcotics. At the end of the week, Healy invites Sage back to his house, where the two continue the cycle of sex and drugs.

However, the arrangement soon falls apart. Disputes arise about how much Sage is to be paid for having sex. The dispute comes to a head one day when Sage is riding in the back of Healy's van. He stops, gets in the back with her, kneels on top of her, grabs her shirt, and tells her to "get out of my truck . . . get out of my life."[7] When Sage sasses him, Healy beats her with a flashlight, strangles her with a plastic tie strap, and stabs her to death. He disposes of her body in the Chicago River. Police discover her corpse several days later.

Detectives question Healy, since he had been seen with her during the past week. After an interview at police headquarters, Healy fails a polygraph test and eventually makes a statement, incriminating himself in Sage's murder. He is arrested and, on December 29, 1992, indicted for first-degree murder.

At Healy's arraignment, he requests a bail hearing, which is set for January 20, 1993. Healy's attorney files a discovery motion (a demand to obtain records and information from the other side), and the court gives the state forty-five days to complete discovery. Healy's attorney requests a return to court on March 16 after discovery is complete. The state requests blood, saliva, and hair samples from Healy, and the judge allows six weeks to complete the analysis. The judge asks Healy's attorney if a May 6 court date is acceptable. Counsel responds, "I have no problem with any date in May, Judge."[8]

Because the Speedy Trial Act sets limits on how long a trial can be delayed without the defendant's agreement, the judge in this case wants to make sure he understands what the defense counsel is saying. He specifically asks whether the date is "a by-agreement date or are you saying you want time to file your motions, too?" The defense counsel responds again, "Any date in May, we will be here."[9]

On May 6 the state requests additional time because the state forensic lab has not yet finished analyzing Healy's samples. Due to scheduling conflicts between the two attorneys and the judge, the court eventually proposes the date of August 26. The judge asks the defense counsel if this date will work for him. Counsel answers, "Whatever date is convenient for you."[10] On August 26 an additional extension for analysis is similarly requested and granted. Healy's attorney suggests the date of September 17. At no point in the process does Healy or his counsel object to any of the delays in the trial.

By September 17, 185 days have passed since the initial hearing. The prosecution has finally obtained its forensics report, but the court decides to give the defense time to file pretrial motions and sets October 14 as the date by which all motions must be filed. Healy files the motions by the October date; among them is one for permanent dismissal because delays have violated the Speedy Trial Act of Illinois. Under the act, Healy is entitled to have a trial within 120 days from when he is taken into custody, unless he agrees to a delay. The trial judge strongly feels that there has never been any indication that the extensions occurred without agreement. Indeed, his court reporter's documents, which were available to the defense counsel, contain explicit annotations that show the defense's agreement to all extensions. The judge denies the motion. At trial, Healy is convicted of first-degree murder and sentenced to thirty years in prison for the brutal murder of Laura Sage.

On appeal, however, the appellate court judge accepts Healy's argument that his speedy trial rights have been violated and unconditionally dismisses his conviction. This judge honors the tricky deceptions of the defense counsel, as if the criminal justice process is a game to be won by the cleverest players. Sage's brutal murderer is free. Healy is released back into society a free man.

No doubt each of these judges would have a reasoned explanation in support of the decision he or she made, as would the appellate judges who constructed the rules being applied here.[11] That is, there is no reason to think that these judgments are being made in bad faith. The explanation for the decisions that the ordinary citizen is likely to come to is more basic and more frightening: too many judges have lost an understanding of the criminal justice system as being in the business of doing justice. Actual fairness is seen as being replaced in the judges' minds by a mess of technical rules. And justice has dropped out of the equation as being of little importance.

SUPPRESSING RELIABLE EVIDENCE

A common practice that is seen by ordinary citizens as regularly perverting justice is the suppression of evidence even if it is highly reliable. Every time this occurs, the criminal justice system is seen as announcing to the community that it values other things as more important than doing justice. The system announces that it is prepared to distort the "truth" presented at trial in order to promote some other interest. And these distortions are perceived as being preferred no matter how serious the offense, no matter how trivial the violation, and no matter that the competing interest, such as controlling police and prosecutors, could be promoted as effectively or even more effectively in a less justice-frustrating way.

The Fifth Amendment of the Constitution provides that no person "shall be compelled in any criminal case to be a witness against himself, nor be deprived of life, liberty, or property, without due process of law." From this broad language, the courts have created a specific, demanding rule that may exclude from use at trial even highly probative and reliable incriminating statements if they were made during interrogation while a defendant was in police custody.[12] The concern is that suspects in custody can be coerced into incriminating themselves. Thus, before suspects in custody can be questioned, they must be "Mirandized": they are told that they have no obligation to talk to police; that if they say anything, it can be used against them in court; that they have the right to have counsel present; and that one will be provided if the suspect does not have one. To help enforce this rule, courts will exclude statements made to police who have not given a suspect a Miranda warning. No Miranda warning is required and no exclusion of incriminating statements occurs if the defendant is not in custody at the time or if the statements are made spontaneously rather than in response to police questioning. These are the court-constructed rules offered to operationalize the constitutional admonition that a person not be compelled to incriminate himself.

But just as the courts made up the original rule, they have also created the definition of what counts as being in custody or what counts as being a response to an interrogation. The suppression of reliable evidence commonly can occur if any of the countless technical niceties of Miranda rules have not been satisfied, no matter how trivial the violation and no matter the absence of any actual unfairness to the defendant.

Murder Confession Suppressed Because an Officer Did Not Regive the Miranda Warning after Placing Incriminating Evidence in Front of the Defendant

On December 5, 1975, in Queens, New York, eighty-four-year-old Lillian Sher is sitting in her home when Alfio Ferro and Thomas Lewis break in.[13] They subdue Sher, tightly bind her hands and feet, and stuff a piece of cloth into her mouth to prevent her from crying for help. Ferro and Lewis then loot the residence of valuables, including some furs. When they flee, they leave Sher bound. With the cloth firmly lodged in her throat, Sher dies of asphyxiation. Authorities find her body six days later.

The investigation puts Ferro and Lewis on the list of possible suspects, and police bring the pair to the station for questioning in connection with Sher's murder. They are questioned separately, and each man is read his Miranda rights. Ferro refuses to answer any questions. Lewis confesses. An officer drives to Lewis's house and retrieves the stolen furs that Lewis has told them about. Without saying anything, the officer places the furs in front of Ferro's cell, "a foot away from him. With nothing else said, Ferro immediately asks to speak with an Italian detective."[14] He tells the detective that Sher's neighbor approached him and told him that she wanted to have Sher robbed as a matter of revenge. She asked if he or anyone he knew would be interested in doing the job, to which Ferro responded he did. After confessing, Ferro pleads to the detective, "I just can't do a lot of time."[15] The officers then book Ferro for homicide and robbery.

At trial, Ferro's confession to the police is a key piece of evidence. The jury finds him guilty of robbery and second-degree murder.

On appeal, Ferro challenges the admissibility of his confession. He claims that it should be suppressed because the police should have read him his Miranda warning a second time when they placed the stolen furs in front of him. The Court of Appeals of the State of New York agrees to his claim and overturns his conviction. The court also rules that if Ferro is tried again, his confession must be hidden from the jury. Knowing this would make a successful retrial unlikely, prosecutors are compelled to let the murderer plead guilty only to robbery. His time served while awaiting trial is his only punishment. As the trial ends, Ferro immediately walks free with no punishment for his murder of Lillian Sher.[16]

A similar justice-frustrating distortion of the truth is seen to occur when important incriminating physical evidence is suppressed at trial because of some technical violation of the intricate search and seizure rules. Like the Fifth Amendment, discussed above, the Fourth Amendment's broad language—"the right of the people . . . against unreasonable searches and seizures, shall not be violated"—has been translated by the courts into a complex set of rules governing when police may search or arrest a suspect. More importantly, the courts have added their own rule that a police violation of these intricate rules will result in excluding from trial the evidence seized—the so-called exclusionary rule—no matter how serious the offense, no matter how trivial the violation, and no matter that the violation causes no actual unfairness to the defendant.

Multiple Murderer-Torturer Released to Kill Again because He Was Held Too Long for Questioning about His Suspicious Behavior

In 1982 and 1983 thirty-year-old Larry Eyler has picked up and then tortured, mutilated, and murdered eighteen young men.[17] Police have come to suspect Eyler in the killings and have begun trying to follow him during his nighttime drives, but they have insufficient proof on which they can arrest him for the murders. Early one morning, a state highway trooper, who is unaware of the investigation, happens upon Eyler parked on the side of the highway. The trooper makes a U-turn and intercepts Eyler as he and his passenger, now back in Eyler's pickup, are attempting to leave. Unknown to the trooper, Eyler is in the process of coaxing an intended victim, Daryl Haywood, into the woods with a promise of money for sex. Eyler has brought along his usual torture kit of rope and tape. The trooper becomes suspicious when Eyler seems evasive in his answers to questions and seems to try to hide the kit he is carrying when the trooper first sees him.

The trooper radios his headquarters to ask about Eyler, and his call is overheard by the investigators who had been following Eyler earlier that night but lost him. They rush to the scene and bring Eyler and his truck back to the station for further investigation. Haywood confesses that they were about to have sex for pay. Eyler gives the police permission to take his boots, which the investigators have noticed matched the imprints left at the previous murder scene. He also gives permission for them to search his truck, in which they find clothesline and surgical tape like those used in previous murders, as well as a bloody knife.

Police do not arrest Eyler but instead release him and his truck later that day. However, they do obtain a warrant to search his apartment, where they find handcuffs, credit card receipts, and phone records that tie him directly to previous murders, as does subsequent laboratory analyses of the seized evidence. Police then arrest Eyler for the murders.

However, the court orders his release and orders that all evidence

Fig. 4.1. Larry Eyler was captured and then released from police custody, 1984. (Courtesy of Illinois police)

be suppressed. According to the judge, the officers had the right to stop Eyler but did not have sufficient probable cause to take him into custody. In the view of the judge, Eyler had effectively been arrested the moment they took him into custody and the evidence at hand did not justify the quasi-arrest for murder. The judge suppresses not only the evidence that had been taken with his permission but also the evidence obtained in a search of his apartment under warrant because the warrant was based upon the earlier evidence. Thus, all of the incriminating evidence from Eyler's house must be excluded under the doctrine of the "fruit of the poisonous tree." Although the evidence of multiple murder-tortures is overwhelming, Eyler is allowed to walk free.

As he watches Eyler get into a car and drive off, an outraged Lake County sheriff, Robert Babcox, complains, "He's freed to kill. Hell, it's only a matter of time."[18] Sheriff Babcox is right. Several months after his release, Eyler returns to his killing habits, murdering several more people, including a brutal attack on a fifteen-year-old male prostitute, Danny Bridges. Once he is in Eyler's control, Bridges is tortured. Death comes when Eyler, using a butcher knife, cuts into Bridges's abdomen and back, until he perforates Bridges's heart and left lung. Eyler uses a hacksaw to cut the boy up into eight separate pieces, which he drops into a Dumpster.[19]

DECISION MAKERS BLIND TO JUSTICE

The criminal justice system vests enormous discretion in decision makers—sentencing judges, members of parole commissions, and governors (exercising their pardon power)—to determine the punishment that is just and appropriate for an offender. Yet, in practice, many of these decision makers are seen as apparently indifferent to the importance of doing justice, and some of them exercise their punishment discretion in ways that the ordinary citizen would find to be an appalling failure of justice.

Parole boards have the power to release prisoners early but do not always exercise this power in a way that ensures that justice is done and the community protected.

Previously Paroled Twice, Once for Homicide, Kills Yet Another During a Drug Deal

At age seventeen, Cornelius Ferguson shoots and kills a man in a Chester, Pennsylvania, bar.[20] Convicted of third-degree murder, Ferguson serves a stint in prison, where he is known for being extremely hostile toward prison guards, including threatening to kill and seriously injure them. After five years, he is paroled.

Within a year of his release, he shoots and wounds another man. He is again arrested and found guilty of aggravated assault and the criminal attempt to commit murder. Although the criminal attempt charge is eventually vacated, Ferguson is sent back to prison for the assault.

In 1991 Ferguson is again released early on parole, even though he has already shot two people, killing one of them and violating his parole by shooting another.

Just as after his first release, Ferguson immediately obtains a firearm and within a year is involved in another shooting. In June 1991 he shoots and wounds another Chester resident. Police charge him with the assault, but, inexplicably, he is allowed to keep the gun.

Two months later, Ferguson and another man, Tyrone Hyland, go to the Tri-State Mall in Claymont, Delaware, to meet Troy Hodges, a twenty-two-year-old college student. Hodges is accompanied by a seventeen-year-old friend. The meeting is to consummate an illegal drug transaction, in which Hodges will pay Ferguson and Hyland $10,000 for a half kilogram of cocaine. However, Ferguson and Hyland plan to simply rob Hodges rather than deliver the narcotics.

Hodges leaves his friend in his car and takes two plastic bags filled with $5,000 each to Hyland's car. Hodges gets into the front passenger seat beside Hyland. Ferguson is in the back. The three begin discussing the cocaine deal, but the discussion quickly turns into a heated argument. Ferguson points a cocked gun at Hodges's head. As the car drives slowly in the vicinity of the mall and the argument continues, Hodges attempts to exit the car, but Ferguson shoots Hodges point-blank in the back of the head. He then pushes Hodges out of the moving car and onto the pavement. Stumbling, Hodges makes it a few feet before he collapses and dies from a massive hemorrhage.[21]

Many judges also are seen as exercising poor judgment, often biased by personal or local prejudices, sometimes blaming the victim, and at other times showing sympathy for offenders far beyond what the facts of the case can justify.

Two Racists Who Hunt Down an Asian Man and Kill Him with a Baseball Bat Get Probation

A week before his wedding, Vincent Chin, a young Chinese American, is enjoying his bachelor party with friends at the Fancy Pants Lounge, a suburban Detroit club, on a summer evening in 1982. As the party goes on around the elevated dance floor, where club dancers strip to hard rock music, Chin encounters two recently laid-off autoworkers, Ronald Ebens and his stepson Michael Nitz. Ebens, a seventeen-year veteran supervisor at the local Chrysler plant, erroneously assumes Chin is of Japanese descent. Upset about losing his job and blaming the auto industry's decline on the Japanese, Ebens, followed by his stepson, approaches Chin.[22]

"It's because of you little motherfuckers that we're out of work," Ebens yells at Chin, referring to the growing success of Japanese imports in America.[23] Anti-Japanese sentiment, especially among autoworkers, is rampant in the Detroit area. The local United Automobile Workers (UAW) Union headquarters has a large billboard outside its offices that reads, "300,000 laid off UAW members don't like your import. Please park it in Tokyo."[24] These are the sentiments that fuel Ebens as he continues to berate Chin with racially charged epithets, including "jap," "chink," and others. Ebens's verbal attacks escalate into a brawl, in which Nitz joins his stepfather. Ebens picks up a chair and swings it at Chin, who successfully deflects it into Nitz.

Fig. 4.2. Vincent Chin in his early twenties. (Courtesy of Helen Zia/ Estates of Vincent and Lily Chin)

The Fancy Pants Lounge bouncer stops the hostilities long enough to eject the trio from the club, but the confrontation continues in the parking lot. As Nitz stands bleeding, Ebens runs to his car to retrieve his baseball bat. He returns and moves forward to strike at Chin and his friends, who flee.

The father and stepson get into Ebens's car and begin cruising the neighborhood, searching for Chin. They pick up an unemployed man on the street and give him twenty dollars to help find those "Chinese guys."[25] Twenty minutes later, Ebens, Nitz, and their newly hired man spot Chin and his friends two blocks away outside a McDonald's.

Ebens gets out of his car, baseball bat in hand, and begins striking Chin repeatedly. Chin manages to stagger a few feet away before collapsing in the street. Ebens follows and stands over his victim. Chin looks at his friends, who are nearby, and utters his last words: "It isn't fair. . . ."[26] Ebens strikes Chin twice more, bashing in Chin's skull. Police arrive and stop the laid-off autoworker, but Chin is already brain-dead. The doctors officially declare him dead four days later at Henry Ford Hospital.

Ebens and Nitz are charged with second-degree murder. The duo is popular in the auto industry–centric Detroit, especially among those living in their Eastpointe neighborhood. After both men are released on bail, prosecutors offer them a plea bargain. If they plead to manslaughter, they may still serve fifteen years in prison but will sidestep the potential life imprisonment that second-degree murder will entail. Ebens and Nitz take the deal. Chin's mother, who fled Communist China to come to America, is never consulted.

At sentencing, a probation officer provides the judge with a presentencing report recommending a prison term at minimum. However, the judge ignores the officer's recommendation and sentences Ebens and Nitz to three years of probation. They are also ordered to pay a $3,000 fine and $780 in court fees. When asked about his verdict, the judge explains, "These weren't the kind of men you sent to jail. . . . You don't make the punishment fit the crime: you make the punishment fit the criminal."[27]

Husband Who Drugged and Raped His Wife for Years Gets Home Detention as Judge Tells Wife She "Needs to Forgive"

In 2005 in Indianapolis, Indiana, David Wise begins to drug his wife, Mandy Boardman, either by slipping a substance into her drink before she goes to sleep or by placing pills directly in her mouth while she sleeps.[28] Boardman later reports that there were times when she woke up feeling like "her body had been 'messed with,'" but during this time she is unaware of the rapes.[29]

In 2008 she comes across videos on Wise's cell phone of him raping her while she is in a drug-induced state. She makes a copy of the videos to have tangible proof that Wise repeatedly sexually attacked her from 2005 to 2008. She files for divorce, but she does not immediately take the videos to the police because she does not want her children to suffer the humiliation of a public display of the videos or the shame of seeing their father in prison.

After the divorce, however, Wise harasses her. She reports the incident to the police. In 2009 Boardman becomes involved with another man and becomes engaged. Wise threatens to kill her new fiancé. Boardman files for a protective order against Wise and later shows the police the videos that she had found back in 2008. The police investigation lasts until 2014.

In April 2014 the fifty-two-year-old David Wise is formally charged with rape and criminal deviate conduct for repeatedly drugging and raping his wife. A jury finds him guilty of rape and five counts of criminal deviate conduct, each of which carries a term of between six and twenty years in prison. Prosecutors seek a forty-year prison sentence.

Judge Kurt Eisgruber, however, gives a suspended sentence with eight years of home detention. Wise will serve no prison time for his repeated rapes of his wife. The judge also tells Boardman that she "needs to forgive her attacker."[30]

The sentence and the judge's advice to Boardman spark outrage within the victim, the prosecution, and the greater Indiana community. Boardman calls the sentence and the judge's comments "a punch to the gut." She adds, "[Wise] will continue to harass me and cause me as much pain in my life as he can. . . . I don't feel like he deserves to sit at home and watch TV and eat ice cream. . . . He deserves to spend many years in prison." Catherine O'Connor, the president of a support center for victims of domestic violence, says, "When these crimes don't appear to be taken seriously, then we'll be worried that victims will be worried to come forward to report these crimes." A local law professor explains, "Many people don't even report sexual assaults and rape because they're afraid of stigma, because they're afraid of being locked into a legal proceeding with a person they're scared of. But if he's going to get sentenced to house arrest, basically, what's the incentive?"[31] The editor of the *Indianapolis Star* writes that the sentence "is a slap in the face to all victims of sexual abuse."[32]

Pardon decisions by presidents and governors can be a method to right legal wrongs, but they also can be a source of perceived failures of justice. Chief executives are sometimes seen as ignoring justice to obtain some political advantage or personal benefit.

Puerto Rican Terrorists Who Attacked the United States 120 Times Are Pardoned by the President before Election in Which Hispanic Voters Are Key

The Fuerzas Armadas de Liberación Nacional (FALN) is a Puerto Rican terrorist organization formed in the 1960s dedicated to bringing Communism to Puerto Rico, by force if necessary.[33] The group's primary focus is on what they see as the foundations of capitalism in the United States. On January 24, 1975, a member of the FALN stuffs ten pounds of dynamite in a suitcase and places it in the entrance hallway of the historic Fraunces Tavern in New York City. A group of Wall Street bankers are dining on the second floor of the restaurant when the massive explosion rocks the building at 1:29 p.m.

When firefighters arrive on the scene, they describe it as "utter havoc," with dismembered people and pools of blood covering the rubble on the ground.[34] A FALN member calls the Associated Press and claims the explosion to be the work of the FALN. Harold Sherburne, Frank Connor, and Alejandro Berger are killed instantly; James Gezork lives until he reaches the hospital, but he cannot be saved. More than fifty other people are injured.

On August 3, 1977, another FALN member places a bomb in a building on Madison Avenue in New York City that explodes at 11:30 a.m. Another bomb placed in the Mobil Building on East Forty-Second Street explodes one hour later. Charles Steinberg is killed, and eight other people are injured. The FALN warns that its members have placed additional bombs in other buildings around the city, including the Empire State Building and the World Trade Center. Panic ensues, and nearly one hundred thousand workers are evacuated from buildings downtown. To increase the terror, FALN members call numerous bomb threats into police.[35]

In all, the organization is responsible for over 120 attacks across the United States between 1974 and 1983.[36] The federal government eventually captures and convicts a number of FALN members, who receive prison terms ranging from 35 to 105 years.[37]

The FALN movement and prisoners have an appeal for some members of both the Puerto Rican and the greater Hispanic communities who would like Puerto Rico to be independent of the United States. While this group is a minority in Puerto Rico—in 1999 2.6 percent of the island's population voted to sever its association with the United States—the movement nonetheless resonates with some voters sympathetic to the poor in Puerto Rico.[38]

In 1999 Hillary Clinton is running for the US Senate for New York, and Vice President Al Gore is running for president to succeed Bill Clinton. Hispanic voters are seen as key in the New York race and also in the presidential race, in which Florida is thought to be a pivotal state. This turns out to be a bit of an understatement.

On August 11, 1999, President Clinton, stating that he feels that their continued incarceration will not serve any purpose,[39] grants clemency to sixteen of the FALN members who were convicted in the earlier terrorist attacks.[40] The pardoned members have been linked to more than one hundred bombings or attempted bombings since 1974 and have been convicted of offenses ranging from bomb making to conspiracy to armed robbery to firearms violations.[41]

Clinton's actions are met with criticism by many groups, including the US Attorney's Office, the FBI, the Federal Bureau of Prisons, and the former victims of FALN terrorism.[42] Joe Connor, the son of one of the victims who died in a FALN attack, says, "[My dad] didn't have any qualms with the Puerto Rican people as such. He was just a working guy. He was eating lunch with friends and his life was valued less than that of the election campaign of the president's wife and Al Gore. It's disgusting."[43]

DEFENSES FOR THE GUILTY

Sometimes it is not the poor exercise of discretion by decision makers or misguided judicial procedures that produce perceived failures of justice. Some formal liability doctrines, many of them judicially created, offer guilty offenders a complete defense against criminal liability, no matter how serious the offense or how blameworthy the offender. That is, the legal "defense" often applies no matter how clear the offender's guilt nor how serious the crime.

The judicial interpretation of the Constitution's Double Jeopardy Clause, part of the Fifth Amendment, is sometimes seen as stretching that defense far beyond what fairness or other societal interests can justify.

Prior Acquittal Obtained by Perjury Bars Torture-Murder-Rape Caught on Film

It is 1988 in Louisville, Kentucky. Brenda Schaefer has become afraid of Melvin Ignatow, whom she has been dating but with whom she would like to break up.[44] Ignatow is unhappy about her desire to break up and arranges a final meeting with Schaefer. He also arranges with a former girlfriend, Mary Ann Shore, to help him with what he plans to do to Schaefer at this final meeting.

Fig. 4.3. Melvin Ignatow with Brenda Schaefer, 1988. (Courtesy of the family of Brenda Schaefer)

Ignatow complains to Shore that Schaefer is a "frigid" personality. He wants Shore to help him with a "sex-therapy" session, which he wants to hold at Shore's house.[45] Ignatow also asks Shore to help him dig a hole in her backyard that is big enough for a person. When Shore resists, Ignatow assures her that he just wants to scare Schaefer. The pair test Shore's house to gauge whether screams can be heard outside. In preparation for the meeting, Ignatow brings to Shore's house a wooden paddle, a camera, film, plastic garbage bags, a vibrator, lubricating jelly, tape, a pair of gloves, rope, and a bottle of chloroform.

Ignatow, using a ruse, gets Schaefer to Shore's home. Ignatow sits Schaefer down on the couch and explains his sex therapy idea. Schaefer attempts to leave, but Ignatow forces her back down on the couch. Ignatow tells her that "she [needs] to have this because she [is] just very cold-natured, and he needs that sex."[46] Ignatow has written a checklist of all his planned steps on a yellow piece of paper. Over several hours he tortures the young woman. Schaefer cries during the assault and begins screaming when Ignatow beats her with a wooden paddle. Ignatow pours chloroform onto a handkerchief and covers Schaefer's mouth and nose until she appears to be dead. Uncertain whether she is dead, Ignatow ties a rope tightly around her neck and chokes her. Ignatow folds Schaefer's body into a fetal position and secures it tightly with ropes. With Shore's assistance, he wraps Schaefer in garbage bags and buries her in the backyard.

Joyce, Schaefer's coworker, eventually provides investigators with some key information. She knows a hairstylist who has cut Ignatow's hair. The stylist says she knows a woman named Mary Ann Shore who has confided in her about Ignatow's controlling nature and her inability to get over her relationship with him. Robert Spoelker, who pays Shore to babysit his children, tells authorities that Shore had taken September 24 off from work. A background check reveals that Shore has five outstanding arrest warrants for bad checks.

Shore is questioned by the police and takes a polygraph test, which she fails. When Officer Jim Wesley confronts her with her test results, she becomes agitated and refuses to say more. Wesley allows her to leave and arranges for an officer to follow her. That night, the officer watches Shore and Ignatow as they walk in the rain. The officer notifies Wesley, and an unmarked police car pulls up next to the couple and asks them to come to the station. At the station, Wesley grills Shore, demanding to know the full story, but Shore refuses to say what she knows. Wesley senses that Shore wants to say something, so he pulls out all the stops, threatening her with prosecution for the bad checks. She still refuses to talk, and at 12:45 a.m. on February 14, 1989, Shore is fingerprinted and put in jail for the outstanding bad-check warrants. She is released on bail.

Some months later, Shore is called to testify before a federal grand jury. US Attorney Scott Cox asks Shore how many times she had seen Schaefer before her disappearance. Shore replies each time that she had seen Schaefer only once. When Cox later asks what Schaefer looked like the time Shore saw her, she responds, "You mean the last time?"[47] When Cox points out the discrepancy in Shore's statements, Shore turns pale and leaves the jury room. On January 9, 1990, Shore confesses to the FBI and the police that she was present when Ignatow killed Schaefer at Shore's house. Leading the police into the woods behind the house, Shore shows them the area where the body is buried. In return for her cooperation, the authorities agree to limit her charges to tampering with physical evidence.

The following day, the police bring a cadaver dog, and within fifteen minutes the dog picks up a scent. Digging where the dog indicates, the police find a large bag that stores four overlapping plastic bags containing Schaefer's body. A second smaller bag is also unearthed that contains Schaefer's clothing. Decay has erased the facial features, but a forensic odontologist identifies the body of Brenda Schaefer through her dental records.

While police are digging up the body, Shore, wearing a concealed microphone provided by the police, meets with Ignatow and talks of her fears of being found out. Ignatow orders her to resist investigators' requests for a lie detector test and explains how unlikely it is that the body can be found. Ignatow is then arrested and charged with murder, kidnapping, sodomy, sexual abuse, robbery, and tampering with evidence.

On December 3, 1991, Ignatow's jury trial begins. Mary Ann Shore, who the day before pleaded guilty to tampering with physical evidence, testifies as to what happened on that night. Ignatow also testifies, giving a very different story. At the conclusion of Ignatow's trial, on December 21, the jurors begin deliberating. Most believe that Ignatow is involved, but they see Shore as a less believable witness, primarily because Ignatow's attorney portrays her as a vindictive ex-girlfriend. Jurors consider the recorded conversation between Shore and Ignatow to be ambiguous, and Ignatow's testimony has offered innocent explanations for much of the evidence.

Ignatow is acquitted. Walking from the courtroom as a free man, he tells the media, "This is the best Christmas present I ever had."[48] On February 3, 1992, Mary Ann Shore is sentenced to the maximum allowable sentence of five years in prison for tampering with physical evidence.

On October 1, 1992, Ronald and Judith Watkins, who have moved into Ignatow's old house, are having new carpet installed. As part of that process, they remove the vent cover on the heating duct. Behind it, they discover film and jewelry, which they turn over to the FBI. The film includes one hundred photographs of "sexual acts, sadomasochistic bondage, disrobing, and torture of Brenda Sue Schaefer," providing conclusive physical proof of the horrendous things Melvin Ignatow did to Schaefer.[49]

However, even though Ignatow has gained his acquittal by committing perjury in court, the court rules that the double jeopardy bar prevents prosecutors from retrying Ignatow. Ignatow's horrendous murder-rape-torture of Brenda Sue Schaefer is punishment-free.

Another defense that is seen as letting blameworthy offenders go free is diplomatic immunity. No matter the seriousness of the offense, the number of offenses, or the clarity of the offender's blameworthiness, diplomatic immunity can protect an offender even from arrest.

Serial Rapist Finally Caught Walks Free with a Smile Because of Diplomatic Immunity

On January 8, 1981, "Jane" (not her real name) heads home after grocery shopping. Grocery bag in hand, she walks across the street to her apartment building. She stops in the entryway of her building, as always, to check her mailbox before unlocking the inside door. Before the door locks behind her, a young man, who will be identified later as Manuel Ayree, catches it and enters the building. Short but powerfully built, he is dressed nicely in a tie and well-pressed slacks and is carrying keys in his hand. Jane assumes he lives in the building. He leisurely climbs the stairs behind her, lighting a cigarette on his way up. He follows her up to her apartment and approaches the door across the hallway from hers.[50]

As soon as she unlocks her door, Jane feels him press against her back. In a thick accent he says, "Do everything I say or I'll kill you. I have a gun."[51] Jane tells him that she will do anything he wants and pleads with him not to kill her. Although her heart is pounding and her mind is racing, she manages to appear calm so as not to agitate the man. As they enter the kitchen, he grabs a steak knife. Once again, he threatens her, prodding her stomach with it. She offers him money to leave her alone. He ignores the offer and asks if she lives alone. She lies and says that she does not. "If you don't tell me the truth, I am going to kill you. Do you live alone?"[52] he demands. She admits to living alone as she hands him the few dollars she has in her wallet. She hopes that he will leave now. She thinks about telling him that she has a venereal disease to deter any sexual assault, but the words do not surface. He orders her into the studio. The convertible sofa is still open from the previous night. He tells her to take off her pants and lie facedown on the mattress. He pulls down his own pants and enters her anus. She screams from the pain and starts crying. When he withdraws, he wipes himself with her blanket.

Ayree orders Jane to get under her bed and tells her to go to sleep and never wake up. At this point, she is sure that he means to kill her, but then she hears him walk out the door and down the stairs. She picks herself up and eventually telephones the police. She is taken to the emergency rape unit, where she is questioned by police and examined by nurses. After a sleepless night at her friend's apartment, she receives a telephone call from Detective Pete Christiansen asking her to meet him at her apartment. There, she recounts the horrors of the previous night.

Later that winter, Ayree victimizes Carol Holmes, a freelance proofreader in New York, using a similar modus operandi. He enters her building with her before the outside door closes behind her, then approaches her and presses something against her back, warning her that he has a gun and forcing her up the stairs to her apartment. There he grabs a knife off the table and places it under her chin, threatening to kill her if she disobeys. He orders her to take off her clothes and lie down on the mattress in her living room, where he has forcible anal and vaginal sex with her. He then pulls up his pants and heads for the bathroom. She follows him, completely naked, hoping to make him feel uncomfortable enough to leave. He lights a cigarette and burns her with it. Suddenly, they hear a door slam and loud footsteps. Carol recognizes the sounds as a neighbor descending the stairs. Ayree panics and flees. Still naked, Carol runs after him, screaming, "Stop him, stop him; he raped me."[53] There is no response as Ayree escapes. An ambulance takes her to the rape unit of Lenox Hill Hospital, where she is questioned, examined, and given medication. At the police station, she is questioned by Detective Christiansen.

Following the attack, Carol begins to have nightmares of men breaking into her apartment and attacking her. She hears reports that her rapist has been seen by others in the neighborhood, which heightens her fears of another encounter with him. She becomes obsessed with finding her attacker. Every afternoon, Carol scours the neighborhood with her boyfriend, Bruce.

Meanwhile, Detective Christiansen's frustration builds as the rapes continue. Nearly all the rapes occur in the same area, and each time, the rapist's methods are the same: he follows a woman into her apartment building, pretending to be a fellow resident, then forces her into her apartment and rapes her. At least ten such rapes, in addition to Jane's and Carol's, have now been reported. By February 1981, with help from Carol, Jane, and other victims, Detective Christiansen is able to come up with a composite sketch of the rapist. He hands copies of the sketch to undercover agents and tells them to concentrate on the Yorkville neighborhood.

That Friday, Carol and Bruce set out on their daily search for the rapist. They pass a grocery store on the corner of Eighty-Ninth Street and continue past the Carnegie Animal Hospital and the Stuyvesant Square Thrift Shop around the same time that Manuel Ayree leaves his apartment building and walks across Eighty-Ninth Street toward Second Avenue. He is spotted by two undercover policemen in a yellow taxi. They recognize his face from the composite sketch Detective Christiansen gave them. At the same time, Detective Christiansen is heading south on Second Avenue in his unmarked police car. After parking his car on the curb at Eighty-Ninth Street, he gets out and walks over to the corner pay phone. Ayree passes the Carnegie Animal Hospital and the Stuyvesant Square Thrift Shop while the taxi creeps along behind him.

Carol and Bruce, meanwhile, decide to turn around just as they approach Eighty-Eighth Street. As soon as they turn around, Carol sees Ayree walking toward them. She stares at Ayree as he walks by them and tells Bruce that Ayree is the rapist. Immediately, Bruce grabs Ayree, and a fight ensues. Carol rushes to the pay phone on the corner of Eighty-Eighth Street and tells the operator to call 911. The police in the taxicab, as well as Detective Christiansen and two more undercover agents posing as joggers, arrive on the scene. Ayree is shoved into the back seat of the taxicab and taken to the police station.

At the police station, Ayree demands to be released, announcing that he has diplomatic immunity. (Diplomatic immunity allows some diplomats who are serving their own nations to be protected, even from arrest, for violations of their host country's laws. The country of origin can remove an individual's immunity if it chooses—thereby permitting the host country to prosecute the individual—but has no obligation to do so.) Detective Christiansen moves quickly, calling the other victims to come and identify Ayree as their attacker. Christiansen has little luck contacting the victims, but he finally reaches Jane at work. Upon hearing that Ayree has been caught, Jane runs out of her office and heads toward the station. However, members of the Ghanaian mission arrive sooner and identify the rapist as nineteen-year-old Manuel Ayree, son of the third attaché to the mission. Carol confronts the group, recounting her horrible experience. Jane arrives at the police station, where she is introduced to the Ghanaians as another of Ayree's victims. In a viewing room, Jane tells the detective to have Ayree say, "Is it in you ass?"[54] When she hears his voice, she knows for sure that Ayree is the rapist.

About forty-five minutes after arriving at the police station, Manuel Ayree walks out, a free man. "I told you I had diplomatic immunity," he says, snickering. He laughs tauntingly as he walks by Carol on his way out.

On Tuesday morning, a press conference is held in which Ghanaian officials announce that Manuel Ayree will be leaving the United States and will not return. They also announce that the case will be fully investigated in Ghana. He is never investigated or brought to trial in Ghana.

Another doctrine seen as letting offenders go free is the entrapment defense. As with the exclusionary rule discussed earlier an offender can get a free pass if a police officer blunders, even if it is clear that the offender would have committed the offense without the officer's involvement. (The entrapment defense cannot be raised unless the authorities were involved. If an ordinary citizen influences a defendant in the exact same way, the offender would have no entrapment defense.) Consider an example of the kind of case that is likely to upset people.

Sexual Predator Shows Up to Have Sex with a Fourteen-Year-Old but Walks Free because Police Arranged the Meeting

For seven months in 2011, the Volusia County Sheriff's Office in Florida organizes a massive sting operation to catch online sexual predators targeting young boys and girls.[55] The police dub the plan Operation Cyber Sting, in which officers use online chat rooms to make contact with predators and lure them to a location where they think they will have sex with children.

Detective April McCray takes part in the sting operation. During an online chat with forty-four-year-old Florida native Michael Llorca, she invites him to meet with her and her "baby sister" Amber, who is fourteen. McCray asks Llorca if her little sister's age is a problem for him. On the contrary, Llorca writes, "Send me some pics and let's talk!"[56] In later communications Llorca says that he is going to teach Amber, the fourteen-year-old, a number of sexual positions.[57] McCray tells Llorca to meet them several days later at a home in Deltona where both sisters will have sex with him.

On the arranged day, Llorca jumps in his car with his two young daughters and drops them off at his brother's house. He then drives to the house in Deltona, where he parks his car in the driveway. He rings the doorbell, but when the door swings open, he is greeted by two officers, who arrest him.[58]

In December 2013 Llorca faces trial for three felonies arising from the incident: use of a computer to solicit, seduce without a parent's or guardian's consent, traveling to meet a minor, and unlawful use of a communications device. He successfully argues that he was entrapped by the authorities, and he receives the defense and walks free.

The prosecutor is appalled; Llorca was clearly told that the girl was fourteen and, with that knowledge, got in his car and drove to their home. He reminds the court what was and what was not in the emails: "You are not going to read anywhere where he says '14 are you crazy? That's illegal. Goodbye. I'm not interested.' That's not in there."[59]

One final doctrine of this sort are statutes of limitations, which require cases to be brought to trial within a certain length of time after the crime. The amount of time varies by the severity of the crime and by jurisdiction. Statutes of limitations can block justice, even for serious offenses, even if the community remains upset about the offense, and even if the offender has continued in his criminal ways ever since the original offense. This doctrine is a common source of disillusionment.

Murder Mitigation to Manslaughter Triggers Statute of Limitations and therefore Bars all Liability

In 2002 Samuel Ciapa is a small-time pot dealer in western New York State.[60] He is in a dispute with two other drug dealers, Alan Tomaski and Michael Hesse. On August 16 the men lure Ciapa to a reservoir, a place where people gather to drink during the summer outside Buffalo. When Ciapa arrives, Hesse overpowers him and holds him down while Tomaski savagely and repeatedly stabs him and then strangles him to death. Tomaski and Hesse tie Ciapa's body to a cinder block and throw it into the reservoir.

When the police discover Ciapa's body, Tomaski has already fled to West Virginia. From 2002 to 2005 Tomaski spends some of his time in New York and the rest in West Virginia, where he is incarcerated on multiple occasions for various minor offenses.

The case goes cold for nearly eight years. Eventually, Tomaski emerges as a suspect, and the police obtain a warrant to search his New York home and obtain additional evidence. On June 10, 2010, Tomaski and Hesse are charged with second-degree murder. Hesse agrees to testify against Tomaski and is allowed to plead guilty to the lesser charge of first-degree manslaughter. Tomaski pleads not guilty, and the case goes to trial.

Before the trial begins, the prosecution asks the judge to instruct the jury on the legal meaning of both the offense of second-degree murder and the lesser offense of first-degree manslaughter. The defense objects to including the lesser offense, thinking that they have a better chance of getting an acquittal if the only choice presented to the jury is murder or not guilty. The jury finds Tomaski guilty of the lesser offense of first-degree manslaughter, and he is sent to prison.

On appeal, Tomaski's attorney asks that his conviction be reversed and that he be permanently discharged. He argues that while there is no statute of limitations for murder, which is the primary offense for which he was charged, New York does have a statute of limitations for manslaughter, the lesser offense for which he is ultimately convicted. Under the statute of limitations, the defendant must be charged within five years of committing the offense, excluding anytime during which he was not within the state of New York. In fact, Tomaski was charged seven years and ten months after the offense and had been out of the state for two years and five months. Thus, the state missed its opportunity to prosecute him by five months. Even though Tomaski had opposed giving manslaughter instruction to the jury at trial, the appellate court directs that he should be given an unconditional and permanent discharge.

As with the previous rules and practices, advocates of these rules could give an explanation in support of such defenses for guilty offenders. Some of these doctrines can claim to promote legitimate interests, but it is also frequently the case that people would want those interests promoted in some less justice-frustrating way.[61] More importantly, every time a guilty offender is given a defense there is a hidden cost. Each such case may be seen as announcing the criminal justice system's apparent indifference to the value of doing justice—giving offenders the punishment they deserve, no more and no less.[62]

Should the law care that its reputation for giving importance to doing justice is damaged? The previous chapter has already shown the danger of the shadow vigilantism sparked by perceived failures of justice, and parts III and IV will give more detail about why the system should very much care about getting a reputation for regularly producing failures of justice.

Part II

THE DANGERS OF EVEN MORAL VIGILANTISM

Readers have hopefully come to see that vigilantism is something considerably more nuanced than the evil incarnate that its Ku Klux Klan paradigm might suggest. Some vigilantes may well be morally if not legally justified in what they do, as chapter 2 illustrates.

One may be tempted to mark out these two importantly different categories as "moral vigilantes" and "immoral vigilantes," but as will become apparent in this part, such a simple distinction may not be possible. First, as chapter 5 will show, it is not so easy to construct a clear, workable code of conduct for the moral vigilante. There remain fuzzy lines.

Further, even if one could construct a clear, detailed code of conduct, it is an inevitable weakness of vigilante action that, once the red line of criminal prohibition has been crossed, it is easy for even the well-meaning vigilante to lose track of where the boundaries of moral justification lie, as chapter 6 illustrates. Finally, and perhaps most compellingly, even if the vigilante is successful in staying within the boundaries of moral justification, it is commonly the case that his or her conduct nonetheless may remain problematic for the larger society, a theme that chapter 7 explores.

The bottom line is that official action is always to be preferred over vigilante action. But it does not follow that the moral vigilante must simply suffer in silence. First, this may not be possible. Strong feelings of disillusionment may spark action no matter what the law threatens. Further, asking moral vigilantes to suffer in silence is a poor crime-control strategy because it can provoke shadow vigilantes to undermine the system, as chapter 3 explains (and part III will detail).

But more importantly, suffering in silence ought not to be asked. The government has clear obligations with respect to safeguarding its citizens under its social contract with the people it governs, and it is not free to simply choose not to perform them. The criminal justice system ought to take seriously its obligation to assure that justice is done and crime avoided whenever possible so that people are never put in the position of having to consider moral vigilantism.

5

TEN RULES FOR THE MORAL VIGILANTE

If people are confronted with a criminal justice system that seems grossly insensitive to the importance of doing justice, what are they to do? Is it possible to define what would and would not constitute moral vigilante action—to define a *vigilante code* that sets the preconditions for and the limits of legitimate conduct?

If a group were contemplating vigilante action, here are ten rules one could suggest to members of such a group or community to help them choose action that stays closer to what is morally defensible. Vigilante action is never legally justified (if it were, by definition it would not be vigilante action), but if a group follows these ten rules, its conduct might at least be viewed by outsiders as being nearly morally justified.

1. DON'T ACT UNLESS THERE IS A SERIOUS FAILURE OF JUSTICE

Any vigilante action will be disruptive. It cannot justify itself unless it produces more benefit than the disruption itself costs. For example, a pattern of petty thefts by youngsters in a marketplace is not likely to justify the social disruption of vigilante action, unless that action is itself of little or no disruption, even if the police are lazy and indifferent and could solve the problem if they chose to do so.

2. DON'T CAUSE MORE HARM THAN IS NECESSARY AND JUST, AND AVOID INJURY TO INNOCENT BYSTANDERS

Part of doing justice means recognizing that society has an interest in minimizing damage to all, even unlawful aggressors. If a person's safety and property can be protected with a punch, it ought not to be defended with a gunshot. Clearly, harm to innocent bystanders ought to be avoided at all costs. Consider an example of how easy it is to violate this rule.

The Legion of Doom

In 1984 Paschal High School in Fort Worth, Texas, is facing a problem of petty theft from student lockers and drug use by some students.[1] The problem does not go unnoticed, nor is it resolved. The school principal appoints a group of students, called the Ambassadors, to serve as hall monitors and to report suspicious activity. This intervention does not fix the problem. Students continue to express frustration at the inability of school officials to stop the problem, noting that "we could get a jacket stolen or something. You could be walking down the hall and [the thief] would have your jacket on. You could prove it, but they (school officials) wouldn't do anything about it."[2]

Not seeing any other ways to stop the problem, a subset of the Ambassadors, joined by several other students, forms a group called the Legion of Doom. Its members are seen as model students from affluent families; some are star athletes, while others are members of the school's honor roll.

By December the Legion of Doom concludes that it must undertake its own independent campaign. Initially, the group is interested in "trying to scare some of the kids they suspect of being involved in drug pushing and stealing."[3] The Legion focuses its attention on a group known as Fire It Up, fellow students known for putting partying above all else.

The Legion leaves warning notes for the targeted students. The notes have no more effect than previous efforts. Now, more frustrated than before, Legion members escalate their activities. They begin carrying firearms to school as a means by which to intimidate the troublemakers. Bringing guns to class does not end their efforts. They build a pipe bomb and a homemade rocket launcher and shoot out the windshield of one student's car. Legion members also kill and disembowel a cat, leaving the bloody remains smeared on the seats of another student's car. The body of the dead cat is draped on the steering wheel.

Fig. 5.1. The turf that the Legion of Doom sought to protect, 1985. (Courtesy of Wikimedia Creative Commons, Dark Serge at English Wikipedia, licensed under CC BY 3.0)

While these acts are clearly illegal, the Legion's members see themselves as preventing further decline to their society, harm to innocent students, and chaos in the school.

With the advent of these more violent activities, law enforcement authorities begin to investigate the group's activities. After some serious investigation, the evidence is presented to a grand jury. An indictment for thirty-three separate counts is brought against eight members of the Legion for their vigilantism-fueled activities. The charges include destruction of property, firebombings, aggravated assault, and illegal weapons possession.[4]

If the Legion members' conduct is judged against the ten rules for the moral vigilante, that conduct would seem to come up short, having violated rules 1 and 2. While the locker thefts and minor drug dealing are regrettable and must have been frustrating, they do not rise to the level of violence and victimization that would justify the vigilante campaign. Further, the nature of the Legion of Doom's campaign, which risked bodily injury to both the suspected offenders and innocent bystanders, is clearly not proportionate to the threat of a stolen jacket.

3. DON'T ACT UNLESS THERE IS NO LAWFUL WAY TO SOLVE THE PROBLEM

The law often allows citizens to use force in defense of unlawful aggression against themselves, others, or property. Individuals should stay strictly within the requirements of this legally authorized force if that response will provide the needed protection against lawlessness. Unfortunately, the emotional state sometimes common within a vigilante group, together with limited faith in the criminal justice system, often produces a violation of this rule.

The Last Lynching in California

San Jose, California, in the early 1930s is a fairly unremarkable city born out of the California gold rush. It boasts a population of eighty thousand and is thriving despite the Great Depression. One family in particular, the Hart family, has prospered greatly. Alex Hart, a married man with four children, has built a reputable chain of department stores and by 1933 runs one of the city's two largest. The Hart family is well-known and well-liked in the community. In November Alex's son, Brooke, returns home after graduating from the University of Santa Clara and begins work as vice president of the family business.[5]

On the evening of November 9, 1933, Alex is waiting outside one of the stores for Brooke to pick him up and then drive home, but Brooke does not arrive. Unknown to Alex, at that moment two men, Jack Holmes and Thomas Thurmond, are in the process of abducting Brooke, something they have been planning for six weeks.

Around 6:00 p.m., Holmes and Thurmond sneak up behind Brooke and force him at gunpoint into their car. They drive north, stopping on a bridge near the southern end of the San Francisco Bay. After placing a pillowcase over his head and using bailing wire to tie cement blocks to his torso, they bludgeon Brooke with one of the cinder blocks and toss him into the water below. Knowing that the tide is low, Thurmond pulls out his gun and shoots Brooke several times to be sure that he is dead.

Around 10:30 p.m., Thurmond calls the Hart family and demands a $40,000 ransom. Over the next week, many ransom demands arrive, but the family is unable to act because there is no evidence forthcoming to prove that Brooke is alive. Finally, on November 15 authorities trace a phone call to a local pay phone and are able to arrest Thurmond. It does not take long before Thurmond implicates Holmes and confesses his own role in the kidnapping. Holmes is initially reluctant to confess but, faced with the evidence of his deeds, eventually does.

Citizens across the country, including those in San Jose, are already sensitive to the problem of kidnappings for ransom, such as the kidnapping and murder of Charles Lindbergh's infant son and nearly three hundred other kidnappings in 1931. Additionally, Congress and state legislatures seem unable to do anything about the problem. It is this state of public frustration and fear that fans the flames of rage as the story of Brooke's kidnapping becomes public.

Magazines from east to west use the compelling narrative to boost sales, newspapers intensify their coverage of the story with each new piece of information, and that constant attention keeps the story in people's minds. On November 16 local newspapers are able to obtain copies of Thurmond's and Holmes's confessions. San Joseans are shocked by the horrific details of Brooke's murder. Not trusting the government to quickly and fairly punish those responsible, as well as not wanting a trial that would torment the family further and mock Brooke's memory, Californians across the state begin to seriously talk about vigilante justice.

Angry crowds in San Francisco gather in the streets near where Thurmond and Holmes are being held, shouting, "Lynch'em! Lynch'em!"[6] The *San Francisco Chronicle* declares that the only thing to do with the murderers is to promptly hang them but legally. Since the 1850s, newly formed cities in the American West were quite comfortable with lynching as a proper and just way for communities to fight back against heinous criminals.

The pressure to act in San Jose continues to build. On November 24 psychiatrists, under direction of the court, examine Thurmond and Holmes in anticipation of a possible claim of insanity by the defense. On November 26 local hunters discover Brooke Hart's mutilated body. With the discovery, a crowd gathers outside the jail's barricades, demanding that Thurmond and Holmes be handed over to them. The crowd grows to three to five thousand men, women, and children. Local government officials begin calling in reinforcements to contain the angry mob, but Governor James Rolph refuses to call up the National Guard because he believes that the citizens are doing the right thing. Rolph knows that not everyone agrees with his view. The governor cancels a political trip to Idaho to prevent political rivals from calling out the National Guard in his absence.

Police try to quell the angry mob with tear gas, but that proves ineffective. Due to the high number of women and children, police decide that they cannot use more forceful measures against the crowd, which ensures that the masses will ultimately overpower them. Breaking through the police barricades, the mob uses items found at a nearby construction site as battering rams to break through the jail's entrance, beating and knocking down police officers in the process. Other prison inmates fear for their lives as the hallways become flooded with angry citizens.

Thurmond and Holmes are quickly located. They are kicked and beaten, then dragged by the mob to nearby St. James Park, where a crowd of thousands, including children on their parents' shoulders, watch as the prisoners, nearly naked from having their clothes torn from their bodies, have nooses placed around their necks and are hanged from tree branches. The two men die six minutes apart. One member of the mob sets Thurmond's hanging body ablaze, burning his corpse for the entire crowd to see.

Fig. 5.2. Vigilantes hung the kidnappers of Brooke Hart, 1933. (Courtesy of the Library of Congress)

A few days after the lynching, Governor Rolph announces that he not only approved of his citizens' actions but also will pardon anyone involved in the lynching if he or she is charged. Rolph defends his actions: "Had I called out the troops to beat down the crowd, terrible consequences would have resulted. Should good citizens be shot down to protect a couple of fiends for whom there are no words adequate to describe?" Rolph argues that the lynching is "the best lesson California has ever given the country."[7]

President Franklin D. Roosevelt and former president Herbert Hoover condemn the lynching, while reaction across other parts of the country and in the media is mixed. Charges are brought against seven leaders of the mob, but despite the leaders openly boasting about their deeds, the grand jury decides to take no action against them. The judge, Timothy Fitzpatrick, states, "There was no element of doubt in this case. . . . [T]he men had confessed. While ordinarily we cannot condone such happenings, from a judicial standpoint, I can only say, in my own personal opinion, they did a damned good thing."[8] The tree from which Thurmond and Holmes were hanged is cut down, as citizens had begun to strip the tree of its branches and bark to keep as mementos.

Under the ten rules for the moral vigilante, it is hard to see how rule 3 is not violated. Given the strength of the evidence, which is cited by many of the vigilantes and their supporters, it seems clear that the men would have been convicted at trial—or at least there is no apparent reason to think otherwise according to the then existing facts. In other words, justice could have been achieved without the unlawful vigilante action, and official action ought always to be preferred.

4. DON'T ACT ALONE

The vigilante is one who acts for the community, not himself; vengeance is not vigilance. If a person's conduct is to reflect community views, that fact must be demonstrated by having the vigilante action be group action. The larger and more broadly based the group, the better. Open membership in the group would be ideal. There may be practical limits on how public some discussions can be, but the guiding principles, such as the adoption of rules (such as these rules as a charter), ought to be sought and approved by as large a group as possible.

5. BEFORE ACTING, BE SURE OF THE FACTS, AND TAKE FULL ACCOUNT OF ALL RELEVANT MITIGATIONS AND EXCUSES

Perspective vigilantes must understand that they are in a credibility contest with the official criminal justice system. To win the battle for hearts and minds, the vigilantes must actually do justice better than the system is doing it, not worse. Doing justice requires taking account of the mitigating or excusing factors in a case, not just the aggravating factors. A vigilance committee can as easily discredit itself by showing an indifference to mitigations and excuses as the criminal justice system disgraces itself by showing indifference to giving offenders the punishment they deserve. Consider a case that illustrates the point.

The Beating of Steve Utash

It is a brisk, sunny afternoon in Detroit on April 2, 2014. White suburban tree trimmer Steve Utash hops into his pickup truck for a drive through an East Side neighborhood.[9] As he is driving slowly along, a ten-year-old African American child suddenly steps in front of his truck, and Utash is unable to stop in time. Utash hits the child, injuring one of the young boy's legs. Utash immediately jumps out of his vehicle to help the youngster but is soon confronted by a group of bystanders who have quickly gathered.

A group of around two dozen young men who are nearby decide to enact their own justice. The men attack Utash as he is kneeling down tending to the boy and proceed to take turns savagely punching and kicking him. They strike all parts of his body as he writhes on the ground in agony.

When the dust settles, the fifty-four-year-old Utash is in critical condition. He is rushed to the hospital, where he is put into a medically induced coma. He wakes up ten days later but needs long-term therapy to recover. He is released from the hospital a month and a half after his beating.

Clearly, the vigilantes here have violated at least rule 5. They did not take the time to get their facts straight, or if they did, they failed to take into account important factors such as whether the driver was truly responsible for the boy's injuries or whether it was an unfortunate accident. The injury to the child was accidental: it was the boy who stepped in front of the truck, and therefore the accident was beyond Utash's control. The vigilantes also probably violated several other rules, including rules 2 and 3. They had little if any reason on this occasion to think that the criminal justice system would not fairly punish any wrongdoing.

Unfortunately, many of the people who tend toward vigilante action do it for emotional reasons rather than as part of a thoughtful plan. Getting their facts straight commonly gets lost in their rush to be renegades. Consider the cases of the animal rights activists who, under cover of night, open the cages of semidomesticated minks to release them into the wild to save them. Unfortunately, once freed, the animals quickly die from exposure, starvation, road traffic, drowning, and attacks by other animals. Not having been raised in the wild, the animals are ill prepared for freedom. As a result of such releases, minks by the thousands have died in Illinois, Minnesota, Wisconsin, and England.[10]

6. SHOW RESTRAINT AND TEMPERANCE, NOT ARROGANCE OR VINDICTIVENESS

The goal is to be responsible, even if the government is not. A vigilante is not the wrath of God but just a means of shaming the government into doing what it ought to do: namely, take justice seriously. Vigilantes should not just adhere to the moral vigilante rules but make it clear that they are adhering. Unfortunately, examples of violations of this rule abound.

Pittsburgh Prison Guards

Starting in 2009, a group of eight correctional officers at the State Correctional Institution–Pittsburgh join forces under the leadership of Harry Nicoletti to punish sex offenders who are sentenced to the officers' prison.[11] The eight men feel that it is their duty not only to keep watch over these prisoners in F Block but also to make their time in prison as miserable as possible.

When one sex offender is brought to the facility after being convicted of raping an eleven-year-old girl, a guard announces the details of his conviction to the other prisoners, thereby signaling to them that they are free to punish the new prisoner. The guards also undertake their own forms of torture and harassment. They "order inmates to defecate and urinate into inmate's food [and] place defecation and other bodily fluids into inmate's food."[12] The guards also perform "swirlies" on these inmates, forcing them to put their heads in toilets and then flushing them.

The guards' torture crosses the line into sexual abuse as well, especially by the leader, Nicoletti. On one occasion, inmate Rodger Williams is relaxing in his cell when Nicoletti enters and orally and anally rapes Williams. He then "doled [him] out to other corrections officers and a [prison] inmate into forcibly committing sexual acts."[13]

In January 2010 Nicoletti approaches another inmate and gives him three choices: to be anally raped, to perform oral sex on Nicoletti, or to fondle Nicoletti's genitals. If he does not choose one of the three options, he is told that Nicoletti will beat him and file "fraudulent misconducts" against him.[14] The man chooses the third option. In another instance, Nicoletti sodomizes an inmate as he slaps him. After finishing, Nicoletti threatens to tamper with the inmate's food. For the next two weeks, the prisoner survives on toothpaste out of fear that Nicoletti will poison him.

Nicoletti assaults as many as twenty inmates during his time as a correctional officer. The other members of his vigilante group also attack a large number of prisoners, often using broom handles to sexually assault them.

The guards' conduct is not vigilance but rather vindictiveness. (Indeed, in this instance, one suspects that Nicoletti, at least, was a sexual predator who used vigilantism as a cover.) The moral vigilante is pushed into action because an indifferent government has made clear that there is no other path of justice, but some immoral "vigilantes" are simply thugs in disguise.

7. WARN THE GOVERNMENT THAT IT IS IN BREACH OF ITS SOCIAL CONTRACT WITH ITS CITIZENS, AND GIVE IT AN OPPORTUNITY TO FIX THE PROBLEM, UNLESS IT IS CLEAR THAT SUCH A WARNING WOULD BE USELESS

Ideally, this means laying out the specifics of the system's failures of justice, as well as giving the authorities the time and opportunity to make things right. It is always preferable to have the official criminal justice system do justice, no matter how well respected a vigilance committee may be. (More on this in the following two chapters.) Admittedly, in some instances, the failures of justice may be overwhelmingly obvious to all, and a special notification to the government would be senseless.

8. PUBLICLY REPORT AFTERWARD WHAT YOU HAVE DONE AND WHY

Failure to publicly take responsibility for your vigilante actions simply adds to the problem of perceived lawlessness. The community cannot judge the justness and reasonableness of a vigilance committee's actions unless it is given the details of what has been done and why. Such public reports may not always be feasible, but they ought to be done whenever possible.

9. RESPECT THE FULL SOCIETY'S NORMS OF WHAT IS CONDEMNABLE CONDUCT

Do not act in pursuit of justice for an offense unless it is clear that the larger society sees the offender's conduct as truly condemnable. Taking action based upon a peculiar view of the world lacks the basis for moral vigilante action. (More on this in chapter 7.) For example, mainstream America believes that while animals ought not to be treated cruelly, it does not share the view of some animal rights activists that animals cannot properly be farmed or eaten or used for medical research. Some activists demand that animals be given the same rights as those accorded to humans, and they feel justified in breaking the law to defend this stance.

Similarly, some people in the antiabortion movement feel strongly enough about their cause that they believe they are justified in committing serious criminal offenses. For example, in 1982 the operator of an abortion clinic, Dr. Hector Zevallos, and his wife, Rose, were kidnapped by the Army of God with demands that President Ronald Reagan publicly denounce abortion. The FBI intervened, and Dr. Zevallos and his wife were released after being held for eight days in an abandoned ammunition bunker 120 miles from their home.[15]

No doubt the activists in these and other causes felt strongly about the rightness of their views. However, it is equally clear that they knew themselves to be in a small minority of the larger society. They are certainly free to try to change the society's views—and perhaps someday they will succeed—but until that day comes they cannot in a democratic society substitute their own values for those of the larger society and claim that their lawbreaking is that of a moral vigilante.

10. IF IT BECOMES CLEAR THAT THE PROBLEM CANNOT BE FIXED THROUGH VIGILANTE ACTION, THEN WITHDRAW FROM FURTHER ACTION

If it becomes clear that the criminal justice system literally cannot be changed no matter how dramatic and thoughtful the vigilante action, then further action toward that goal cannot achieve its purpose. Vigilante action must be a temporary and transitional state that moves the system to fix itself, not a permanent substitute for official conduct.

A final suggestion to the prospective vigilance committee: if you cannot abide by these rules, don't act. Justice is important, and it ought to be pursued. But vigilante action that does not take account of the preconditions and limitations that morally justify it is doomed to do more harm than good to the community and, ultimately, to the cause of justice. Certainly, many of the vigilantes in chapter 2 can make a plausible argument that the criminal justice system's failures to do justice morally authorize them to engage in some conduct that is technically criminal and legally unjustified. The 1851 San Francisco vigilance committee would seem to satisfy most of these ten rules. And many other cases—Deacons for Defense, Lavender Panthers, and Pink Gang of India—may satisfy many if not all of the requirements, although the details of each of their specific criminal acts may vary. On the other hand, many well-meaning vigilante cases, some discussed above and some in the following two chapters, will fail the test.

While one can sympathize with the frustration of all of those who suffer from the government's breach of its social contract, those who act beyond the boundaries of moral vigilantism will in the long term do more harm than good.

6

MORAL VIGILANTES BREAKING BAD: COMMUNITY DRUG WARS

Below are four instances of vigilantes trying to deal with a drug-use epidemic that they see destroying their community but that the criminal justice system seems unable or unwilling to address. None of these four groups appear to be acting out of personal self-interest. Their motivation appears to be saving their neighborhood and the vulnerable people living there.

But even when vigilantes are morally justified at the start, once the bright line of lawful conduct has been crossed, it is not so easy to know where to stop if the first efforts fail. Being a little more aggressive is a natural response, but, having already broken the law, it is easy for a series of "a little more" to go too far.

REVEREND DEMPSEY FIGHTING THE 1960S HARLEM HEROIN EPIDEMIC

Reverend Oberia Dempsey, pastor of Upper Park Avenue Baptist Church in Harlem, New York, in 1962, is troubled by the escalating violence and human misery caused by the growth of the narcotics trade in his neighborhood. In his view, Harlem is overrun with at least forty thousand dope addicts, and the authorities are indifferent to removing the drug pushers that cause so much damage.[1] "Citizens fear to venture out after dark," Dempsey says. "Church members are afraid to go to their meetings at night. The law seems to be in the hands of the muggers and robbers. There's panic among the people."[2]

He sees the pushers' dealings and the officers' apathy as a direct affront to African American freedom and civil rights. "There are forces still bent on keeping Afro-Americans down," he warns, and the drug game is a conspiracy to do just that.[3] In response, he forms the Anti-Drug Committee of Harlem, based out of his church, focusing on advocacy and grassroots campaigns.

These initial efforts include a 1962 rally of black associations, church groups, and other community organizations to protest the police and their ineffectiveness in dealing with Harlem's destructive drug problem. Dempsey also hangs banners outside his church; some read, "all dope peddlers and gangsters get out of harlem & new york city." Others plead with authorities to "return harlem back into the hands of decent people."[4] Dempsey thinks increasing awareness of Harlem's plight will provoke an official response.

The groups' activities have a limited effect, however—on the pushers and on the authorities. By 1965 Dempsey has given up his nonconfrontational approach in favor of a more aggressive, militant solution. He transforms his group into a vigilante patrol consisting of community members, including seven former police officers. Many of the members carry guns on patrol, with Dempsey using a .21-caliber revolver. The "pistol packin' pastor" brands his activities Operation Confiscation, the newest initiative consisting of two hundred citizen patrol members committing to "watch for pushers, summon police, and where they are not forthcoming immediately, make citizen arrests."[5]

The group harasses suspected dealers and encourages residents to go after pushers. If anyone has problems with the dealers and is afraid of reprisals for reporting them to the police, Dempsey tells that person to let him know. He will deal with the problem.[6]

Dempsey's efforts go beyond his confrontations with drug dealers. Dealers and cops are only part of the problem. The reverend also blames local landlords—he routinely refers to them as slumlords—for their refusal to install effective locks on apartment doors, which he believes contributes to the success of the drug dealers. Dempsey calls on community members to withhold rent from any slumlord who fails to act in combatting the drug trade.

In 1969 Dempsey petitions Robert Morgenthau, New York's US attorney, demanding, "If something isn't done immediately, people are going to arm themselves. There's going to be a lot of bloodshed."[7] Dempsey advocates for stricter penalties for drug dealers, including "death by firing squad" for anyone trafficking dope.[8]

Dempsey's demands reverberate throughout the community. A young social worker at the time tells a reporter that the most effective way of dealing with the community drug problem is to "kill the pusher." This is already happening, according to the social worker, but the police and news media simply report the homicides as dealer-on-dealer violence. "The word is seeping through black ghettos," the reporter observes, "that vigilante action—up to and including 'elimination'—may be the only way to halt the growing use of heroin among black youths."[9]

By the early 1970s, Dempsey has succeeded in gaining national attention. *Ebony* magazine interviews him in 1970, publishing an article entitled "Blacks Declare War on Dope."[10] Dempsey's efforts and newfound popularity make him a likely target for retribution. After a drug gang attacks him in 1971, he vocally encourages all citizens to arm themselves. "People in Harlem," he says, "should find the heaviest baseball bats around or any other type of weapon that's sold legally to ward off those hoodlums."[11]

The reverend's efforts, and the rising crime problem in the wider New York City area, ultimately spur local politicians to action. By 1973 New York is shifting away from its prior position of relying on treatment to deal with the drug epidemic and its associated violence. Officials finally respond to Dempsey's pleas with the enactment of the now controversial Rockefeller drug laws, mandating severe sentences for mere drug possession.[12] Harlem's neighborhoods have run out of patience with the local drug problem and welcome the harsh penalties for anyone involved with the narcotics scourge.

A HYSTERICAL RESPONSE? THE ROSA LEE STORY

Reverend Dempsey and his supporters are obviously fearful of the effect of drugs in their neighborhood and outraged at the official inability or indifference that lets the problem grow. Are they hysterical, fighting an imagined problem or exaggerating its harmful effects?

Consider the human stories that they see in their neighborhood each day multiplied a thousand times over as drugs take in one neighbor after another. Those neighbors then open the door for others to follow in a sad, endless cycle.

Rosa Lee Cunningham, a mother of eight from Washington, DC, was born into poverty and survives mainly on welfare.[13] Even though Rosa Lee has sold heroin for many years, she has only recently started using.[14] Rosa Lee quickly becomes hooked and develops an expensive habit that demands to be fed from the family's already small resources.[15]

To finance her addiction, Rosa Lee resorts to stealing and hustling. She teaches her children how to shoplift. Rosa Lee also resorts to prostitution. This may be how she contracts HIV, which later develops into AIDS.[16]

Rosa Lee regularly shoots heroin alongside four of her children, sharing intravenous needles with them. Three family members work as prostitutes, and they all share needles. It is no surprise that HIV spreads among the Cunningham clan and thus potentially to their clients. Two of her children eventually develop full-blown AIDS.[17]

Besides funding her children's drug addictions, Rosa Lee also involves them in the drug trade itself. Rosa Lee runs illegal "oil joints," places where heroin addicts can buy or inject themselves with heroin, sharing unsterilized needles.[18] She employs her five-year-old granddaughter to do the legwork in some heroin deals.

The vast suffering of her family speaks to the impact of drugs. Her husband is beaten to death with a hammer by a woman with a cocaine addiction with whom he had had a relationship. Of Rosa Lee's six children who become addicts, one dies from AIDS, and three others end up incarcerated. Her fifteen-year-old grandson, Rico, is killed in a drug-related shooting. Rosa Lee dies from AIDS complications.

Multiply the Rosa Lee story by thousands, and they depict a neighborhood in serious trouble. Reverend Dempsey and every other civic-minded person had reason to be afraid. Heroin use exploded in the late 1960s and early 1970s, when Reverend Dempsey was trying to salvage his neighborhood. Most drug users started between the ages of fifteen and twenty-one, and half were addicted within two years.[19] This "heroin generation," as it is called, is estimated to have included somewhere between eight hundred thousand and four million people.[20]

THE 1980s COCAINE EPIDEMIC

In the late 1980s came the explosion in the use of crack cocaine. Statistics from the period show that 83 percent of arrestees in Manhattan tested positive for cocaine use, as did 65 percent of those in Los Angeles and Washington, DC, and over 50 percent of arrestees in Chicago, Dallas, Houston, New Orleans, and Birmingham.[21] A 1990 Philadelphia study found that 81 percent of males and 78 percent of females arrested tested positive for drugs, most often cocaine.[22]

The effects of drugs on crime can be staggering. In Philadelphia in 1991, police reports indicate that narcotics are involved in 50 to 70 percent of all crimes.[23] In a Baltimore study, the average addict committed crimes on 248 days each year.[24] The same study revealed that 243 of the male addicts each committed an average of two thousand offenses over an eleven-year period; taken together, the group was responsible for five hundred thousand crimes.

But the damage from drugs goes beyond its effect on crime. It has been reported that 70 percent of all child abuse and neglect cases involve substance abuse by the parents.[25] Half of all pediatric AIDS cases result from injection drug use or sex with injection drug users by the child's mother.[26] Thirty percent of all traffic fatalities involve drug use.[27] Two million people in 2010 went to emergency rooms for situations brought on by illicit drug use.[28] Every year, forty-five thousand cocaine-exposed babies are born.[29]

The overall societal costs of drug abuse are staggering, and they continue to grow each year. In 1998 the total cost to taxpayers nationwide was $373 billion. By 2000 the cost had grown to $484 billion, which means that on average every American taxpayer is paying $500 a year for the costs associated with illegal drug use by others. This includes $61 billion a year for crime and criminal justice costs, $11 billion a year for added healthcare costs, and $120 billion a year in lost productivity.[30] And the problem continues to grow. In 1979 just over 7,000 deaths were attributed to drug-induced causes; by 2011 the number had grown to 43,544.[31]

Against the background of rampant drug use and its destructive effects, the outrage and fear of Reverend Dempsey's supporters may seem well-founded. One can see how their frustration with the system's failure to stop the destruction of their community by drugs and drug dealers could provoke them to action.

One can also imagine their dilemma when their initial efforts are not effective in stemming the threat. Should they push a little harder? Should they perhaps step a bit further over the law's line of authorized conduct to see if that might be enough to solve the problem that the system seems helpless to solve? To them, the social contract seems to have been clearly breached. How far can they go to take care of the problem themselves?

Reverend Dempsey's struggles with Harlem's 1960s' heroin problem are replayed for crack cocaine in the 1980s. But the groups in these instances—in Philadelphia, Detroit, and Baltimore—each take different paths in addressing the problem. The community group in Philadelphia, for example, takes a somewhat more aggressive approach than Reverend Dempsey.

HERMAN WRICE BATTLING DRUGS IN WEST PHILADELPHIA

The Mantua neighborhood of West Philadelphia is hit hard by the crack cocaine epidemic.[32] An economically depressed area known as the "Bottom"—40 percent of its population survive below the national poverty line, and its infant mortality rates are among the worst in the country—Mantua has an assortment of abandoned houses taken over by local drug dealers and their customers. The dealers and addicts drift through the neighborhood, leaving syringes, glassine bags, and other paraphernalia in parks that a few years earlier were the province of small children. But the makeshift crack houses bring more than just noise and blight. They usher in increased crime and introduce more young people to the drug trade, often starting at eight and nine years of age. The open criminality and increasing decline of the neighborhood is met with the unwillingness of officials to do what is needed to stop the slide.

In 1986 Herman Wrice, an African American who has successfully run rehabilitation programs for drug addicts in other states, moves back to his home city of Philadelphia. Wrice, a former gang member until his wife was almost killed in a shootout, advocates for direct community involvement in stopping crime. Instead of continuing to wait for the police or the city to take action, Wrice suggests that neighbors as a group confront the criminals, especially the drug dealers. Although he starts by running a Mantua sports league, hoping to get youth involved in something other than drugs, he quickly realizes that more is required. Fed up with the drug dealers' influence over the neighborhood's youth, he forms Mantua Against Drugs (MAD) to put his philosophy in action by confronting drug dealers and driving them out of the community permanently. "Stand up to them," he believes, "and they'll leave."[33]

After recruiting a group of concerned residents, Wrice and his MAD organization begin to target known crack houses. In large groups, and wearing the group's trademark white hard hats, members picket outside the drug dens and attempt to block customers from entering. Sometimes they spend the night in front of the crack den singing and chanting to embarrass the occupants and remove any pretense of their existence being unnoticed. "Up with Hope," they yell out. "Down with Dope."[34] The confrontational methods sometimes provoke violence—shoving matches and a few brick-throwing battles.

Another MAD tactic that turns out to be quite effective is to pressure utility companies to cut service to the crack houses. When the dealers and their clientele leave, the group quickly boards up the houses to prevent reentry. In those cases where police do arrest drug dealers, MAD members attend their bail hearings. They commonly interrupt the defense counsel's presentations and even try to intimidate the locally elected judges into setting higher bail. MAD also makes wanted posters of local drug dealers. The group selects a different dealer each week—their "Dealer of the Week"—and fills Mantua with the lucky person's face.[35]

As the group's successes become known, similar antidrug groups form around Philadelphia, often working together in larger numbers to rally and march in areas known to be drug-trade hotbeds. In one incident, calling themselves the United Neighbors Against Drugs, twelve of the city's antidrug groups, including MAD, amass three hundred people to march down Dauphin Street, a road surrounded by blocks of graffiti-spray-painted buildings, stripped-down cars, and collapsing row houses, with drug pushers roaming freely.[36] The drug-ravaged street is the type of waste that Wrice wants people to take notice of. As Wrice put it, MAD will "march all over this city" to fight the scourge of drug dealers.[37]

MAD's efforts seem to pay off, perhaps in part because they eventually embarrass local authorities into taking the drug problem in Mantua seriously. The 1,644 felonies reported in Mantua in 1989 drop by 40 percent by 1993.[38]

Wrice sometimes took a short step over the line of legality to get the results that he got, but what if a longer, more aggressive step over was required? Consider the situation facing antidrug community groups in Detroit.

Fig. 6.1. A mural tribute to Herman Wrice, 2006. (Photo by Jeremy Burger, 2006. Mural by David McShane and Eurhi Jones)

BURNING CRACK HOUSES IN DETROIT

Heavily armed gangs willing to push the drug trade with brutal and bloody violence accompany the crack epidemic in 1980s Detroit.[39] The crack houses bring the predictable uptick in crime but also common, random gunfire. The neighborhoods most affected are areas where kids once played pickup baseball on side streets and where residents would sit on their front steps trading gossip. After the gangs move in, venturing outside is limited to only essential outings.

Outraged at the failure of local authorities to deal effectively with the problem and the toll it is taking on families, two local men, Angelo

Parisis, an unemployed landscaper, and Perry Kent, an unemployed mechanic, organize an effort to get the police's attention. They campaign to persuade authorities to rid the area of open criminality, but the effort is futile. The police largely stay away, and the crime continues.

The duo decides the community must confront the gangs themselves. But while the confrontational chanting and singing worked well in Philadelphia, here it might be more likely to result in gunshots than fleeing drug dealers. After discussions among concerned neighbors, a new course of action is decided upon: to burn the crack houses down. Residents take up a collection to buy canisters and gasoline. Parisis and Kent take what the community provides them and burn down their first crack house in October 1988.[40]

Authorities charge the pair with arson and even consider pressing conspiracy charges against the neighbors who contributed to the fund. In support of the two, a local resident starts a fund to help pay for their defense, noting, "Ninety percent of the people in this block support them. When they set the fire, everybody in the neighborhood knew they were going to do it and they knew why they were going to do it."[41] Even those few neighbors who do not necessarily approve of the method agree that what the men did was beneficial, or, at the very least, they see it as the understandable result of the failure of local officials to fix the problem. As one neighbor put it, "I don't agree with their means. . . . But I don't want a crackhouse in my neighborhood. They did what they had to do."[42]

The jury agrees with the majority of residents. Despite overwhelming evidence and an acknowledgment that the two men did burn down the house, the jurors refuse to convict the men. Parisis and Kent are acquitted of all charges.

Other communities in Detroit quickly follow suit. In 1988 approximately one hundred drug-related fires are reported in the city, most of which residents are known to have caused or are suspected of to have caused. Arson is not the only method that proves successful in driving drug dealers away. Neighbors wielding pipes and baseball bats routinely clear crack houses of dealers and druggies by force. These altercations often are a precursor to a fire in the building later that evening.

Fig. 6.2. Crack houses were burned in many cities. (Courtesy of James Jeffrey, Flickr.com)

The community responds with overwhelming approval. Passing motorists witnessing crack house bonfires or fleeing dealers often honk their horns in celebration, and crowds of onlookers are known to form and applaud the destruction. In a *Detroit Free Press* poll, 87 percent of respondents find the actions of community groups justified. A supportive resident has only one regret: "I just wish'd they do it to more houses."[43]

The self-described "lynch mob," however, has some local officials and national commentators worried. They fear the city's problem with drugs and violence will only escalate with the vigilante action. The criminals may use the community attacks as a justification for retaliation. Other officials argue that the residents who rationalize the attacks and the jurors who acquit them hold primitive notions of justice that will not lead to a stable, safe environment. Dr. Mark Moore, a professor at Harvard, put it like this: "We're seeing a shift to public justice, and that's a very scary situation."[44] Instead, the house burnings and mobs will only push the downtrodden communities into anarchy. The communities largely ignore the objections. As one resident explains, "But what are you going to do? We have to be vigilantes."[45]

Clearly, Detroit's house-burning approach creates greater potential for a disaster than MAD's group confrontations in Philadelphia, but the sufferings and dangers as a result of drugs in Detroit seem to be worse. The residents see their actions as one of the only effective means of communicating the seriousness of the problem to authorities. If police and local authorities would actually step in, the mob would no longer be necessary. Because they refuse to step in, however, the neighbors see their actions as necessary and justified to protect their families.

From the larger societal perspective, it would be better for law enforcement to deal with the crack houses rather than leaving it for the neighborhood to deal with them. An official enforcement action could prevent not only the risks of confrontation but also the encouragement of vigilante action by others inspired by the burnings.

This Detroit episode shows how desperate a neighborhood can become when the social contract seems broken, but it turns out that things can get even worse. Baltimore's reaction to the drug problem was at times even more extreme than Detroit's.

BALTIMORE'S BLACK OCTOBER MOVEMENT

Baltimore is engulfed in a serious drug problem in the 1970s. Authorities do little to fix the rampant violence and drug dealing. Disillusioned with the ineffective official response, some community members decide to fix the problem themselves. Their method: kill the drug dealers.[46]

Graffiti appears on inner-city walls heralding the start of the movement: Off the Pusher. Fatal action is urged as the only way to get drugs and their ancillary problems out of the community. A group calling itself Black October forms, dedicated to imperiling the lives of dealers.[47]

In 1973 the organization informs the *Baltimore Sun* that Turk Scott, a freshman member of the Maryland House of Delegates and local heroin trafficker, is to be found in the basement parking lot of his apartment building. "This is Black October," the anonymous caller tells the reporter working the newspaper's city desk. "Fucking Turk Scott's a gone motherfucker. . . . He's in the fucking parking garage for Sutton Place. Left something for him."[48]

Delegate Scott has been awaiting trial on eight indictments involving his attempt to sell forty pounds of heroin worth at least $10 million. Police find his body where Black October said it would be. Multiple shooters have shot Scott. Spent shotgun shells, bullet casings, and Black October flyers surround the body. The flyers issue a warning: "These Persons Are Known Drug Dealers. Selling drugs is an act of treason. The penalty for treason is death!!! Black October."[49]

Six days after Scott's murder, members of Black October strike again. A call to the same newspaper directs it to another body. In a similar style to Scott's murder, twenty-two-year-old George Evans is shot to death by Black October members. Authorities find Evans, another local dealer with a criminal record for narcotics offenses dating back over a decade, on the ground in front of his home with one bullet hole in his chest and another in his back. As with Scott, Black October's flyers are strewn around the young man's dead body. This time, the leaflets read, "This person is a known dope dealer. He has made his living off people for a long time. He too has paid the penalty for treason. There is no hope in dope. Off the pusher. Black October."[50]

The group also sends a statement to the same Baltimore newspaper claiming that it will use any means necessary to rid the city of pushers. Black October members express their frustration with the apathy of local police, stating in a letter to the editor, "It is necessary now, after years of depending on corrupt police, to solve our problems by any means necessary or available. . . . Ninety percent of black-on-black crime is drug related." The letter concludes, "Dope must go. Save black children. Off the pushers."[51]

The group is quoted in a *New York Times* article as saying, "The violence we are organizing and using to destroy this Frankenstein monster we feel is necessary and justified."[52]

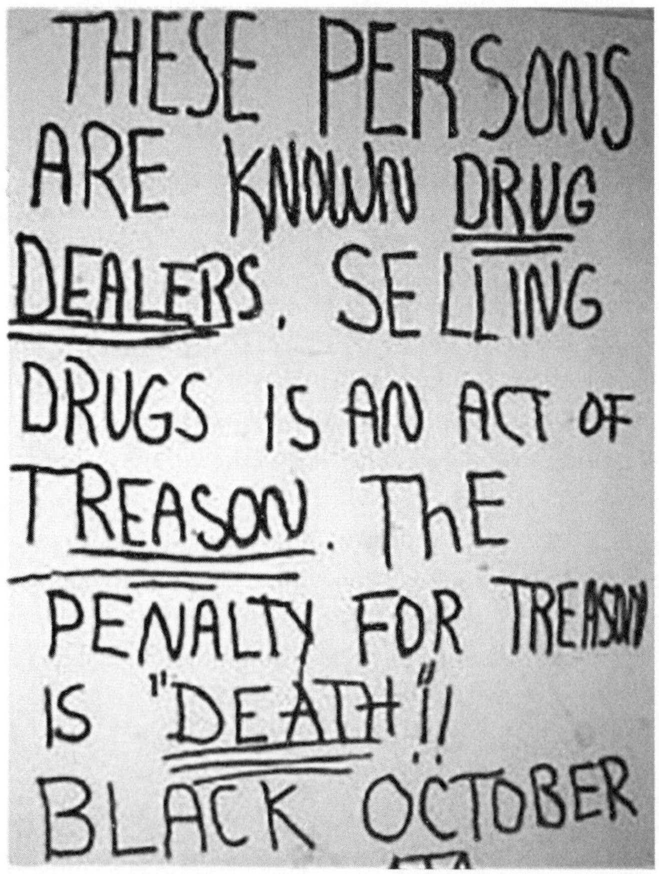

Fig. 6.3. Black October poster left at crime scene makes clear the group's motivation, 1973.

The organization follows its initial killings with a manifesto. The statement includes ten "Black Laws" punishable by death. These "laws" prohibit selling drugs to African Americans, raping African American women, killing progressive African American leaders, and working as a police informant against African Americans. The group also argues that, given the authorities' ineffectiveness, killing drug dealers is the only way to solve Baltimore's drug problem. The murders of Scott and Evans are, in Black October's opinion, necessary for that purpose.

The authorities' investigation into the drug dealers' deaths nets only one member of Black October: Sherman Dobson, a college student with no criminal record and a member of a Baltimore family that is highly involved in the civil rights movement and other community activities. While Dobson awaits trial, the community reaction is mixed. Some are happy someone is doing something to fix the city's drug problem. One commentator praises the organization's action: "It is my opinion that Black October is doing the most beneficial job of combating and eradicating the distribution of drugs into the community."[53]

After the trial and fourteen hours of deliberation, the jury deadlocks on Dobson's murder charge. Instead of murder, the jury settles for a compromise verdict: taxi hijacking. Four weeks before Scott's murder, Black October hijacked a taxi, presumably rehearsing the upcoming crime.

Baltimore is not alone in this violent response to drug dealing. A social worker in Washington, DC, tells the press that the most effective solution to the drug problem is "killing the pusher."[54] An apparently organized group in New York undertakes a campaign of killing drug pushers, sometimes by throwing them off building rooftops. Ten are killed in a period of eighteen months.

Clearly, assassinating dealers is a huge step beyond burning crack houses. The practice would seem to violate many if not most of the rules that might morally justify vigilante action. Particularly distressing in the Turk Scott murder is the fact that he was awaiting trial for drug dealing.

Apparently, those involved did not trust the courts to deal effectively with the problem, even after they had a large-scale dealer in hand.

Taken together, these cases show how easily what begins as moral vigilante action slides into immoral action. When morally defensible efforts are ineffective, the next logical step is to do a little more until something does work. If harassing dealers does not stop them, then burning down their place of business seems a logical next step, and if that does not work, then pushing them off a roof or shooting them certainly will.

Once vigilantes cross the line of lawful conduct, there are few obvious signposts telling them not to go a little further. Unfortunately, it is in the nature of vigilantism that, having left behind the signposts of legality, there inevitably arises the danger of the slippery slope.

7

HOW BEING RIGHT CAN RISK WRONGS

If a vigilante group is careful to stay within the rules of moral conduct, can it say that what it is doing is, in the larger scheme of things, best for society? The answer to that simple question turns out to be a bit complicated. Can something that is moral for the individual actor, given his or her situation, be problematic in its implications for the larger society? And if so, what, if anything, should a society do about the moral vigilante in such a situation?

THE PROBLEM OF TRAINING AND PROFESSIONAL NEUTRALITY

Ranch Rescue

In the late 1990s American ranchers are struggling to make a living along the Mexican border, especially on the ranches traversed by the avenue of choice for immigrants entering the United States illegally. These ranchers have long complained to the US Border Patrol about its failure to stem the flow of undocumented immigrants. The ranchers feel that their property is under a state approaching siege. Those illegally crossing over are said to regularly kill ranchers' livestock; pull down their fences, allowing cattle to stray and get injured; steal or damage their trucks and equipment; and break into their houses. Far worse, the easy and unchecked flow across the border invites heavily armed drug smugglers. The drug smugglers are a real threat to the ranchers and their families.[1]

Getting no meaningful response to their repeated pleas, several of the ranchers organize Ranch Rescue, an organization that seeks to do what the government refuses to do. Volunteers patrol the border using the same kind of equipment and tactics as the Border Patrol. The group typically detains the trespassers and turns them over to the Border Patrol. By 2006 Ranch Rescue, according to the group's count, has stopped more than twelve thousand illegal entries.[2] Other organizations, such as Arizona Guard, are born from this same motivation.

The members of Ranch Rescue are taking on the job, but they are hardly the best people to perform this role. They do not have the training to screen suspects properly or to detain them most effectively without harm. But even with better training, the members of the group would not be a particularly good substitute for professional law enforcement officers doing their job in an appropriately detached way. The ranchers are the most interested of parties. They are defending their own property and families. And therefore, they are far more likely to have an emotional response to the intruders that one might expect to see in a person defending against personal threats. Mistakes and overreaction seem inevitable in such a situation.

Roger Barnett, one of the founders of Ranch Rescue, and Casey Nethercott, a member, are both civilly sued by undocumented immigrants for making angry threats and for the use of force while detaining them. Nethercott loses his ranch in the civil lawsuits.

While the group is effective in reducing illegal entries and successful in dramatizing and humanizing the illegal entry problem—the number of Border Patrol agents is eventually doubled—the loss of Nethercott's ranch was an ignominious end to an action aimed at saving ranches.[3] Even if the moral vigilante gets it right in all respects, the vigilante action creates a risk of mistakes that would not exist if that action had been undertaken instead by the fully trained and equipped, unbiased official law enforcement.

What conclusion should we draw from this? Where does this leave the would-be moral vigilante? Should prospective vigilantes not act, even if they might be morally justified in doing so, because law enforcement officers, if they were willing to put forth the effort, could act more effectively? If that were the conclusion, then even moral vigilantes ought never to act because official law enforcement, with sufficient motivation, can almost always do it better. By that logic, moral vigilantes should defer to the government that has broken its social contract with them simply because that government *could* have fixed the problem. That analysis seems like a nonstarter on its face. The fact that the government *could* have done it better only emphasizes the extent of its breach of trust with the citizenry. The government *should* have done it better but chose not to. That would seem to support, not undermine, the moral vigilante's right to act.

A better conclusion to the dilemma might be that the risk of error created by the moral vigilante is one more reason why the government should avoid breaching the social contract and should never tolerate situations that would justify moral vigilantism. The government ought to take more seriously its obligation to do justice and to protect citizens.

Unfortunately, the moral vigilantes' lack of training and professional detachment is not the only set of problems they create for society.

THE DISPLACEMENT PROBLEM

The Crown Heights Maccabees

In 1964 Crown Heights, New York, is awash in rampant crime and violence. The Hasidic Jewish community is a highly homogeneous group surrounded by cultures and people vastly different from themselves. Crime in their few well-defined blocks and those around them is high and growing quickly. (For religious reasons, the community is tied to the location.) Most crime is committed by persons from outside the immediate neighborhood. Yeshiva students seeking religious training are regularly attacked and robbed. Home invasions have become increasingly frequent, and several have recently turned violent. People fear rapists and muggers to such an extent that many residents have become wary of even walking in the street. Shops begin to close earlier and open later.[4]

Fig. 7.1. The Hasidic community in Crown Heights, New York, formed a neighborhood watch group in 1964. (Courtesy of Wikimedia Creative Commons, Diluvi.com, Anna i Adria, CC BY 2.0.)

Local resident, Rabbi Samuel Schrage, seeks additional police patrols, even using his connections to arrange a meeting with then New York mayor Robert Wagner, but his repeated pleas are ignored. Not satisfied to let the problem go on any longer, Schrage turns to the community. He feels that the Jewish people have a history of self-defense, and he wants the community to step into the void. They will need to take on their own crime problem. Schrage forms the Crown Heights Maccabees, a neighborhood watch group—one of the first of its kind—with four squad cars, a radio network, and other equipment, all funded by the community. The patrols are set up in such a way that no block of the neighborhood is ever without surveillance for more than two minutes. More than one hundred residents volunteer and are given training on how to handle situations that might arise while they are on duty.

The Maccabees' goal is to be a deterrent force. A typical exchange follows this pattern: a young man is observed peering into shop windows after hours. He appears to be forming a plan while checking the area. The Maccabee patrol pulls up. No one gets out of the car. The man looks at them, they look at the man, and he leaves the area. Not a word is spoken. Simply watching is not always enough, and while the Maccabees are willing to ask the police for help, it is not always forthcoming. There is no strict hands-off policy, and Maccabee volunteers often end up in confrontations.

As the Maccabees' neighborhood watch program becomes known, fewer offenders find it worthwhile to come to the neighborhood to commit crimes. The results are dramatic. From December 1963 to December 1964 crime falls by 90 percent.[5] Some cases are instructive as to the power of the deterrence: a serial rapist attacking women in the areas around those patrolled by the Maccabees never attacks within their area.

The striking success of the Maccabees becomes a problem for their neighbors. Many of the robberies and rapes that are deterred by the Maccabees are simply displaced to the surrounding neighborhoods. The crime rates in the surrounding areas go up as those within the Maccabees' area go down, producing an ever-growing disparity. The adjacent areas are predominantly African American and Puerto Rican. The crime rate disparity and claims of racial profiling by the Maccabees increase racial tensions, sometimes to the boiling point.

It could be argued that the surrounding neighborhoods should simply organize the same kind of neighborhood watch that the Maccabees have organized. This argument may seem persuasive if we were to view the world in terms of groups, as many people tend to do—i.e., "us versus them." But the government's obligation is to each individual, and most individuals living in the higher crime areas are in no position to organize a neighborhood watch program as effectively as that of the Maccabees. The Maccabees are a cohesive group that view living in the area as a religious imperative.

If the government had taken more seriously its obligation to keep all of its citizens safe, if it had not left the Jews in Crown Heights or the African Americans or the Puerto Ricans or any other group to fend for themselves, it could have avoided the crime disparity and the racial tensions. Only a society-wide crime-control program can be truly effective, and vigilantes can rarely provide this.

Where does this leave the moral vigilante? Do the residents of Crown Heights lose their moral justification for vigilante action because it will push the crimes to adjacent neighborhoods? That will strike many people as being seriously unfair: the residents of the neighborhood must suffer because the residents of adjacent neighborhoods are unable or unwilling to organize as effectively? The better solution is for the government to take more seriously its obligation to provide safety and justice. The authorities should avoid ever putting the Jews of Crown Heights, or any other group, in a position where they must take on the role of moral vigilantes.

Here, then, are two problems inherent in the conduct of moral vigilantes: the risks created by their lack of training and professional detachment, and the risk that their conduct will simply shift the crime elsewhere with no net societal benefit.

It turns out that moral vigilantism presents other societal problems as well.

BLURRING THE LINE OF CONDEMNABILITY AND THE PROBLEM OF MINORITY VIEWS

Once the line of legality is crossed, it is less clear where to stop. What begins as moral vigilantism can easily spill over the moral boundaries as the momentum of the campaign carries a group too far—as evidenced by the community drug wars in chapter 6. But even more problematic than this, vigilante action—particularly action that initially provokes community sympathy—blurs the line of what can and should be condemned. The vigilante action itself, especially when approved by the community, tends to legitimize lawbreaking. What the law makes criminal may no longer be seen as the best guide of what is truly condemnable, and once the legal boundary is no longer seen as the moral boundary, the legal boundary loses its effectiveness and, at the same time, it becomes harder to find the moral boundary.

The Animal Liberation Front

Beginning in the 1960s, animal rights activists work to raise public awareness concerning the improper treatment of animals. There is often a good deal of public outrage against the kind of animal cruelty that the activists expose. This exposure includes not only describing the torturous treatment animals undergo when they are raised for sale for food but also exposing instances of abuse in laboratories, such as baby chimpanzees locked inside steel boxes or an infant monkey with its eyes stitched close for a blindness experiment.[6]

In the 1970s hundreds of US-based groups campaign on behalf of animal welfare. In many cases, such advocacy leads to new legislation and some levels of incremental change. However, for some members of the animal rights movement, such change is too little and not fast enough.[7]

The Animal Liberation Front (ALF) represents the more extreme end of the movement. It focuses on "direct action," a euphemism for committing illegal acts of varying degrees of violence in order to save animals or otherwise convey the group's message. Although the exact year the ALF starts operations in the United States is unclear, as early as 1979 individuals who identify themselves with the ALF and its mission break into New York University Medical School and release animals.[8] This is followed by a spate of similar incidents, some violent.

According to the Department of Justice, between 1979 and the present, ALF-affiliated individuals are responsible for more than fifteen hundred incidents of trespass, vandalism, arson, and thefts committed in the name of animal rights. The damage they have caused, primarily arson, is well into the millions of dollars.[9] Other forms of violent action include sending letters booby-trapped with razor blades to scientists affiliated with research using animals, and the use of improvised incendiary and explosive devices against property and, occasionally, against the homes of researchers.[10] In 1987 ALF members set a veterinary lab on fire at the University of California, Davis, and in 1992 ALF members, including an activist by the name of Rod Coronado, firebomb a research lab in Michigan.[11]

Researchers are also threatened, leading them to request a temporary restraining order against ALF sympathizers who publish names and addresses of researchers to help target them for harassment. The group also breaks a window in a researcher's house and floods the ground floor of her home, and it sets multiple explosive or incendiary devices under researchers' cars or at their front doors.[12] In other instances, ALF members have contacted researchers using animals for their research, stating, "Let this message be clear to all who victimize the innocent [animals]: we're watching. And by axe, drill, or crowbar—we're coming through your door. Stop or be stopped."[13]

Fig. 7.2. Animal Liberation Front poster advocates illegal action to aid animals. (Courtesy of Flickr.com)

The ALF rails against the general public and particular targets for engaging in "speciesism." One member explains that speciesism is "the belief that nonhuman species exist to serve the needs of the human species, that animals are in various senses 'inferior' to human beings, and therefore that one can favor human over nonhuman interests according to species status alone."[14]

Continuing support for the ALF is made possible by a public relations branch that acts within the bounds of the law to provide information about ALF deeds and propaganda for the cause of animal activism. These websites speak of "direct action" actors in laudatory terms and compile reports on aggregated instances of direct action on a semiregular basis. The organization also publishes various forms of materials intended to assist individuals interested in the ALF's movement: one ALF activist who has been arrested for arson has with him an ALF-created document that states that violence to protect animals is justified, nonviolence should be rejected, and actors should "use any and every tactic necessary to win the freedom of our brothers and sisters. This means they cheat, steal, lie, plunder, disable, threaten, and physically harm others to achieve their objective."[15]

As part of its online media campaign, the ALF also publishes guidelines on how to do the following: engaging in "direct action," avoiding prosecution, jamming locks, and making improvised explosive devices. The guide is provided both as a technical manual and as a summary of the ideological position of the group while also exhorting its members to participate in live animal liberations at laboratories, fur farms, and factory farms.

The ALF and affiliated actors and cell groups continue to operate, for example, by torching a dozen cattle trucks in Fresno, California, in 2012. The ALF states that "despite guards, a constant worker presence and a razor wire fence, the enemy is still vulnerable. There is a lot of stuff that needs to be destroyed, and we can't count on spontaneous combustion and careless welders to do all the work."[16]

The public abhorrence of cruelty to animals and the government's apparent failure to prevent it helped animal rights activists gain some initial support. And that support in turn helped the activists justify their initial use of vigilante action, which continued even when their program expanded well beyond the notion of animal cruelty condemned by the larger community. It is not an uncommon dynamic. Once a group passes the signpost of the majority view, it is not difficult to drift further and further from the mainstream. (This, of course, was one of the reasons in support of the majority-rule requirement set out in rule 9 in chapter 5.) In most cases there is no single obvious idea that distinguishes the nearly majority view from the extremist splinter-group view.

It is no surprise that this problem regularly arises in the context of vigilante action. The people most inclined toward vigilante action are people who usually have a greater motivation to act because they have an exaggerated view of the importance of the interest that they promote. Alienated people often feel that they have less to lose when they reject the status quo. With strong beliefs comes an exaggerated sense of the importance of the government's failures. In the case of the animal rights activists, for example, it is their exaggerated view of animal rights that both motivates them to vigilantism, which the community might initially support, and propels them to extremes that the community does not support.

INSPIRING OUTSIDE EXTREMISTS

The unhealthy relationship between vigilantism and extremists appears in other forms as well. Even if a vigilante group stays within the boundaries of what society considers moral action, its lawbreaking conduct may inspire others outside the group to go far beyond those bounds. No matter how scrupulous the group is about remaining moral, its members may have little control over those who see their example and are moved to act in more extreme ways. Indeed, the stronger the group's public credibility, perhaps earned by staying within moral bounds, the more inspired outside extremists may be, believing through magical thinking that they too are cloaked with the mantle of moral justification. Consider two examples.

Project Perverted Justice

In 2002 a group of computer-savvy volunteers, led by a man adopting the nom de guerre of Xavier Von Erck, form Project Perverted Justice in the belief that pedophiles are using expanding web technologies to better lure children for abuse. Consisting of former abuse victims, retired law enforcement officers, and civilian volunteers, the group finds and monitors online chat rooms where pedophiles are trying to make connections with teenagers. Once they identify a trolling predator, group members seek to embarrass him with his spouse, family, employers, or the community by posting his chats with the teenage girls. More aggressive forms of action include arranging to meet the man and filming his embarrassment when group members, rather than a young teen, appear for the meeting.[17] (*Dateline NBC*'s wildly successful reality TV show *To Catch a Predator* was in partnership with the group.)

In one instance, a twenty-nine-year-old Portland, Oregon, man surfs Yahoo! chat rooms in which teenagers hang out. He strikes up a conversation with "misspunkgirlie13," who identifies herself as a fourteen-year-old Portland girl. The man quickly steers the conversation toward sex. "I'm 29, your [sic] 14 and adorable," he writes and then continues flirting.[18] He emails her a photo of his penis and a pornographic video and arranges to meet later at her apartment once her mother has gone.

The man drives an hour to the girl's house, where he is greeted not by a fourteen-year-old girl but rather by two large men with baseball bats and a camera. They chase him back to his minivan and scold him for soliciting sex from a young girl as they film his flight. By the end of the day, the group has posted the man's contact information along with the chat conversation and the retreat video to its website, Perverted-Justice.com.

The organization allows anyone ensnared by one of its ruses to post a reply letter justifying his actions. Most men swear that they have learned their lesson and just want the site to take down their information so others will stop harassing them. A twenty-year-old trapped by the group complained, "People pm [private message] me all the time and tell me that they are going to find me and hurt me, threaten to kill me, and etc. . . . i cry at night sometimes cause i fear for my life, since people seem to see what I look like, im very scared."[19]

Group members have been accused of falsely representing themselves and of endangering those persons whom members publicly claim to be pedophiles. Some critics also accuse the group of endangering the lives of the very children it claims to protect by bringing the predators into the neighborhoods. And since the aggressive tactics rarely result in convictions, at least according to some law enforcement officials, the actions only lead to embarrassment but not incarceration of the would-be assailants. Police investigators undergo extensive training on how to chat online with potential offenders in a way that will build a strong criminal case. Perverted Justice volunteers do not undergo any such training, nor does the group perform background checks on any of the participants.

Authorities caution the group not to make law enforcement's job more difficult. Sgt. Nick Battaglia, head of a child exploitation unit in San Jose, California, says, "Their hearts are in the right place, but the law needs to be enforced by someone who is qualified to enforce them. They need to be very careful. . . . If they're insinuating that someone is committing a criminal offense and putting their photograph and personal information online, they could be held liable in a civil suit."[20]

As of 2017 the group claims that its actions have led to six hundred chat-based convictions and that it has information-sharing agreements with hundreds of local police agencies, as well as the Department of Homeland Security.[21]

While people may disagree about whether the Project Perverted Justice program is ultimately beneficial or harmful, it is clear that its publicity elevates the public's emotional level of outrage against child sex abuse, and, most importantly, many people will see it as demonstrating that citizens can be as effective as law enforcement in exposing pedophiles. In seeming to legitimize such citizen conduct, the group is that much more likely to inspire more extreme conduct by others.

In 2005 Michael Anthony Mullen, incensed by a recent case he had heard about, pretended to be an FBI agent and arranged to "interview" three sex offenders living together in Whatcom County, Washington. When one of the "interviewees" left the meeting, Mullen shot and killed the other two.[22] His actions could inspire others to take similar extreme methods.

Operation Rescue

Although abortion is legal in the United States, it remains a highly controversial issue: some consider abortion to be a matter of free choice and women's rights, while others see it as little more than state-sanctioned murder of unborn children.[23]

Among the more militant groups is Operation Rescue, a pro-life protest group founded in Texas by Randall Terry in the mid-1980s. Terry and Operation Rescue are known for illegal protests in front of abortion clinics and for training individual pro-life advocates in "boot camp" to turn them into the "shock troops" of the pro-life movement. The training includes instruction on how to trace license plate numbers of clients and doctors at the clinics, how to jam their phone lines, how to picket, and how to videotape those who enter clinics. The group is also known to deliberately block entrances and display grisly photos and exhibits of dead or aborted fetuses to those who visit the clinic.

In the 1990s midterm abortions are controversial, but of particular concern are late-term abortions. Performed in the last trimester of a woman's pregnancy, late-term abortions require what many see as a horribly cruel procedure. A flashpoint of the debate is Dr. George Tiller, an abortion doctor at a clinic in Wichita, Kansas, who is one of the few medical professionals in the country willing to provide the controversial procedure at the time. Tiller performs such procedures rarely, typically for reasons that include the health of the mother or development issues of the unborn fetus.

Furious at Tiller's apparent willingness to commit murder for profit, as they see it, Operation Rescue members target Tiller and his clinic. In 1991 Operation Rescue organizes an event called the Summer of Mercy, during which members plan to shut Tiller's clinic down by blocking entrances and harassing those who enter. The group also keeps close tabs on Tiller and the clinic's patients and staff to the point where pro-life protesters boast that "we know when Tiller's using the bathroom."[24]

Their tactics include near-constant day-and-night harassment by protesters, which leads the clinic to seek legal and law enforcement help. Nearly forty police officers have a full-time job trying to keep the pathway to the clinic's entrance open.[25] As a result of the protesters' refusal to obey police orders, a federal district court issues an injunction against the protesters on July 23, 1991, but they ignore it. The next day, protesters crawl under Tiller's van, preventing him from entering the clinic's driveway.

For nearly six weeks, Operation Rescue defies federal court injunctions and blockades the clinic, doing everything from chaining themselves to fences to bussing in protesters every morning. Protesters are not deterred by arrest; some activists are jailed six times in the course of the protests, while many protesters have to be physically carried away by police officers. By the time the protests end, nearly twenty-six hundred people have been arrested for blockading the clinic. In total, the mass protest prevents twenty-nine abortions and lasts forty-two days. Tiller's clinic does not cease operations.[26]

During the protests, participants are usually released on their own recognizance and simply rejoin the human blockade, so Wichita enacts a city ordinance imposing a two-thousand-dollar bail for individuals blocking access to local businesses. In 1994 federal authorities enact the Freedom of Access to Clinic Entrances (FACE) Act.[27] The FACE Act makes it a federal offense to block access to a clinic entrance by means of intimidation, threat or actual use of force, or physical obstruction; it also increases penalties for blocking clinics from two to three days in jail in most cases to up to eighteen months in jail and a twenty-five-thousand-dollar fine. As a result of the FACE Act, as well as Supreme Court cases of the same period, illegal blockades cease to be a workable strategy of the pro-life movement. Operation Rescue abandons the tactic.

Operation Rescue continues to issue its heated statements condemning Tiller and other abortion providers, and it continues to run a boot camp for its members and other pro-life protesters in the hopes that they will "go home and make babykillers' lives miserable."[28] The group also issues "wanted posters" of abortion providers, supplying names, pictures, and addresses of abortion doctors to pro-life advocates. No longer able to blockade the entrance to Tiller's facility, activists stalk him, search his trash, harass his employees by providing their identities to local businesses, and confront Tiller at his home and church.

Although Operation Rescue itself is not implicated in overt violence, its inflammatory rhetoric inspires others more inclined toward violence.[29] In a 1993 assassination attempt, Tiller is shot twice by a woman with ties to antiabortion groups. Scott Roeder is another militant inspired by Operation Rescue. He is a donor to the organization who posts on its online message board. In 2007 he calls Tiller's clinic "the concentration camp of Mengele of our day [who] needs to be stopped."[30] In May 2009 Roeder confronts Tiller in the lobby of Tiller's church, where he is serving as an usher, and shoots him in the head, killing him instantly.

The original organizers of Project Perverted Justice would no doubt be appalled at the notion of murdering a sex offender. Should they have known, however, that their highly public campaign might stir up all manner of backlash against sex offenders? (Recall the Pittsburgh prison guards in chapter 5 who were similarly inspired.) Even if organizers understood this possibility, should it invalidate their moral justification for stepping in because they believe that the government has failed to take seriously its obligation to protect its vulnerable children and teenagers?

But Operation Rescue presents an importantly different case. Its organizers' public rhetoric might be taken as inviting extremists to do more than what the organization itself is willing to do and as indicating to extremists that they have the organization's private approval even if not its official public support. This seems a stronger case for holding the organizers morally accountable for the subsequent murder of Tiller.

As the cases in this chapter make clear, there is no substitute for the government providing protection and doing justice. Under the right circumstances, vigilantes can do it with good short-term results and perhaps even in a moral way, but the larger society will often suffer. The only solution to the problem is for the government to take more seriously its moral obligation to hold up its end of the social contract and to avoid at all costs putting citizens in a position where they must be moral vigilantes if they are to obtain protection and justice.

Part III

THE SUBVERSIONS AND PERVERSIONS OF SHADOW VIGILANTISM

The loss of moral credibility through perceived gross failures of justice can provoke ordinary people (chapters 8 and 9 below) and officials within the criminal justice system itself (chapter 10) to take action to force from the system the justice that the system seems reluctant to impose. And, as we will see in part IV, the manipulations and distortions of the system by which this is done—through what might be called acts of *shadow vigilantism*—commonly provoke their own distorting response, leading to a downward spiral of disillusionment and subversion (chapter 11).

8

COMMUNITY COMPLICITY WITH VIGILANTES

Part II focused on the people who, frustrated with perceived failures of the criminal justice system, take the law into their own hands to impose the justice that the system is unwilling or unable to impose. But as we hinted in chapter 4, these *classic vigilantes*, as they might be called, are not the real problem. It is the reaction of the broader public that can be more troublesome.

To gain a sense of how the same vigilante impulse that inspires the classic vigilante can influence a broad cross section of the larger community, consider these two case studies.

A FRUSTRATED NEIGHBORHOOD HIDES A KILLER

The Assassination of William Malcolm

In 1981 William Malcolm is living in East London with his wife and her two children, a six-year-old stepdaughter and a nine-year-old stepson. He sexually abuses both of his stepchildren on a regular basis. He is caught, and during the trial it comes to light that he has been abusing his stepdaughter since she was three years old. Malcolm is given a two-year jail term.[1]

Since England does not, at this time, have a pedophile registry system or laws that allow restrictions to be placed on convicted sex offenders' movements, when released in 1984, Malcolm returns to the same house and resumes life with the same two children whom he was convicted of abusing. Before the end of the year, he is again charged with abusing his stepchildren, as well as other young victims from the neighborhood;

again he is convicted and sent to jail. Upon his second release, Malcolm moves in with a new girlfriend and her five children.

Malcolm continues to abuse children. In one instance, he tracks down a former victim who testified against him in a previous trial and rapes her again. He tells her that she is "asking for it" because she helped send him to jail.[2]

In 1994 Malcolm is once again charged with sexually abusing children. The charges involve thirteen different children, including children who are living with Malcolm. Among the charges are multiple instances during which children are "tied to a bed and forced to perform sex acts."[3] Details of some incidents include Malcolm placing his shoeless young victim in a bedroom and then spreading carpet tacks on the floor outside the room so he can be alerted if the victim tries to escape. It is also reported that Malcolm frequently beats his victims with a belt.

Prior to prosecution for the latest charges, Malcolm undergoes a psychological evaluation, which determines that he is a sexual psychopath. The report describes him as having pedophile tendencies of a "strongly sadistic nature."[4] Social workers suggest that he is "incurably psychopathic and violent."[5] At trial, the judge describes the crimes as "unspeakable" but concludes that there can be no trial for the new offenses because his two previous convictions make it impossible for him to receive a fair trial.[6] The judge explains that victims of the offenses cannot realistically be expected to testify without mentioning previous abuses they have suffered from him and that this type of testimony will be prejudicial to the defendant. Malcolm is released from custody without restriction.

The victims and neighbors are not happy with the court's refusal to even try Malcolm. A female victim expresses disbelief: "The judge says he is not going to get a fair trial because of his history, but surely it's that history which proves what a dangerous man he is."[7] A male victim complains, "I didn't have a childhood. I was petrified of him."[8] In court, furious cries of "kill the pervert" come from the public gallery. Upon being set free, Malcolm receives death threats.

Malcolm moves to a block of flats in Manor Park that overlook a common area where children frequently play. Sharing the apartment with him is his current girlfriend and her children, three of whom are under the age of six. By lying about his background, Malcolm obtains a job across the street from a primary-grade school. Residents of Manor Park are outraged when they learn that Malcolm lives there. One neighbor explains, "You can't do what he did without creating an awful lot of enemies."[9]

On February 18, 2000, at around 10:00 p.m., Malcolm answers the door of his flat and is shot in the face. No one else is home at the time. Neighbors rush out when they hear a gunshot and find him lying on the floor still breathing but bleeding profusely. An ambulance arrives, but Malcolm is pronounced dead on arrival at the hospital.

The case is not different from others considered previously in which vigilantes take the law into their own hands when the law shows itself unwilling to punish serious wrongdoing. But what happens next illustrates another dimension of vigilante action.

News of Malcolm's killing is greeted with jubilation. As one neighbor explains, "I'm quite happy that people like him are out of this community. I can understand quite clearly why someone would want to have him out of the way."[10] Another neighbor reports, "Nobody will feel sorry, except maybe his relatives. I was shocked when I heard someone had been shot on the doorstep like that, but when I heard it was him I was relieved." In fact, Malcolm's relatives are not feeling sorry about the killing. Andy, Malcolm's brother, says, "I want to shake hands with his killers. . . . He was vermin, I'm glad he is dead. . . . Our entire family wants to say how glad we are that Bill is no longer on this earth. As far as I'm concerned, my brother was lower than the rats in my barn." Malcolm's former stepdaughter, now an adult, who was raped repeatedly since her earliest childhood, is ecstatic when she receives news of the killing, saying, "Hearing the animal is dead is the happiest I've ever felt." While she knows that, as one of his victims, she is a suspect in his killing, she insists that she personally was not involved, saying, "It was none of us [but] I wish it had been me who killed him."[11]

Police investigators question Malcolm's former victims and relatives, as well as the people in the neighborhood. They run into a wall of silence. The next-door neighbor reports seeing a pair of white males of average height and average build leaving the premises after the shooting. Although the entire neighborhood seems to have known about Malcolm and has been outraged by his living there, the next-door neighbor, whose son was killed by a pedophile in 1994, claims not to have known that Malcolm had ever sexually abused children. The police are nearly certain that the neighbors know who has done the killing and that many of them have information that could help in the investigation, yet no one comes forward, and those who are interviewed do not provide information.

Months after the murder, investigators are no closer to apprehending the killer or killers. It is clear that Malcolm's murder is a crime that the neighborhood does not want solved.

The doctrines of disillusionment, such as those illustrated in chapter 4, can spark all manner of classic vigilante action, including acts like the killing of William Malcolm. Where the criminal justice system has shown itself to be unable or unwilling to do justice and provide protection, a vigilante may be inspired to step in and take on that role. Earlier chapters are full of such cases.

But the Malcolm case illustrates a new dimension to the vigilante impulse: where people act not by taking on the task of doing justice themselves but rather by helping to protect the vigilante by refusing to help authorities in their efforts to investigate and prosecute the vigilante conduct. The community here is essentially serving as an accomplice of the vigilante, or at least an accessory after the fact, as the law might call it. They are not willing to go into the streets to do the justice, but they are willing to take the smaller, less aggressive step of refusing to help authorities, probably motivated by the same impulse that provoked the classic vigilante.

Such vigilante complicity appears in a wide range of forms, some even more public and more aggressive than in Malcolm's case.

AN OUTRAGED COMMUNITY COLLECTIVELY ATTACKS A BULLY AND SHIELDS HIS KILLERS

The Killing of Ken McElroy

A resident of Skidmore, Missouri, in the 1980s Ken McElroy is a local thief, bully, and sexual predator. He rarely holds a job but always has plenty of money from stealing anything he can get a fence to buy. He is an active livestock rustler, and as a result, for years Skidmore County has the highest incidence of cattle rustling in the state.[12]

McElroy's sexual preferences are for young girls between the ages of twelve and fifteen. Married three times but never faithful, he attracts one young girl after another, keeping them compliant first by attention and support in this poor rural area, then by intimidation and abuse. He fathers more than twenty children with different girls.[13]

If family or friends of one of the underage girls objects, McElroy responds with an aggressive intimidation campaign. In one instance, a twelve-year-old girl in eighth grade is his current target. She soon becomes pregnant, drops out of school, and moves in with McElroy. Sixteen days after their child is born, she goes home to her parents to escape McElroy's regular beatings. McElroy brings her back at gunpoint and beats her, then returns to her parents' home, shoots their dog, and burns their house to the ground. Unsurprisingly, most people are too intimidated to report McElroy to the police, and even when they do, little happens, perhaps because the police are also afraid of him.[14]

Whenever McElroy is charged with an offense, he arranges for one of his coon-hunting buddies to offer an alibi and works to intimidate any witnesses. In one instance, when a neighbor complains of his trespassing,

McElroy shoots the man with a shotgun, wounding him. The wounded neighbor insists that charges be filed, but between the shooting and the trial McElroy parks outside the man's house to stare at him on nearly one hundred occasions. When the trial takes place, it plays out in the same way that previous trials have in the past: McElroy is acquitted by an intimidated jury after one of his buddies presents the usual false alibi. Free to exact revenge, McElroy shows up at the complainant's farm and shoots at him with a rifle as he drives his tractor in a field.

Fig. 8.1. Ken McElroy, killed by the people in his town, 1981. (Courtesy of Harry MacLean)

One episode finally brings things to a head. Some of McElroy's many children are accused of stealing from a local grocery store owned by Louis and Bo Bowenkamp. After an argument, McElroy is refused further service and is banned from the store. As usual, McElroy engages in an aggressive response: he begins a staring vigil outside the store and outside the Bowenkamps' home. Also, as usual, the police refuse to do anything. When McElroy twice fires a shotgun at the Bowenkamps' house, they insist on filing a complaint, but nothing is done about it. McElroy returns two nights later, firing again, with the same nonaction by authorities.

On July 8, 1980, McElroy confronts Bowenkamp outside his store and shoots him with a shotgun, hitting him in the neck. McElroy is arrested and charged. Freed while awaiting trial, McElroy continues his campaign of intimidation, including threatening a minister and a local sheriff who might be witnesses against him.

Despite his usual witnesses, who swear in court that they happened to be driving by just at the moment that McElroy shot the elderly man in what they testify was self-defense, McElroy is finally convicted of second-degree assault and sentenced to two years in prison. The town's citizens breathe a collective sigh of relief. Perhaps the McElroy reign of terror is finally over.

But McElroy is released on bail pending appeal, and a hearing to consider revoking his bail is delayed repeatedly. When McElroy shows up at a local bar ranting that he will kill the Bowenkamps, the townspeople arrange a meeting to discuss how to deal with the situation and set up a watch to protect the store owners.

McElroy hears of the meeting and drives to a nearby bar, with his wife in the passenger seat. He goes inside, buys cigarettes, then climbs back into his truck and sits. A group of about forty-five people assemble. He starts the truck, then lights a cigarette. Six shots ring out from multiple directions, striking and killing McElroy. His young wife is taken from the truck to the safety of a nearby bank. The foot of the dead man has fallen onto the accelerator, and the engine roars on its way to nowhere.

Amazingly, despite the large group of people present at the time of the shooting in broad daylight, no one is able to provide information to investigators (with the exception of McElroy's latest young wife, who was seated in the truck at the time of the shooting). A state investigation is followed by an FBI investigation ordered by the US Department of Justice. Nearly one hundred interviews of apparent witnesses and local residents are conducted, but no one seems willing to provide information to investigators.

Explains Cheryl Huston, whose elderly father had been shot by McElroy and who watched the killing of McElroy from her family's grocery store, "We were so bitter and so angry at the law letting us down that it came to somebody taking matters in their own hands. . . . No one has any idea what a nightmare we lived." The case remains unsolved.[15]

This sort of vigilante complicity can include not only refusing to help authorities investigate and prosecute but also publicly supporting the vigilantes, as in talking with the news media to explain their motivation and to promote their point of view.

COMMUNITY SUPPORT FOR GROUP LAWBREAKING PROVOKED BY LESS SERIOUS WRONGS

The Destruction of the Venice Pagodas

Venice, a neighborhood in Los Angeles, California, is known for its two-mile-long promenade along the Pacific Ocean.[16] The boardwalk has long attracted an eclectic mix of people, including street performers, tourists, and sun worshippers. A tourist attraction during the day, it draws a less respectable crowd at night. A series of wooden pagodas with benches along the boardwalk provide tourists and neighbors with a welcome place to sit out of the sun, but at night the same shelters serve as a prime place for local gang members to deal drugs. These structures allow dealers to hide their drugs in a place nearby so they can control the drugs without personally holding them, then signal a confederate to retrieve a certain amount once a buyer pays.

The neighborhood has repeatedly appealed to police to deal with the drug problem or at least to remove the pagodas so that the drug dealing will move to less prominent places, reducing the extent of the trade, but their pleas have no effect. Frustration builds until one local resident finally takes matters into his own hands, ramming the structures with his pickup truck until they are destroyed. With the pagodas gone, the drug dealers move away.

Over the objection of residents, the city rebuilds the seating and tables, this time constructed in concrete. The newly installed gathering areas are popular with tourists and the local merchants who sell to them, but, as expected, the shelters are once again a hit with the drug dealers, who now have a nicer location in which to deal drugs at night. As a local resident puts it, "Once the picnic tables went back in, it re-created the problem."[17] Although local community members regularly call the police to report the drug dealing, the police rarely respond because, in their view, there are bigger crime problems elsewhere.

Fed up with the lack of police response, local residents decide to again take matters into their own hands. One weekend in August 1994, a group of residents in ski masks arrives at the site, post a lookout for police, and take sledgehammers to the new benches. Organizers have informed the neighbors beforehand that the demolition is going to occur so that the loud demolition noises will not prompt calls to the police. Apparently, someone missed the message and called the police, but the police simply ignore the call as being of insufficient importance.

When the sun rises on Monday morning, all of the new structures have been destroyed, to the cheers of the large crowd of onlookers. Local drug dealers are unhappy with the destruction, and that same morning they send their people swarming into the local apartment buildings, demanding to know who destroyed their hangouts.

The people who demolished the benches justify their actions by citing the refusal of law enforcement to deal with the problem. As one of the perpetrators describes the group's sledgehammer escapade, "We've got a bunch of nineteen-year-old kids running this street. The fear is unbelievable. . . . We have the silent approval of the whole community. People were cheering—we even had a woman take a few swings." Another resident explains, "Sometimes you have to tear the house up to get the rat out. We have complained and complained and complained to the police and they will not stop here. . . . It was intolerable." Others who are less enthusiastic about the destruction nevertheless concede that "the guys who did this may have some legitimate complaints."[18]

Fig. 8.2. Venice Beach shelters such as these were destroyed by neighbors, 1994. (Courtesy of Nan Palmero, Flickr.com)

Despite the fact that eighty or ninety people witness the demolition and that one of the perpetrators is interviewed at the time by the press, investigators can find no one willing to help them with their inquiries. As one investigator marvels, "It is just amazing to me that there were three or four people out there busting up tables and none of the residents saw anything."[19] Because no one in the neighborhood is willing to help, no prosecution is ever brought.

This public support for vigilantes is only one of a wide variety of ways in which the vigilante impulse can express itself in conduct short of classic vigilantism. As will become apparent in the following two chapters, these more covert expressions of the vigilante impulse can be more pervasive, more dangerous, and more destructive to justice and effective crime control than classic vigilantism ever was or could be.

9

THE COMMUNITY AS SHADOW VIGILANTES

A vigilante shoots child abuser William Malcolm in the face, and the neighbors refuse to help authorities investigate. Several vigilantes shoot bully Ken McElroy while he is surrounded by a large crowd, but none of the many witnesses are willing to identify the shooters to investigators. Residents of Venice watch a group of vigilantes spend the weekend destroying the seating areas that drug dealers use to ply their trade, yet the police must read about the events in the newspaper.

The vigilante impulses that drive some people to take the law into their own hands inspire others to act in less visible ways, as with the refusal to report an offense or to help investigators. These vigilante sympathizers may not be willing to go into the streets themselves, but their subversion of effective law enforcement is commonly provoked by the same frustrations with the system that drive classic vigilantes. Rather than becoming the punishers themselves, these *shadow vigilantes*, as discussed in chapter 3, promote the same goals through a variety of other means by which they subvert or distort the criminal justice system.

Imagine that the community members watching the shooting of McElroy are sitting on a trial jury for the case. Does anyone doubt what the result would be? Or what would be the likely outcome if the killing of Malcolm reached a grand jury on which sat people from his neighborhood? The same shadow vigilante impulse that produced their refusal to assist investigators is likely to express itself when they are jurors, grand jurors, and even voters, or whenever they have an opportunity to affect the operation of the criminal justice system.

Consider, for example, the reaction of citizens, in particular jurors, to the case of "Subway Vigilante" Bernhard Goetz, discussed in chapter 3.

The citizens on that jury refused to convict Goetz in part because they viewed his actions as an understandable, if excessive, reaction to the criminal justice system's failure to provide the safety and justice to which they believe citizens are entitled.

Goetz is by no means a unique case but rather is representative of a common phenomenon. For example, in a Minot, North Dakota, case, four men came to Jeremiah Tallman's home to confront him about an incident from earlier in the day. They exchanged angry words while standing in the entryway and were told to leave; they did leave when Tallman cocked the slide of his gun. As they walked away, one pounded on a trailer and another broke a window. Tallman then shot one of the men in the back several times, killing him. He was acquitted of all homicide and assault charges.[1] He hardly satisfied the legal requirements for self-defense, but jurors were particularly accommodating because they saw him as resisting aggressors.

Empirical studies show strong support among laypersons for the use of defensive force against aggressors and for the excuse of defenders who make mistakes in using defensive force. The community views on this point are dramatically different from the stated legal rules. Summarizing a series of studies, the book *Justice, Liability & Blame* concludes, "In all of these studies, the community judges that these justifications are more compelling than the legal codes are willing to grant. Respondents frequently assign no liability in cases to which the code attaches liability. Even when respondents assign liability, they typically assign considerably less punishment than would be suggested by codes."[2] According to a survey of judges, prosecutors, and defense attorneys, if self-defense is raised at trial, it commonly succeeds more often than any other kind of defense. The respondents in three major surveys estimated, respectively, that the defense succeeded 76 percent, 47 percent, and 46 percent of the time.[3]

In the Goetz case, it was the trial jury that exercised its nullification power in support of the vigilante. In other words, the jurors overlooked the law and found in favor of Goetz because they considered his subway shootings to be understandable given the rampant crime at the time and Goetz's own previous victimization. But that kind of shadow vigilante protection of those who resist wrongdoers can be seen at nearly any point in the criminal justice process where citizens are involved.

GRAND JURY RELUCTANCE TO INDICT FOR THE UNLAWFUL USE OF DEFENSIVE FORCE

Joe Horn Shoots His Neighbor's Burglar

On November 14, 2007, Joe Horn is a sixty-one-year-old retiree living in Pasadena, Texas.[4] He is having a relaxing day when he looks out the window and sees two suspicious-looking men approach his next-door neighbor's house. (The two men are Diego Ortiz and Miguel de Jesus, and they are intending to rob the neighbor's house of its cash and jewelry.) Horn watches as the two men break into the house, and then he immediately dials 911.

When the operator answers, Horn reports the situation and asks, "I've got a shotgun; do you want me to stop him?" The dispatcher tells Horn to stay in his house, saying, "Ain't no property worth shooting somebody over, OK?" During the call, Horn keeps an eye on his neighbor's house as the burglars are robbing the place, and he repeatedly expresses his frustration that this type of crime is happening in his neighborhood. After the burglars finish stealing cash and jewelry from his neighbor's home, Horn sees them running out the front door. Realizing that they are going to escape with his neighbor's valuables, Horn tells the operator, "I'm gonna kill him." Despite the operator's repeated pleas to stay in the house, Horn picks up his shotgun, loads it, and steps outside the front door. As the criminals are running across his lawn, he shouts, "Move, you're dead," and when the robbers continue to run, he fires three shots and strikes them both in the back, killing them.[5] Horn runs back into the house and tells the dispatcher what has happened. The police arrive on the scene and find the bodies but do not arrest Horn.

Authorities eventually file charges against Horn for murder. In mid-June 2008 the grand jury convenes in order to hear two weeks of testimony from witnesses, including Horn. On June 30 the jury deliberates and decides not to indict Horn. Horn is relieved that he will not have to face charges, and there are many community members who feel he acted rightly. District Attorney Ken Magidson says, "In Texas, a person has a right to use deadly force in certain circumstances to protect property . . . and that's basically what the grand jurors had to deal with." Horn's attorney, Tom Lambright, says, "Joe is not some sort of wild cowboy. He was trying to help the police. He was put in a situation where he didn't have a choice."[6]

The same frustration with the apparent ineffectiveness of the criminal justice system can show itself in shadow vigilante jury nullification in any case in which a defendant resists a wrongdoer and is then prosecuted by authorities. This includes not just civilian actors like Goetz but also police officers. Consider the jurors' reaction to the police beating of Rodney King.

JURY NULLIFICATION FOR LAW ENFORCEMENT OFFICERS

Acquittal of the Officers Who Beat Rodney King

Los Angeles in the middle to late 1980s is one of the more dangerous cities in America. The period from 1984 to 1990 is known in LA as the "crack epidemic." Crack first enters South Central LA in the early 1980s. Many children are left to grow up without parents because of addiction. Crime steadily rises.[7] From 1985 to 1990 the city averages nearly 2.5 murders, six rapes, and almost ninety robberies every day.[8]

The heavy demand for crack cocaine also helps local gangs such as the Crips and the Bloods to increase their financial strength and recruiting power, which in turn brings an increase in gang violence. Prior to the 1980s, the gangs have had limited participation in drug trafficking. But beginning in 1983, the Los Angeles gangs and their fifty thousand members begin to get a stranglehold on the streets, taking control of the narcotics industry.[9] For citizens, the most dangerous time of day may be the early afternoon, when the most dangerous criminals are on the streets: armed teenagers just out of school. By 1991 crime in Los Angeles has reached its pinnacle. Police officers struggle more than ever to control the streets. Murder and violent crime rates reach all-time highs.

On the night of March 2, 1991, Rodney King watches a basketball game with friends while drinking quite a bit of alcohol in suburban Los Angeles.[10] When the game ends, King and his two friends decide to take the 210 Freeway into downtown LA to try and meet some girls. King drives a bit erratically, probably because his blood alcohol level is 0.19, well above the legal limit, and he has been smoking marijuana. California Highway Patrol (CHP) officers notice King's speeding and reckless driving and begin to follow him. King, who is on probation for a robbery offense, does not want to go back to prison. He hits the gas and increases his speed to 115 mph. With the CHP right behind him, the high-speed pursuit heads down the freeway.

When his vehicle is cornered, King finally stops; his two friends quickly exit the vehicle and surrender to police. King takes a more combative approach. He refuses to exit the vehicle. When he does finally exit, he begins waving at the police helicopter that is overhead. Police backup arrive in the form of three LAPD squad cars: Officers Laurence Powell and Timothy Wind in one car, Theodore Briseno and Rolando Solano in the second car, and Sgt. Stacey Koon in the third.

King's erratic, even bizarre, behavior leads the officers to believe King is on PCP (or angel dust), a drug commonly associated with violence. King grabs his buttocks in a manner that a CHP officer believes indicates that King is reaching for a weapon, so she immediately draws her gun and asks him to get on the ground. Sergeant Koon, who knows that the threat of violence from all parties is escalated with the presence of a gun, orders guns to be holstered. He also orders his four officers to perform a tactical "swarm" technique to subdue King without the use of weapons.

Right around the time that the physical struggle between the LAPD officers and King begins, George Holliday, the manager of a plumbing company, begins videotaping the interaction from his apartment ninety feet away. After the struggle begins and after it is clear to officers that King is resisting arrest, they fire their TASER gun twice at King, but the powerful voltage does not subdue him. He continues to wrestle, gets back up off the ground, and rushes toward the officers. Police officers start using "power strokes" against King's limbs with their batons to subdue him, but still King continues to struggle and stand back up. Koon orders his officers to "hit his joints, hit the wrists, hit his elbows, hit his knees, hit his ankles."[11] Ultimately, the LAPD inflicts nearly fifty blows and several kicks on King before dragging him on his stomach to the side of the road to wait for paramedics to arrive. King's medical examination reveals numerous injuries, including a fractured facial bone, a broken right ankle, and multiple bruises and lacerations.[12]

The incident receives almost no publicity until Holliday releases his eighty-one-second videotape to a local news station two days later. CNN picks up the story, and it spreads like wildfire across the nation. The video sparks outrage among many who see it as yet another example of police brutality against a minority group. An LA poll taken soon after the tape's release indicates that 92 percent of participants think authorities used excessive force.[13]

Two weeks after the incident, a grand jury indicts four officers—Powell, Wind, Briseno, and Koon—for use of excessive force. Due to the publicity surrounding the case, in July the California Court of Appeals unanimously grants the defense's motion for a change of venue while also removing the original judge because of evidence of his bias toward the prosecution. In November a new judge decides to try the case in Simi Valley, a conservative and predominantly white city that starkly contrasts with the makeup of Los Angeles. Nearly a year after the incident, on March 5, 1992, a jury consisting of ten whites, one Asian, and one Latino hear opening arguments from the prosecution, arguing that the use of force was excessive.

Seven weeks of testimony are presented (Rodney King never testified). The jury studies the eighty-one-second Holliday videotape. When it is all over, the jury votes to acquit.

Jurors report that they only needed one day to decide to acquit the officers of the main charges against them. However, they needed an additional six days because they remained deadlocked on the assault charge against Powell.

Many experts believe that race played a role in the jury's decision, but many of the jurors dismiss that notion. One juror points out the obvious, that the two other men in the car, both of whom are black, calmly surrendered and had no force used against them.[14] One female juror notes, "In my opinion, based on all of the evidence that was presented to us, it is not a racial thing. I am not unhappy with the verdict; that's the only verdict that could have been reached."[15]

The juror's statement suggests that, given the violent conditions in LA at the time, the jury was not afraid to give police officers some flexibility in their use of force. Jurors seemed to be giving police more power in policing the streets than the state's law would allow. Stanford constitutional law professor Gerald Gunther notes, "This jury seemed unwilling to put any decent limits on police discretion, and I think that's the flat-out bottom line on this. The beating that King took was not justified even on the assumption that he did not turn quiescent as soon as [police] stopped the car and even if they had a basis for using force in the first few blows."[16] Some believe the majority of the jurors had such a "reverence for police officers as guardians of the social order" that the prosecution's use of the shocking videotape may have unintentionally undermined its own case.[17] Some of the jurors may well have thought that the police conduct was in violation of existing law. And yet, they may have felt that the right thing to do was to acquit the officers because the jurors were concerned that existing law did not take proper account of the need for the force nor did it give enough room for an understandable mistake in a fast-moving situation.[18]

This broad leeway given to police officers is reflected in the data. According to a Cato Institute study, the prosecution, imprisonment, and other sanctions of police officers occur at a much lower rate than for civilians facing similar charges.[19] In some cases, according to the Cato data, officers are acquitted even in the face of clear evidence such as multiple witnesses or videotape. For example, in September 2009 a Spokane, Washington, jury acquitted an officer of assault for kicking a suspect in the face, though other officers present confirmed that he had done so.[20] In another Washington State incident in 2010, an officer was acquitted after he was videotaped striking a fifteen-year-old girl who, when told to remove her basketball shoes, kicked toward the officer's fellow deputy.[21] The first trial resulted in a hung jury, while the second resulted in an acquittal.

Of course, if a case takes on a racial component—as when a white officer is perceived as using excessive force against a black citizen—racial political influences can conflict with the normal sympathy for an officer's mistake, as what occurred to some extent in the Rodney King case. On the other hand, even though the Black Lives Matter movement has done much to sensitize the public, the police officers involved even in cases that make the headlines are rarely punished. Grand juries refused to indict the officers in the killings of Eric Garner (2014), Michael Brown (2015), and Tamir Rice (2015). None of the officers involved in the killings of Freddie Gray (2016), Terrance Cruther (2016), Sylville Smith (2017), Samuel DuBose (2017), or Philando Castile (2017) were found guilty at trial. (Similarly, neighborhood watch supervisor George Zimmerman was acquitted at trial for his 2012 killing of Trayvon Martin.)[22]

Empirical studies confirm these public views: many people tend to be quite forgiving of mistakes made when force is used for law enforcement purposes, certainly much more forgiving than the criminal code itself, and this even applies to citizens when acting in a law enforcement role. As one study concludes,

> In general, the subjects are much more forgiving than the Code of a person's mistakes in using deadly force to affect a citizen's arrest. The Code imposes murder liability if the apprehending person kills an innocent person. A strong majority of the subjects, in contrast, impose no punishment even in the case in which the citizen kills an innocent person in trying to stop a fleeing rapist. Only in the case in which an innocent person is killed in an attempt to stop an offender fleeing from a property damage offense does a bare majority of our subjects judge punishment to be appropriate and, even then, liability is a few months rather than the murder liability that the Code provides.[23]

These striking results help explain why it is so easy for citizens, disillusioned with the justice failures of their criminal justice system, to justify expressing their shadow vigilante impulse through protecting those who use force against wrongdoers.

FRUSTRATION WITH CRIMINAL JUSTICE FAILURES AS GIVING RISE TO PRIVATE POLICING

Shadow vigilantism among citizens also shows itself in the loss of confidence in and reduced expectations of official law enforcement, which has produced the dramatic rise in private security and neighborhood watch organizations. The 2000 National Crime Prevention Survey estimated that 41 percent of the American population lives in communities covered by neighborhood watch. The survey report concludes that "this makes Neighborhood Watch the largest single organized crime-prevention activity in the nation."[24] One writer describes the degree to which private entities have taken over law enforcement functions in this country: "Private security officers vastly outnumber public law enforcement officers, and spending on private security is approximately double the spending for public law enforcement. For the most part, this growth has all occurred within the past three or four decades—only thirty-five years ago, there were more public police officers than private security guards."[25]

Watch groups are not formed in neighborhoods that are content with their law enforcement situation. Neighborhood watch is a literal form of a neighborhood taking on the law enforcement role of the government.[26]

But as chapter 7 made clear, shifting the law enforcement function to citizens commonly creates serious problems. Recall, for example, the members of the Ranch Rescue group who used improper detention methods because they lacked the formal training that police receive. In the case of the Crown Heights Maccabees, their vigilance was effective but tended to push crime into surrounding areas rather than preventing it. Project Perverted Justice, in which an unofficial group stepped in to take on a role traditionally reserved for police detectives, had the effect of inspiring others with more extreme views to take on a similar role. Society would be better off if official law enforcement did its job and did not provoke the shadow vigilante impulse that leads to citizen enforcement.

These same difficulties that we saw in the earlier cases can occur in any situation in which citizens take on the law enforcement role, including neighborhood watch. As noted above, George Zimmerman was the neighborhood watch coordinator for his gated community in Sanford, Florida, in 2012 when he shot Trayvon Martin, a seventeen-year-old African American high school student who was temporarily staying with a family who lived in the gated community.[27] (Zimmerman apparently approached Martin about his presence in the area, and the contact grew into a confrontation in which Zimmerman ended up fatally shooting the unarmed Martin.) It seems unlikely that such a confrontation would have occurred if that community relied upon official rather than private policing.

The local police chief concluded that Zimmerman had a right to act in self-defense and released him. A public national uproar led to the appointment of a special prosecutor, who charged Zimmerman with second-degree murder, but on July 13, 2013, the jury acquitted Zimmerman.

Fig. 9.1. Painting of George Zimmerman, neighborhood watch volunteer who shot Trayvon Martin, 2012. (Courtesy of DonkeyHotey, Flickr.com)

Another danger of leaving neighborhoods to fend for themselves is that their enthusiasm and newfound authority may lead to dropping any pretense of approximating professional police conduct. Some neighborhoods have gone beyond the formation of watch groups. One development is the "Glock Block," where neighborhoods in Oregon, Texas, and Arizona advertise "We Don't Call the Police."[28]

POLITICIANS PROPOSE LAW-AND-ORDER LEGISLATION TO COMBAT PERCEIVED FAILURES OF JUSTICE

But the shadow vigilante's frustration with a criminal justice system that is seen as indifferent to the importance of doing justice plays itself out in much broader civic conduct as well. It means that politicians are provoked to support changes in criminal law and criminal adjudication that are designed to force liability and punishment from an apparently reluctant criminal justice system—even when the reform also risks doing injustice. Consider several examples of this dynamic that have had a significant effect on the American system.

The Abduction and Murder of Polly Klaas

In 1993 twelve-year-old Polly Klaas lives with her mother and sister in Petaluma, California, a small median-income town a few miles north of San Francisco.[29] She is a shy girl who is much beloved by her family and friends. Her favorite subjects at school are music and theater.

On Friday, October 1, 1993, Polly invites her two best friends over for a slumber party. The girls, who are all clarinet players, have formed their friendship in the Petaluma Junior High School band. Because it is a weekend, they are allowed to stay up late talking and playing games. As the girls begin to get tired, Polly starts to leave her bedroom to fetch the sleeping bags from the living room. When she opens the bedroom door she is shocked to find a man standing there with a knife. He immediately threatens all three girls: if they make any noise, he will cut their throats.

Polly offers the man a box with her savings in it, fifty dollars in total, which he refuses. He tells the girls to lie on the floor and then proceeds to tie their hands behind their backs and place pillowcases over their heads. He then grabs Polly and flees. The two girls immediately work to free themselves, stepping through their tied arms, and run to Polly's mother. By 11:00 p.m. the search has begun for Polly Klaas.

The next day the community rallies behind the search efforts. Citizens form patrols that scour the forests surrounding the town. Thousands of posters of Polly are printed and displayed. Purple ribbons, Polly's favorite color, are put up all over town.

The search gains national attention as popular television shows, including *America's Most Wanted* and *20/20*, feature segments about the kidnapping. Hollywood actress Winona Ryder, a native of Petaluma, offers a $200,000 reward for information leading to the discovery of Polly. She tells *America's Most Wanted* that she is offering the reward "because this happened in the community I was raised in."[30]

On November 28, almost two months after Polly was taken, a local resident is hiking around her property with friends when they stumble across disturbing items scattered around several bushes: girl's clothing, a condom wrapper, binding tape, and rags with knots in them. Fearing that these items may be related to Polly's abduction, the resident calls the police.

The police link the evidence to Richard Allen Davis. On November 30 Davis is arrested but refuses to talk about Polly. However on Saturday, December 4, he confesses to kidnapping Polly and murdering her, and he tells investigators where they can find her body. In the weeks since her abduction, Polly's family has kept a candle burning in her window. They now extinguish it.

Davis has served time on several occasions for robbery, burglary, rape, assault, and kidnapping. He was released early on parole twice, only to quickly reoffend. After his first parole he kidnapped a woman, sexually assaulted her, was arrested, escaped from prison, kidnapped another woman, and was rearrested after breaking into yet another woman's home.[31] He goes to prison for that laundry list of offenses but six years later is again paroled. When released, he and a criminal partner force their way into a woman's home, threaten to kill her family, beat her, and force her to go to the bank and withdraw $6,000. When that money runs out a few months later, they rob a bank.

In 1985 Davis is arrested again, convicted, and sentenced to sixteen years. But on June 27, 1993, he is paroled again after serving half of his sentence. In October of the same year he is standing in Polly's bedroom with a knife. Had he been required to serve his entire prison sentence, Polly Klaas would not have been within his grasp.[32] Davis was arrested over fourteen times and convicted of many violent offenses before he kidnapped and murdered Polly Klaas.[33]

Almost overnight, support builds for the passage of "three strikes and you're out" legislation, spearheaded by Michael Reynolds, whose daughter had been violently killed by a just-paroled repeat offender.[34]

On November 8, 1994, California Proposition 184, the Three Strikes Initiative, is on the ballot and receives an overwhelming majority with almost 72 percent support.[35] Outrage over the Polly Klaas case is credited with inspiring that support. The new law has mandatory harsh sentences for repeat offenders: "If a criminal has had one previous serious or violent felony conviction, the mandatory sentence for a second such conviction is doubled. After two violent or serious felony convictions, any further felony, non-violent or not, will trigger a third strike." The mandatory sentence is then even longer, typically three times the ordinary sentence, or twenty-five years.[36] (Prior to the bill, judges could factor in previous convictions in imposing longer sentences for repeat offenders, but doing so was not mandatory and was at the discretion of the judge.)

Within two years of Polly's death, twenty-two states followed California's lead in enacting a version of the three strikes legislation. In 1994, Colorado, Connecticut, Georgia, Indiana, Kansas, Louisiana, Maryland, New Mexico,

North Carolina, Tennessee, Virginia, and Wisconsin passed their respective laws. The next year Arkansas, Florida, Montana, Nevada, New Jersey, North Dakota, Pennsylvania, South Carolina, Utah, and Vermont followed suit.[37] When Massachusetts enacted its version of the three strikes law in 2012, it became the twenty-eighth state to have some form of the law.[38]

POLITICIANS PROMOTE MANDATORY MINIMUMS

Beyond the three strikes legislation, politicians have promoted mandatory minimum sentences of all kinds. It is common for criminal statutes to specify a maximum authorized sentence for an offense, but it became politically popular to also provide a minimum sentence. This trend derives not from a single headline-making case like that of Polly Klaas but rather from a stream of what was perceived as outrageously lenient sentences—much like the dozen or so described in chapter 4 and the appendix, such as the sentence to probation and community service for the shopkeeper who shot a teenage girl in the back after wrongly accusing her of shoplifting and the sentence of a fine for the two racist men who hunted down their victim after a confrontation in a bar and beat him to death with a baseball bat.

Dissatisfaction with overly forgiving judges who were given broad discretion nurtured the mandatory minimum movement that took hold during the 1970s, initially in New York when drug and crime rates were rising.[39] Once begun, the movement took on substantial momentum. From 1991 to 2011 the number of mandatory minimum penalties in federal criminal law nearly doubled.[40] More than two-thirds of the states have mandatory minimums for drug offenses.[41] More than 80 percent of the increase in the prison population between 1985 and 1995 was due to drug convictions that triggered mandatory minimum sentences.[42]

Unfortunately, the shift to mandatory minimums essentially guarantees a regular stream of unjust sentences, some grossly so. Every offense or offender presents its own unique situation. A just sentence requires taking into account the seriousness of the offense, as well as the culpability and capacities of the offender. Because of the wide differences among cases, any mandatory minimum will impose an excessive sentence in some cases.

Research studies demonstrate the point. One study of laypersons' shared expectations of justice showed the dramatic conflict between the law's application of mandatory minimums in real cases and the average person's judgments about those cases. In one three strikes case, test subjects gave an offender 3.1 years; in reality, the court was required to give life imprisonment. In a cocaine case, subjects gave 4.2 years, while the court was obliged to give life without parole. In a marijuana case, the subjects gave 1.9 years, while the court was compelled to give fifteen years to life.[43] The unfortunate irony here is that these cases are seen as grossly unjust even by the lay public who elected the politicians who put the mandatory minimum sentencing rules in place.[44]

To illustrate how badly wrong the system can go with mandatory minimums generally and three strikes statutes in particular, consider the case of Shane Taylor.

Twenty-Five Years to Life for Possessing Drugs Worth Ten Dollars

At age eleven, Shane Taylor is living on the streets of Los Angeles.[45] He had previously been bouncing around from house to house, often staying with friends and relatives. After a few years on the streets, he develops a methamphetamine addiction, initially out of curiosity and as a respite from his otherwise bleak life.

Around age sixteen he meets Shelly Hayes. The two begin dating and before long have fallen in love. Hayes sees the good in Taylor. Taylor in turn appreciates that Hayes does not use drugs and is trying to make a life for herself by going to night school. Taylor is drawn to that positive path. However, in 1988 he is arrested for two burglaries that he committed to feed his drug addiction and spends time in prison. Neither of the burglarized homes was occupied, and Taylor took something from only one of the houses. He serves his time in prison and says he "learned [his] lesson."[46] After his release, he marries Hayes, and the two begin their life together.

When Hayes tells Taylor that she is pregnant, he is overwhelmed with joy. He is certain that he wants to be a good father and to get his life together. He starts working full-time as a prep cook, earning money to support his family. His daughter, Alisha, is born into a loving home, and Taylor has never been happier. He holds a steady job, is a good husband and father, and together he and Hayes strive to raise their daughter.

In 1996 Taylor and Hayes's brother take a small retreat together as a break from their normal hardworking lives. They drive up toward the Sequoia National Park, where they find a scenic overlook, pull over, turn on the car radio, and open a few beers. A police officer driving past also decides to pull over and see if either of the young men is underage. Unfortunately, Taylor has not quite managed to completely give up meth. The police officer finds 0.14 grams of the drug in a plastic bag tucked into Taylor's wallet. The drugs have a street value of under ten dollars.

Taylor is convicted of illegal narcotics possession. When he shows up for sentencing a month later, Judge Howard Broadman is surprised to see him: "I never expected to see you again, frankly. I thought a lot about you. And I said, 'Jeez, if I were him, I'd do research and find out what country didn't have extradition laws,' because I don't think I'd have showed back up."[47] Taylor has done what the law requires of him and is hoping to get a sentence of a year or two and treatment for his drug problem. To his shock and horror and that of his family, Taylor is sentenced to twenty-five years to life for his ten dollars' worth of drugs. Because of his burglary and the attempted burglary more than eight years ago, the minor possession offense becomes his third strike and requires a mandatory minimum sentence.

Hayes is forced to raise their four-year-old daughter by herself, as Taylor is locked up for the foreseeable future for carrying that meth in his wallet. Years later the judge who was compelled to sentence him attempted, with the help of a private group, to get Taylor's sentence reduced.[48]

This outcome has been the case for thousands of defendants in California and other states that enacted similar—three strikes or repeat-offender legislation. Lester Wallace was a homeless man suffering from schizophrenia who had two nonviolent residential burglaries on his record. When police caught him attempting to steal a car radio, he became an early victim of the three strikes legislation in California, having committed his crime hours after the legislation came into effect. He was sentenced to twenty-five years to life. Curtis Wilkerson was sentenced to twenty-five years to life for shoplifting; his first two strikes arose from some group criminal activities he participated in more than thirteen years before. The property he was trying to steal was a $2.50 pair of white tube socks.[49] Under many three strikes statutes, petty offenders are being incarcerated for long prison terms.[50]

Everyone—offenders and the public alike—would have been better off if this sentencing war had never begun, if the system had restrained overly lenient sentencing, perhaps with sentencing guidelines, and had never sparked the shadow vigilante impulse of voter outrage over such leniency that gave us three strikes statutes and mandatory minimums.[51]

The problem is we now have mandatory minimums, and, as unnecessary as they may be, getting rid of them will not be easy because politicians will worry that voting to repeal them will mark the politicians as being "soft on crime" during the next election.

We will for some time pay the price for our past sins of enacting rules and practices that produce predictable failures of justice, advertising the system's seeming indifference to doing justice. At the very least, we can stop making things worse and begin to repair the system's moral credibility by having the system publicly and persuasively commit itself to the importance of doing justice and to forsake trading justice away unnecessarily or for a less important benefit.

The effect of justice-frustrating sentencing in sparking the shadow vigilante impulse that stoked politicians' calls for three strikes and mandatory minimums can be seen in other contexts as well, in which injustice-producing legislation suddenly becomes popular. Consider other examples with similar dynamics.

POLITICIANS PROMOTE REDUCING THE AGE TO BE TRIED AS AN ADULT

Multiple Robber-Murderer Gets Five Years of Rehabilitation

Willie Bosket is a troubled child.[52] In third grade, he is "having problems in school like pulling fire alarms and fighting with the students and the teachers and stealing school books and materials like colored paper."[53] In 1974, after several run-ins with the law, a judge sends him to Brookwood Center for Boys. He sneaks out to get drunk, skips classes, hits another boy in the eye with a poker, rapes another boy in the shower, steals cigarettes from a vending machine, and drives a truck into a social worker. After being released to a group home in Brooklyn, he quickly runs away, back to his home neighborhood of Harlem.

On a cold spring morning in 1978, Bosket, now around fourteen years old, lifts $380 from a sleeping subway passenger. With that cash, he buys himself a .22-caliber handgun with a holster he can strap to his leg. On Sunday, March 19, 1978, Bosket is again riding the subway, looking for an easy victim to rob. In the late afternoon, around 5:30 p.m., he spots a passenger sleeping. Waiting until they are alone in the car, he nudges the man, Noel Perez, to see if he will wake easily. When there is no response, Bosket starts to remove the watch from the man's wrist. Suddenly the passenger wakes up, startling Bosket, who draws his gun and shoots him in the head twice. As blood pools around the body, Bosket grabs the watch, some money, and a gold ring. Instead of feeling remorse about taking the man's life, Bosket brags about what he has done to his sister, apparently emboldened by the fact that he has gotten away with murder. With no witnesses, the police are unable to identify the killer of Perez.

Later that same week, on Thursday, March 23, Bosket, with his gun strapped to his leg and his seventeen-year-old cousin Herman by his side, sets out to make some money. Having had recent success robbing subway passengers, they head to the closest subway station in Harlem: 148th Street and Lexington Avenue. As they wait for the next train to arrive, they notice a yard worker, Anthony Lamorte, connecting cars to waiting trains. He is carrying a handheld CB radio that is worth quite a bit of money. As they approach Lamorte, he turns to face them and tells them to "get the hell out," since the area is a restricted zone for workers only. When the youths taunt Lamorte, telling him to "come down here and make us get out," he moves toward them.[54] Bosket pulls out his gun and demands the CB radio. As Lamorte turns to run, Bosket fires, hitting him in the right shoulder. Lamorte is able to reach safety and call for help, while the two young men flee.

This failed robbery does not deter Bosket and Herman. Over the next few days, they continue to rob subway passengers at gunpoint. From one man they get twelve dollars after they kick him down the stairs. Another man is shot in the hip when he resists their demands. Bosket is apprehended for shooting the man in the hip but released. With a murder and several violent assaults under his belt and no punishment, Bosket feels invulnerable.

On Monday, March 27, just over a week after his first killing, Bosket and his cousin once again go to the subway station. The car they enter is empty except for one passenger. As the train leaves the station, Bosket pulls out his gun and threatens the passenger, demanding all of his money. When the man tells them he does not have any cash, Bosket kills him. Going through the man's pockets, Bosket finds two dollars.

Worried, the NYPD turns its full attention to investigating the subway killings. When Bosket sees a front-page newspaper article about the killings, he proudly shows it to his sister. The police eventually pick up Bosket and his cousin for questioning. They get the cousin to turn on Bosket in return for lenient treatment and charge Bosket with two counts of murder and one count of attempted murder.

Bosket, who is still not old enough to drive a car, has been in and out of the New York juvenile courts his entire life and knows that as a juvenile he is mostly protected from punishment. While being detained awaiting the hearing, he stabs another boy with a fork, hits a counselor in the face, and chokes a psychiatrist. The judge is shocked by his belligerent behavior. Despite all this, when Bosket pleads guilty to the two counts of murder and one count of attempted murder, he receives a sentence of five years' placement in the Division for Youth, the maximum allowed under current law for a juvenile. The focus for juvenile offenders is rehabilitation. Facing similar charges, an adult could have been sentenced to fifteen years to life.

Politicians are outraged. Reports of the subway killer's violent escapades throughout the media have scared people, and many are shocked to see the perpetrator receive so light a sentence, especially since rehabilitation does not seem to work for this repeat offender. Mayor Ed Koch calls Bosket a "mad-dog" murderer and complains that "it's an outrage that in this town you can kill, you can murder and you can do it a second time and not get the death penalty."[55] New York governor Hugh Carey tells reporters, "There was a breakdown of the system, and it is really on the doorstep of the Division for Youth. The blame is squarely on the shoulders of the department."[56] After stating that "this type of offender should never be allowed back on the streets," he calls legislators to Albany for a special session, during which they will radically revise the juvenile justice system.[57]

The Juvenile Offender Act of 1978 is passed just a month after Willie Bosket receives his five-year placement.[58] The act changes the New York criminal justice system's treatment of juveniles; it becomes the harshest in the country and shifts the principle of punishment away from rehabilitation to a focus strictly on protecting society. The new laws make fourteen- and fifteen-year-olds equally criminally responsible as adults for fourteen listed crimes and makes even thirteen-year-olds criminally responsible for murder.[59]

The defense of immaturity is no longer available for these crimes (which include kidnapping, manslaughter, arson, and burglary); a juvenile will face the same punishment as an adult in the same situation.[60] The act, known as the Willie Bosket Law, becomes a benchmark for other states in dealing with young offenders.

From the mid-1980s to the mid-1990s the number of homicides committed by juveniles has climbed steadily all over the country. By the late 1990s it has stopped increasing but still remains a major issue, especially in cities.[61] During that time, many other states follow New York in lowering the age at which children can be tried as adults in criminal court.[62] Most states allow prosecution in adult court of juveniles who are sixteen years old or younger for some offense.[63]

While one can easily understand the frustration over the criminal justice system's failures in cases like that of Willie Bosket, the reaction again is to support legislation that goes too far and that now guarantees a regular stream of injustices, as the system is now required to ignore the immaturity of many offenders who deserve mitigation or excuse. To illustrate the point, consider the case of Shimeek Gridine.

Seventy-Year Sentence for a Fourteen-Year-Old's First Offense

Shimeek Gridine, growing up in northern Florida, plays Pop Warner football and dreams of being a merchant seaman when he grows up, excited by the stories he heard of his grandfather who had chosen that career path.[64] Gridine works hard in school and achieves good grades. At age thirteen, his mother loses her job. Because money is tight they move to Jacksonville to live with his grandparents.

After school on April 21, 2009, Gridine, now fourteen, and his younger friend, twelve, go to the local barbershop to hang out. Gridine is going through an emotionally hard time, since two family members died in the previous weeks.

As they leave the barbershop, they notice a strange-shaped item lying under a parked car. They crouch down to investigate and realize it is a small shotgun. They pull it out, both thrilled and scared at their new discovery. Just then they see a man across the alley taking the trash out of a restaurant. Thinking he is the owner, these two boys approach him with the gun and demand that he give them all the money he has.

Unamused and seemingly unafraid of the young boys, the man refuses their demands and turns to walk back into the restaurant. As he does this Gridine fires the gun, pelting the man's back, shoulder, and neck with tiny pellets. The two boys quickly run away, scared. The man is taken to the hospital and released that same day.

Gridine and his friend return to their homes and try to act as if nothing had happened. The police investigate, and the boys become nervous and agitated. Gridine tells his grandfather what he has done. Feeling very bad about it, Gridine goes to the Jacksonville Sherriff's Office with his grandfather and turns himself in.

Because he is only fourteen and has no history of violence, Gridine is hopeful that the judge will be lenient. He is charged with first-degree attempted murder, attempted armed robbery, and aggravated battery. Gridine is charged as an adult even though he is only fourteen. He pleads guilty to armed robbery on the advice of his lawyer, who is confident that he will get a much lesser sentence by doing so. Gridine elects to be tried before the judge rather than with a jury on the other charges.

Family members from as far away as New York come down to Florida for the trial to speak on behalf of the boy and to show their support. However, all of this support seems to have a negative effect on the judge, as he declares, "Because you were known to be a good kid, because you have good grades and a good family that loves you, you knew better. Therefore, for the first charge of Premeditated Attempted Murder, I sentence you to 70 years in prison. On the second charge of Armed Robbery, I sentence you to 25 years. You will serve the sentences together."[65] The sentence is thirty years longer than the sentence the prosecution had asked for.

The seventy-year sentence is essentially a life sentence. As Gridine's public defender points out, it extends beyond the life expectancy for an American male. A life sentence for a fourteen-year-old seems to take away the possibility for the youth to "demonstrate growth and maturity" and instead is a decision to simply let him rot in adult prison.[66]

Unfortunately, Gridine's situation is not unique. Since the wave of harsher penalties against juveniles swept the nation, hundreds of children have found themselves tried in adult court and sentenced to long prison terms. These are not all hardened repeat offenders like Willie Bosket. For many, it was their first offense and an act of impulsiveness. In one case, a thirteen-year-old boy who was raised by an alcoholic and cocaine-addicted father who frequently watched pornography in the home went to his neighbor's house and raped the twenty-three-year-old mother. A psychologist found that the youth had "underlying neurological problems that made him more impulsive than other juveniles his age."[67] He was given a sentence of life plus twenty years.[68] In Nevada another thirteen-year-old was sentenced to life without parole after pleading guilty to killing the man who had been sexually molesting him.[69] A twelve-year-old boy in South Carolina was sentenced to sixty years in prison for killing his grandparents after they beat him and locked him in his room.[70]

Outrage over the system's failure to restrain vicious sixteen-year-old repeat offender Willie Bosket led to distorting the criminal justice system so that it now gives essentially life imprisonment to immature first offenders like fourteen-year-old Shimeek Gridine. Young offenders and the public would have been better off if the system had initially taken more seriously its obligation to punish and to protect so that a Willie Bosket case would never have happened.

The best way to avoid the destructive effects of shadow vigilantism is for the criminal justice system to publicly commit itself to the importance of doing justice—giving offenders the punishment they deserve, no more and no less. With that, the system can earn back its moral credibility with the community and can avoid the downward spiral of shadow vigilantism and its distorting effects.

10

CRIMINAL JUSTICE OFFICIALS AS SHADOW VIGILANTES

Chapter 3 discussed the practice of "testilying" in which police officers feel morally justified in lying in court about the circumstances of a search or seizure because they see the exclusionary rule (which disallows use of even the most reliable evidence if a court determines that the search rules are violated) as an immoral undermining of society's obligation to fight crime and do justice. Also discussed there was the case of sexual psychopath Bill Bradford during which police played fast and loose with the court's warrant rules because they saw no other way of effectively stopping this multiple murderer.

These two examples are symptomatic of the larger problem: officials in many if not most parts of the criminal justice system see the system's apparent indifference to failures of justice as a moral justification for manipulating or perverting the system as needed to catch offenders and have them receive the punishment they deserve. Below is another example of subverting the search and seizure rules, followed by examples of other kinds of shadow vigilante subversions in other parts of the system.

EXCEEDING SEARCH AND SEIZURE RULES AND TESTILYING ABOUT IT TO SUBVERT THE EXCLUSIONARY RULE

In the Columbia Heights section of Washington, DC, on the evening of November 1, 1969, five-year-old Penny Sellers and her older sister Denise visit the apartment of their grandfather Robert Dennis. Also present there is a neighbor, William Sheard, who gives the girls candy and lets them play with his puppy, as he has done in the past. Around 9:30 p.m.

the girls have moved on to watch television in the basement apartment of a friend. Penny leaves to go back to Sheard's apartment to play with his puppy again. It is the last time her family ever sees her.

After about an hour, Penny's grandfather asks Sheard if he knows where Penny is and is told that she "had gone up the street with a man." At the grandfather's request, Sheard calls the police. The police arrive at about 11:00 p.m., having been advised to contact "a Sheard."[1] Upon meeting Sheard, officers are informed by him that a child is missing, that he has telephoned the police, and that he had been the last person to see the child. One hour later, police find Penny's body amid debris on the floor of a garage near the apartment building. Penny's genital area is exposed and bloody. A later autopsy reveals that she has been raped, and died due to asphyxiation from suffocation. Police also find her underpants in the alley near the garage and one of her shoes on the back porch of the house next door.

The police chief orders a lockdown of the apartment complex and for all male residents to be questioned. During the questioning, officers are to also make a visual search for blood in the open living areas of the men's apartments. Officers Shuler and Jones are assigned to question Sheard in his apartment, since he is apparently the last person to see Penny alive.

Officer Shuler knocks on the door and identifies himself as a police officer. When Sheard answers the door, the officers immediately become suspicious because Sheard has fresh scratches on his face, looks as though he has just taken a bath, is wearing fresh but heavily wrinkled clothing, and his overall behavior is odd. Believing that Sheard might hide or destroy vital evidence if they wait to get a warrant, the officers are anxious to enter and examine his apartment.

Officer Shuler advises Sheard that a small child has been killed and that Shuler and his partner, Officer Jones, would like to come inside to talk with him. Sheard later testifies that he did not authorize the officers to come into his apartment but that they simply barged in without permission. Officer Shuler testifies that Sheard was "friendly" and said,

"Come in, come in, I'd like to do all I can to find out." Later, however, Officer Shuler testifies during a motion to suppress evidence that he does not remember exactly what Sheard had said. Officer Jones testifies, "Well, he just stepped back. And I don't remember if he said, come in, but I was under the *impression* that we were to enter the room by his attitude."[2]

After the officers enter the apartment, they observe that the room is in a state of disarray: candy is strewn about on the floor, and a large, damp, burned area is evident on the mattress of a bed. One of the officers leaves to summon their superiors, and the other conducts a plain-view search of the area—evidence that is already exposed to view is considered in "plain view" and does not require a warrant to seize it. The officer supposedly finds in plain view a pair of dark-green pants, with bloodstains, sitting on top of a hamper.

Authorities seize the pants and other evidence and take Sheard to the nearby precinct. A benzidine test reacts positively to the stain on the pants indicating that it is human blood. Additional tests of Sheard's right hand and his penis also show positive for blood. Chemical analysis reveals that the blood on Sheard's jacket, the dark-green slacks, the blanket and bedspread, and Penny's dress and slip is type O blood (Sheard's blood is type A; Penny's was type O). Fibers from the bedspread and blanket are discovered on Penny's dress and slip, on all of Sheard's seized clothing, and in scrapings from the heads of both Sheard and Penny.

With the staggering amount of evidence against Sheard, a grand jury indicts him on February 2, 1970, for the rape-murder of Penny. The indictment includes four counts: felony murder, first-degree murder, rape, and taking indecent liberties with a minor. Sheard is found guilty and sentenced to concurrent terms of twenty years to life on the felony murder count and of ten to thirty years on the rape count.

The truth is that the two officers did not in fact find the critical evidence, the bloodstained pants, just sitting out in plain view. Rather, they—and perhaps even their superiors—probably made a conscious choice to exceed the search and seizure rules and to hide their violation because they believed it was necessary to find the rapist-murderer of a five-year-old girl and because the evidence of the crime would otherwise have been quickly destroyed by the perpetrator.

Police officers morally justify their lying in court to compensate for what they see as improper rules that regularly lead to failures of justice—complex rules that have "metastasized into a dizzying array of formalistic doctrines and sub-doctrines."[3] Harvard law professor Alan Dershowitz explains, "Almost all police lie about whether they violated the Constitution in order to convict guilty defendants."[4] Even police officials concede that police lying in court, especially to justify improper searches, is not uncommon.[5] It has earned its own label: "testilying." The term was coined by New York City police officers apparently to help them justify in their own minds why it was different from normal lying under oath—while not legally justified, it was morally justified. "When an officer is deceptive in court, the rationale goes, he is 'not quite lying' but 'not quite testifying truthfully and completely' either. Testilying is seen as a middle ground between pure honesty and pure dishonesty."[6]

One officer caught lying under oath said it was "standard procedure" and used to "counterbalance the loopholes used by drug dealers to evade the police."[7] An empirical study by Myron Orfield, a professor of civil rights law, conducted in Chicago concludes that "virtually all the officers admit that the police commit perjury, if infrequently, at suppression hearings."[8] (Suppression hearings are conducted to decide which evidence will be allowed to be used in trial versus which evidence must be excluded.) The study claimed that up to 76 percent of the officers surveyed had "shaded" facts in order to establish probable cause to search for evidence.[9] Some claim that police commit perjury in 20 to 50 percent of cases where they have to testify regarding Fourth Amendment (exclusionary rule) issues.[10]

Most famous among the examinations of police perjury is the 1994 Mollen Commission report on the New York Police Department: "Police perjury and falsification is a serious problem facing the department and the criminal justice system." Such perjury is "probably the most common form of police corruption . . . particularly in connection with arrests for possession of narcotics and guns."[11]

The Mollen Commission report spoke to the reasons for the officers' willingness to lie: "In their view, irregardless of the legality of the arrest, the defendant is in fact guilty and ought to be arrested." It explained that the officers were frustrated with the legal rules that protected criminals from search and seizure because the rules were perceived as "unrealistic rules of law." Officers also expressed frustration about their "inability to stem the crime in their precinct through legal means."[12] They held a strong belief that perjury was acceptable because it was necessary to stem the tide of crime and because it was "'doing God's work'—doing whatever it takes to get a suspected criminal off the streets."[13]

Other writers have made the same point: "Police view perjury as a necessary means to achieve the ends of justice. Constitutional rules—particularly the Exclusionary Rule—are viewed as technicalities that 'let the criminal . . . go free because the constable has blundered.'"[14] One study found that testilying began soon after cases were dismissed under the 1961 Supreme Court holding in *Mapp v. Ohio*, which created the exclusionary rule.[15] To police, "there is a deep-seated disregard for what they consider to be silly little laws made by a silly little Supreme Court in a backroom far removed from the dangerous streets they are trying to bring order into."[16]

Presumably, judges, like others in the system, are well aware of the testilying. Yet some may share the shadow vigilante sympathy motivating the lying and thus, while no doubt unhappy about perjury in their court, play along and accept the testimony as sufficient to justify the search or the arrest. As Alan Dershowitz reports, when officers offer perjured testimony, the judge "shakes his head in knowing frustration, but accepts the officers' account as credible."[17] A series of interviews revealed that 75 percent of judges, 100 percent of public defenders, and 65 percent of prosecutors "believed that judges sometimes fail to suppress evidence when they know police searches are illegal."[18]

This is a sad state of affairs but in some ways a predictable development as the collection of outrageous results from the law's "technicalities" accumulates (as in some of the cases described in chapter 4 and the appendix). As the law increasingly loses moral credibility failing to give offenders the punishment they deserve, it becomes increasingly easier for shadow vigilantes to justify the subversion of what they see as an immoral system. It is probably no coincidence that testilying is most frequently associated with satisfying the technicalities of search and seizure law. The same officer who feels comfortable lying about which side of a house's threshold he was on when he made a drug seizure might think it abhorrent to lie about a matter related to the actual guilt or innocence of the defendant.

Just as police officers morally justify their testilying, so too do prosecutors manipulate the system out of frustration with what they see as the system's common indifference to doing justice. This view frequently plays itself out for some prosecutors when they are presented with classic vigilantes trying to provide the justice that the system does not. Consider two examples.

PROSECUTOR RELUCTANCE TO PROSECUTE SOME VIGILANTES

No Prosecution of Vigilantes Who Beat a Child Rapist

Jane Doe grows up in the neighborhood of Hubbard Farms in southwest Detroit, raised by her single mother.[19] When Jane is eight years old her mother dies, and neighbors across the street and, in fact, the whole neighborhood pitch in to raise Jane, calling her "a daughter of the community."[20] The community feels particularly protective of Jane in part because she has Down syndrome. She is often seen on her front porch, dancing and singing along with the radio.

On July 8, 2013, at age fifteen, Jane gets her first job at the local Café Con Leche. She walks the four blocks to and from work twice a week. These small shifts are a stepping-stone for Jane to gain more independence. Her employer describes her as a hard worker. Less than two weeks later, on July 17, she does not show up for the start of her shift. Her employer becomes concerned and calls her guardians, who tell him that she has already left for work. When she finally arrives at work, Jane simply tells her boss that she has been with a friend.

Later that night, Jane confides to her adopted parents that she has been raped. Ramiro Sanchez, age forty-three, approached her and asked her to come inside his apartment. Once inside, he disrobed, kissed, and raped her. He then took nude photos of her on his cell phone. After the attack, Jane quickly dressed and went to work, not knowing what else to do. Her parents immediately notify the police. They provide Sanchez's address and his description.

Jane, her parents, and the community anxiously await an investigation and charges to be pressed. It is not until two days later that a rape kit is finally administered. Several days later, on July 26, the parents are appalled to still see Sanchez walking around free. They send out a chain email through the tight-knit community describing the rape and rapist. On July 29 the community receives some reassuring news: a person reports seeing Sanchez being led out of his apartment by police. But just two days later he is released without any charges. Jane's parents are told that the investigation is ongoing, but the community sees apathy and inattention. They are angry. A fifteen-year-old daughter of their community with Down syndrome has been raped, and she needs support.

Fifteen days after the rape, on August 1, community leaders distribute flyers with a "Rapist Warning" and several pictures of Sanchez. Storefronts along the main street of the neighborhood put up the flyers in their front windows. Tensions and frustrations continue to build, and after hearing that the rape kit has not yet even been processed by the state police, the community explodes. A Facebook thread on the incident has a post that states the following: "attention/warning: this piece of shit u see in this flyer raped a 16 yr old girl in our neighborhood!!! . . . me personally, if i seen him, id call the cops then i would beat the shit out of him myself till the cops arrive. i hate worthless scum like this. stand up for your hood."[21]

On Monday, August 5, at around 1:00 p.m. Sanchez is spotted walking along the main street. A man rides up on a bicycle, jumps off, and while beating Sanchez shouts, "You like raping little girls?" Sanchez manages to escape and runs down the street, where he is attacked by a larger group of people. The crowd kicks and beats him until police arrive. Sanchez is taken to the hospital, where he is treated for his injuries. Another post goes up on Facebook describing how "a friend of mine caught him" and claims that this was "great news for southwest detroit . . . well . . . thanks to everyone who shared the flyer and spread the word."[22]

Wayne County prosecutor Kym Worthy does not seek to arrest anyone in connection with the beatings. Jerome Warfield, a member of Detroit's civilian commission that oversees police, says, "We do understand that the neighbors were enraged." He goes on to warn, though, that "vigilantism cannot be accepted when you're impeding upon somebody's rights."[23] The community is torn between praising the actions of the vigilante mob that finally delivered some justice and condemning its members as criminals themselves.[24] Although it is clear who participated in the beatings, no charges are ever brought.

We have previously noted other examples where vigilantes were not charged. Recall George Zimmerman's killing of unarmed teenager Trayvon Martin, discussed in chapter 9. No charges were filed by the local authorities until the national press focused on the racial aspect of the case. The same was true in the case of Bernhard Goetz unnecessarily shooting Darrell Cabey in the subway car, discussed in chapter 3, and of the beating of Rodney King in Los Angeles, discussed in chapter 9. Whatever one may think of how vigilantes should ultimately be dealt with, the potentially controversial circumstances suggest that at least some public examination of the events would be useful. Yet prosecutors regularly forgo filing charges unless forced to do so by media attention or public outcry.

Prosecutor manipulation of the system works in reverse as well, overcharging rather than undercharging a case, where they believe the system has regularly failed in the past to give an offender the punishment he deserved. When prosecutors finally get hold of a justice-avoiding offender, it is not uncommon for them to seriously overcharge the violator's offenses or to exaggerate their claim of what constitutes an appropriate sentence, feeling justified by the system's past failures to do justice. Consider an example.

PROSECUTORIAL OVERCHARGING TO MAKE UP FOR PAST FAILURES OF JUSTICE

Finally Getting Something on a Career Criminal

Edward Augustine, living in New Orleans, has had numerous run-ins with the police, but they rarely end in conviction and punishment.[25] He has a single conviction for attempted possession of a firearm with a controlled dangerous substance. He has been through the "revolving door" of the criminal justice system many times. Police regularly arrest him on drug or weapons charges, but he will later walk back out on the street. Sometimes it is because the police are unable to find witnesses willing to testify against him. In other instances, prosecutors do not proceed because at the time they have limited prosecution resources and "higher profile" cases in greater need of their efforts.[26]

In 2008 the new district attorney, Leon Cannizzaro, has a different attitude. Cannizzaro makes it office policy that no case is too insignificant to try and pursue. He makes it his mission to increase the percentage of cases his office will pursue from 50 percent to 90 percent.

On January 7, 2011, a New Orleans police officer observes a car making an unlawful right turn at a red light. The officer turns on his lights and siren to pull the car over, but the car speeds away. The officer follows the vehicle, and as he pulls up beside it, he sees the driver, Augustine, dumping white powder out of the car window.

The officer chases Augustine for several blocks but stops when Augustine enters a one-way street. Augustine accidentally hits another vehicle. Augustine gets out of his car and flees. The officer pursues him on foot. As Augustine attempts to climb a fence in a nearby alley, the officer Tases him and places him under arrest.

Upon returning to the scene of the crash, the officer learns that Augustine has killed the passenger in the other vehicle, a college freshman who had returned home for the Christmas holidays. The officer also finds numerous packages of heroin in Augustine's possession. It also comes to light that the car being driven by Augustine has been reported missing by its owner, the mother of Augustine's girlfriend.

District Attorney Cannizzaro is unhappy that this career criminal has been allowed to pass through the system on so many occasions without facing any serious punishment. He believes that by not aggressively prosecuting earlier narcotics cases, the system was in effect "creating monsters."[27] He is determined to pursue Augustine aggressively to try to make up for past failings of the office.

He charges Augustine with manslaughter for causing the death in the accident, for which Augustine ultimately gets, at Cannizzaro's urging, a fifty-year sentence. Cannizzaro also charges Augustine with possession with intent to distribute illegal drugs—the drugs he dumped out the window—and, again at Cannizzaro's urging, Augustine gets an additional sentence of fifty years. While Augustine did not have his girlfriend's mother's express permission to drive her car on that occasion, the woman does not wish to press charges. Cannizzaro nonetheless adds this offense to the list and gets another twenty years added onto Augustine's sentence, for a total sentence of 120 years—a sentence several times longer than what even an intentional murder would typically get.[28]

In this form of shadow vigilantism by prosecutors (and judges), the officials feel morally justified in manipulating the system in order to compensate for past failures of justice.

Prosecutorial overcharging is of two sorts: vertical overcharging, in which the prosecutor charges offenses for which he or she has insufficient proof to convict, and horizontal overcharging, in which the prosecutor charges a series of overlapping offenses arising from the same criminal act.[29] In the latter type, prosecutors charge every offense for which a defendant might theoretically satisfy the offense definition, no matter how overlapping the offenses may be. Thus, a prosecutor might take a standard rape case—using force to compel intercourse—and add on "assault, kidnapping, gross sexual imposition, etc."[30] This is made possible because most American criminal codes, in which the state's criminal laws are collected, grow over time to have a vast collection of overlapping offenses.[31]

Legislatures have been constantly adding new offenses, sometimes making the code seven or eight times longer than its original form based on the Model Penal Code, but without substantially expanding the code's coverage.[32] So, for example, most states now have an offense of "carjacking," after a series of newspaper headlines about such conduct. Does anyone doubt that such conduct was already punished severely as armed robbery (as well as auto theft, kidnapping, assault, etc.)? Adding one more offense to charge was an act of potential showmanship, not criminal code improvement.

The forests of overlapping offenses exist in large part because prosecutors have politically promoted them. Prosecutors have put political muscle into supporting a constant stream of new offenses that typically are just added on top of the old ones. To protect this ability to bring multiple charges, they have repeatedly opposed criminal code reforms that would streamline codes and eliminate unnecessary overlaps. For example, in a new criminal law codification undertaken in Illinois in 2003, which had as one of its primary aims the consolidation of overlapping offenses, the recodification was ultimately blocked by the political opposition of prosecutors.[33] The prosecutors instead sponsored a new reform commission that kept the redundancies in the current code.[34]

Prosecutors' moral justification for excessive charging might rest on any or all of several different claims, the same sorts of claims heard from police to justify their testilying. First, the criminal justice process has so many barriers to an offender getting the liability and punishment he or she deserves that such excess is needed just to end up with something that approximates what is really deserved.[35] In other words, the prosecutor feels that by putting on several extra charges he is getting some insurance. That way, no matter what the court does, the defendant is less likely to escape all punishment. With this insurance policy, the defendant may not do the maximum time but he'll get some sanction. Second, it makes sense to try to get more liability and punishment than an offender deserves for the offense because, given the gross ineffectiveness of the system, the current offense may be just the tip of the iceberg of the offenses he or she has actually committed.[36]

Finally, many people care little if the overcharging generates undeserved liability for both present and unpunished past offenses. That is not something that ought to be a concern to prosecutors because the criminal justice system has given up any pretense about being a search for justice. It is simply a system of mutual combat between the defense counsel and prosecutors, with winners and losers, the goal of which is to always win and to never lose. Just as the defense counsel see their job as always getting the least punishment they can for their guilty clients, prosecutors, in a symmetrical fashion, should see their job as getting as much punishment as they can for guilty defendants.[37]

Strategic overcharging might seem to the uninitiated to be too unethical to be done openly. But the increasing game-like features of the system have dulled participants' sensibilities. Indeed, one need only look at similar manipulative conduct by federal judges before the Sentencing Reform Act of 1984 stopped the practice. Federal law at the time required that all offenders be eligible for early release by the United States Parole Commission no later than after serving one-third of their sentence. Judges who were uncomfortable with this early release could, and did, short-circuit the system by simply determining the sentence they really wanted, then tripling it.[38] Thus, offenders would become eligible for release only after serving the full term the judges thought appropriate. Prosecutors may be making similar sorts of strategic manipulations when they overcharge.

It was in part this judicial manipulative practice that contributed to the enactment of the "truth in sentencing" provisions of the Sentencing Reform Act of 1984. People had become increasingly skeptical of the sentences that were publicly imposed because they always ended in early release. The new act requires that an offender serve at least 85 percent of the sentence imposed—an attempt to earn back some credibility for the system.[39]

WHY SHADOW VIGILANTISM IS SO DANGEROUS, MORE DANGEROUS THAN CLASSIC VIGILANTISM

It could be argued that the manipulations and subversions inspired by shadow vigilantism—of both the official sort discussed in this chapter and the citizen sort discussed in the previous chapter—are not something that, as a practical matter, ought to be of significant concern. We can for the most part ignore these problems because they are only a minor part of the criminal justice process. But the truth is that shadow vigilantism is dramatically more damaging than classic vigilantism.

First, the effect of shadow vigilantism is less dramatic but more pervasive. Shadow vigilantism appeals not just to the unusual person or group willing to be a classic vigilante—willing to openly violate the law in serious ways—but also to more ordinary people. Many people who cannot bring themselves to commit explicit lawlessness *can* bring themselves to undermine and subvert, through noncooperation, lying, or other lower-level misconduct, a system that they see as being immorally indifferent to serious wrongdoing.

Imagine all the neighbors in the chapter 8 cases who refused to help authorities pursue the classic vigilantes. As we asked in chapter 9, if those neighbors were sitting on a jury for the vigilantes, would they be likely to vote to acquit? If they were the grand jurors or prosecutor in the case, would they want to avoid bringing charges? If they were voting on a proposal to change the rules that led to the failure of justice, would they vote for the change and for a politician who supported the change? It seems highly likely that they would do so in all these instances. The fact that an entire neighborhood can show its willingness to succumb to a shadow vigilante impulse shows the potential sweep of the problem.

Further, shadow vigilantism is more problematic than the classic form because the criminal justice system cannot effectively deter it in the way it can classic vigilantism. The shadow vigilantes' conduct may be criminal in some cases, but it also may be only unethical or unjust or unfair in others. The failure to report a crime or to assist investigators is commonly not a crime in the United States.[40] And even if it is criminal, it cannot be effectively deterred. If prosecutors have no witness to the crime itself, how can they find a witness to a witness' failure to report the crime?

Even if the shadow vigilantes' actions are not morally justified (under chapter 5's rules), they may well believe that they are.[41] They probably see themselves in the way civil disobedience protesters might see themselves: they know that what they are doing is inconsistent with the law in spirit if not in fact, but they see the violation as morally justified by the law's own immorality in its indifference to doing justice.

Worse, while shadow vigilantism cannot be as effectively deterred as classic vigilantism can, it is at the same time even more damaging than the latter. Classic vigilantism, by operating openly, serves as a public protest against the system's failures of justice—a call to the system to correct itself. In contrast, shadow vigilantism is generally unseen: failure to cooperate with police and prosecutors, not reporting crimes when they are committed, jury nullification; improper exercise of discretion in charging, sentencing, and other criminal justice decisions; and political support for unjust punishment policies. It provides no public call for reform but instead seeks to remain in the shadows.

Further, shadow vigilantism introduces into the criminal justice system serious arbitrariness as well as disparity among cases. That is the level of shadow vigilantism in any given case may be unpredictable, dependent as it is on a variety of factors. That may change from case to case. The officer in one case may be testilying while the officer in an identical case may not be. A witness in one case may refuse to report a crime while the witness in another case may report it. And so on. The operation of the criminal justice system then is rendered wholly arbitrary; identical cases end in very different outcomes.

And this resulting arbitrariness and disparity only contribute in the long run to the system's reputation as being less predictable, more arbitrary, and more unjust. In other words, shadow vigilantism only serves to exacerbate the system's loss of moral credibility, which is what helped trigger the vigilantism in the first place. It invites a downward spiral of lost credibility and therefore increased subversion.

In fact, the destructive dynamic of the downward spiral is even worse than this, as the next chapter details.

Part IV

THE VIGILANTE ECHO

As previous chapters make clear, systemic failures of justice provoke shadow vigilantes to subvert and pervert the criminal justice system in order to force justice from it. But it turns out that the distorting effects go beyond those created by the shadow vigilantes. Their subverting and perverting effects provoke others, those personally affected by the effects, to become more hostile toward the system and to themselves react by trying to subvert the system in their own ways. This cycle of action and reaction continues in a downward spiral of the system's increasingly damaged credibility.

All sides would have been better off if the distorting dynamic of systemic failures of justice, shadow vigilantism, and the resulting blowback had never begun. We would be better off going forward if we could avoid the avoidable failures of justice that echo in shadow vigilantism and its blowback.

11

BLOWBACK AND THE DOWNWARD SPIRAL

Frustrated with the criminal justice system's failures to do justice and provide protection, shadow vigilantes manipulate and subvert the criminal justice process in a wide variety of ways, as illustrated in part III. But those manipulations and subversions provoke their own reaction in the form of blowback from those affected by and distortions produced by shadow vigilantes. And in the end, that blowback reaction tragically serves only to further reduce the chance of justice and safety, contributing to a downward spiral that ends in more crime and less justice.

Consider one example of this dynamic (failure of justice → shadow vigilante response → blowback): disgusted by the failures of justice that regularly arise from the "technicalities" by which serious offenders escape criminal liability, shadow vigilante police officers morally justify testi-lying in court to avoid the technicalities, and shadow vigilante civilians support mandatory minimums to block overly lenient sentencing. But those actions provoke their own reactions.

It soon becomes well-known that police lie in court to avoid the technicalities. The public perception of this in some neighborhoods may not capture the nuance of the officers' justification (as the only means of avoiding a serious failure of justice) and may well contribute to a belief that police lie in court about anything and everything. Similarly, the use of mandatory minimum sentences soon produces a string of injustices in which criminals are given sentences in excess of what they morally deserve. Both of these perceptions seriously damage the criminal justice system's reputation.

The blowback from such shadow vigilantes' subversion of the system's justness is most acute in those communities most affected by the lying and the unjust mandatory minimums. And just as the shadow vigilantes were provoked to undermine the system, so too are those affected by the lying and the excessive sentences, along with their friends and acquaintances. It is no big leap for this alienation from the system to manifest itself in action, such as a vocal opposition to cooperating with police and social ostracizing of or retribution for those who do cooperate. In the minds of those in the neighborhood, subversion of the unjust system is morally justified, just as the shadow vigilantes thought their subversion was morally justified.

But opposition to cooperation with police, including, for example, the social or physical intimidation of witnesses, is a self-defeating strategy for any community. It only strengthens the hand of criminals, gives them greater impunity to victimize, and increases their ability to further intimidate witnesses, creating a downward spiral of victimization and community disintegration.

THE "STOP SNITCHING" MOVEMENT GOES MAINSTREAM

At one time, the social norm against cooperating with police—popularly called the "Stop Snitching" movement—was just an underground cultural attitude. But it has gained enough legitimacy in some communities to be a mainstream popular message. Originally expressed in rap lyrics ("Snitches get stitches!"[1]), the "Stop Snitching" campaign was fed by a 2006 song and DVD titled *Stop Fucking Snitchin'* performed by rapper Ice Cube.[2] The rap DVD grew into a line of apparel using that phrase as its logo, as well as a follow-up DVD, *Stop Snitchin' 2*. The DVDs express threats and violence against witnesses, together with footage of people discussing their desire to kill those who "rat." The rap artist tells people not to cooperate with local authorities.[3] In Newark, New Jersey, T-shirts carry pictures of witnesses who are to be killed, and pilfered witness statements are posted online.[4] Sports stars also give legitimacy to the message: "Asked . . . how many pro athletes from high-crime areas would help identify criminals . . . Baltimore native and NBA veteran Sam Cassell said

'One hundred percent of them would say no. A hundred. If I see five guys doing something [illegal] on the street, I'm going to look the other way and hope I don't see no more.'"[5]

Fig. 11.1. Stop Snitching urban art project, 2013. (Courtesy of TrustoCorpMiami)

Ice Cube and Cassell made clear the norm against snitching that has taken hold on the streets of many American cities, including Newark, Baltimore, Philadelphia, Dallas, and Washington, DC. As legal scholar Jamie Masten explains, "The Stop Snitching movement has found its tipping point and is now infectiously sweeping through the public. . . . This code is being adhered to not only by prisoners, but by thirteen-year-old girls in school, middle-aged neighbors across the street, and ordinary citizens who would rather run away from the police instead of to them."[6]

The phenomenon is intricately woven into the social fabric of many urban communities. As the deputy attorney general overseeing the Essex County Prosecutor's Office in New Jersey explains that "the number of witnesses who remain silent because they fear for their safety is probably less than one-tenth the number who refuse to talk because they fear the social repercussions."[7] People are afraid to help because they fear becoming social outcasts, shunned by neighbors.

Nobody feels the painful effects of the social pressure against cooperation more than those grieving the loss of loved ones. One mother who lost her son to violence has gone door to door in her neighborhood, seeking answers about the murder. But no one will offer her any information. She admits that if she were on the other side of the case, she might not help either. She explains that "snitching, telling on people, isn't something that I personally would involve myself with. People don't want to talk to you if they think you're a snitch. If they were your friends, they're not your friends anymore. You're left totally all alone."[8]

Her neighbors' reluctance to help with the investigation is based on a social norm that has a root in the community's "deep distrust of the local police and prosecutors and politicians. . . . [R]acial profiling, police corruption and the excesses of the war on drugs have made them suspicious of virtually any arm of government."[9] For communities that are disproportionately impacted by these excesses, it is easy to understand why they see the criminal justice system as an enemy to be subverted rather than an institution worth supporting and helping. Harvard law professor Charles

Ogletree expressed it this way: "A lot of white Americans from suburban communities can't understand why people wouldn't talk to law enforcement. But in a lot of inner-city communities, there is so much hostility to the police that many people of color can't fathom why someone would even seriously consider helping them."[10]

Besides a pervasive distrust of the criminal justice system and its officers, many people have more practical reasons for not aiding in investigations. Consider the complicated social and economic realities in many poor, tight-knit communities. One resident, explaining his lack of cooperation with police, says that drug dealers and gang members are often the lifeblood of the local economy. "[M]aybe the parents are out of work and [money from selling drugs] helps them put food on the table," he says.[11] Without the income from their illegal activities, many residents would have a significantly more difficult life.

There is also a concern that, in assisting the police, one's own criminal history may come to light. When police take a statement from someone with a criminal record and run the name, they might find an outstanding warrant. In such cases, the citizen is arrested effectively because he or she offered information to the police.[12] Or a person may have been engaging in illegal activities himself, such as drug dealing, when he witnessed a more serious offense, such as murder.

Those who choose to help the police in spite of these harsh realities often do so clandestinely for fear of danger to themselves or their families. In some cases, they communicate with detectives by leaving notes in trash cans, or asked to be taken away in handcuffs so that "neighbors will think that they're in trouble with the police and not cooperating."[13]

All of these factors have created an environment in many communities in which ordinary citizens would rather help the criminals than have them punished in a criminal justice system they have come to distrust and disrespect. Indeed, ordinary citizens wear shirts with messages that threaten those who cooperate, and children cheer in the streets when police get into car accidents.[14] It is part of the "rules of the game" that one has to follow when living in such a community.[15] As a result, investigators report that when they arrive at a crime scene, bystanders often leave in order to avoid neighbors thinking that they might cooperate with police. Police struggle to receive cooperation in "even the worst crimes."[16]

But, of course, the success of the movement only feeds the vicious cycle by making effective prosecution of serious crimes more difficult, which increases disillusionment with the criminal justice system. With the intimidators winning the battle with authorities over public allegiance, the power of intimidators only reinforces the impunity with which they can intimidate further, and that in turn gives them a freer hand to commit more offenses. In other words, the "stop snitching" response is a recipe for disaster for the neighborhood. The lack of cooperation reduces the system's crime-control effectiveness, which further damages its reputation, leading to less credibility and less cooperation in an endless downward spiral.

THE PREVALENCE OF WITNESS INTIMIDATION IN COMMUNITIES THAT ARE INJURED BY SHADOW VIGILANTISM

In many neighborhoods, social pressures against cooperating with police have legitimized or at least given rise to social ambiguity of gang violence against witnesses, for it is expected that those who fail to follow the social norms of stop snitching will face threats and even outright violence. A gang leader in a Newark jail awaiting trial for murder put it quite clearly. When asked about the existence of a potential witness against him, he flatly dismissed the idea of a witness testifying. "What's Bam-Bam [the potential witness] going to do, take his plea deal, do his 12 years in protective custody? Then what? What's he going to do when he gets out? Where's he going to go where no one will be able to find him?"[17] The threat facing "Bam-Bam" hangs over the head of the entire community. Even a Newark grandmother, who watched her little granddaughter die in a gang shooting, refuses to cooperate with police. When pressed why, she fears she would "have to move out of the country."[18]

One might wonder if better witness protection might reduce the threat, but witnesses still face risk of intimidation and attack in police custody. In 2005, a witness to a murder is in protective custody when someone summons him to the door of his cell. The person sprays the witness with a mixture of water and baby oil that had been heated in a microwave, causing serious burns. When asked why he had done it, the attacker replied that he had heard the person was a snitch.[19]

The statistics on witness intimidation show the growing extent of this alarming trend.[20] A study of witnesses appearing in Bronx County, New York, indicated that at least 36 percent of witnesses had been directly threatened and that among those not explicitly threatened, 57 percent feared that they would be subject to reprisals.[21] A study conducted by the National Youth Gang Center indicated that 88 percent of urban prosecutors have described witness intimidation as a serious problem. In cities such as Baltimore and Boston, prosecutors estimate that witnesses face some kind of intimidation in nearly 80 percent of all homicide cases, while in Essex County, prosecutors claim that at least two-thirds of their witnesses in homicide cases receive direct threats not to testify. The *New York Times* reported in 2015 that roughly 30 percent of shooting victims in New York City refused to cooperate with investigators.[22] As violence against witnesses becomes more prevalent, the mere possibility of being killed is effective enough; no overt threat is needed.

Such pervasive intimidation has dramatically impeded the ability of law enforcement to investigate crimes and limited the number of cases prosecutors can bring to court. One US senator described the problem of witness intimidation this way: "The bad guys are willing to use tactics that the good guys haven't yet figured out how to deal with."[23] An insider report on the Essex County Homicide Squad (encompassing the city of Newark) revealed that police "see an unconquerable fear that keeps witnesses from coming forward and street intimidation that makes some recant. Police can solve a murder. Getting a conviction is a different story. Many killers walk, to kill again."[24] In St. Louis, city prosecutors have had to drop over half of their criminal cases in some neighborhoods because the witnesses, and even victims themselves, refused to cooperate.[25]

Without reliable witnesses, prosecutors are often forced to pursue charges for lesser crimes that can be caught on tape or through police stings. This takes some drug users and petty criminals off the streets but leaves the more hardened criminals to continue in their ways unimpeded. This creates what one public defender describes as a "scary message": the more serious the crime, the easier it is to get away with it.[26] The data bear this startling reality out: between 1998 and 2006, arrest rates for murders in Essex County, for which Newark is the major population base, decreased almost by half, from 81.1 percent to 41.8 percent.[27] During that same period, homicide arrest rates for the state as a whole increased from 84.7 percent to 91.7 percent.[28] (The actual number of murders in Essex County was 90 in 1998 and rose to 112 by 2006.)[29] Baltimore, in explaining its declining arrest rate for murders, has "attributed it largely to an increasing unwillingness from the public to come forward with tips in today's 'Stop Snitching' culture."[30] Regardless, this unfortunate data has led to criticism of police and prosecutors in these cities for letting more and more violent criminals remain on the streets.[31]

Prosecutors have also watched in horror as the witnesses they are relying on in serious crimes turn up dead. In New Jersey, there are dozens of examples of homicide cases set to go to trial, only to have the case collapse after a witness is intimidated or killed.[32] The Essex County Prosecutor's Office sees the problem too. To combat the rising death toll of witnesses and the number of cases that fall apart upon reaching trial, the office has "established an unwritten rule discouraging pursuit of cases that rely on a single witness, and those in which witness statements are not extensively corroborated by forensic evidence."[33]

This unofficial policy is based on two competing rationales. First and foremost, prosecutors want to protect witnesses. The state and county do not have the resources to protect them, and witnesses know this.[34] Some gangs are so notorious for violence against witnesses that police turn down offers of information about them in order to protect witnesses.[35] A member of the New Jersey State Police Street Gang Unit said, "You've got to keep them from disappearing or getting hurt. Can we protect them? Maybe. But God forbid that two years later you have to tell someone their husband or father got killed. I don't want to have to live with that."[36]

Fig. 11.2. The body of Deshawn McCray who was killed to prevent his testifying in a drug case in 2004. (Courtesy of United States Attorney's Office)

The other rationale for the policy is based on practicality. With a crushing load of cases, the prosecutors cannot afford to waste time on cases where there is only a single eyewitness who may recant his or her statement—or worse.[37] Prosecutors also consider double jeopardy. If a case falls apart at trial because a witness does not show or refuses to testify truthfully because of intimidation, the defendant cannot be retried. (Recall the case of Melvin Ignatow, in chapter 4, in which the courts interpreted the double jeopardy prohibition as barring retrial even if the defendant procured his false acquittal through perjury.[38]) With only one chance to convict a murderer, prosecutors want to make certain they have the evidence to do it successfully.

Other cities and counties with comparable problems have adopted similar approaches. Newark's unofficial policy is similar to a formal one adopted by the Baltimore state attorney. She has explicitly barred her attorneys from filing charges in any single-witness case without extensive forensic corroboration.[39] Even the governor of New Jersey has suggested that police should "use civilian witnesses sparingly."[40] While these leaders have the best intentions at heart, their words show that the criminal justice system is being cowed into retreat by the very people it is supposed to restrain, creating a "self-perpetuating cycle of intimidation and helplessness."[41]

These prosecutorial policies necessitated by witness intimidation have resulted in numerous known murderers continuing to walk the streets.[42] It is perhaps no surprise that Essex County, with its unspoken rule that single-witness homicides generally will not be prosecuted, has one of the most dangerous cities in the country.[43] Newark boasted a murder rate of 40.3 per 100,000 residents in 2013, more than three times the average of comparably sized cities, and nearly nine times the national average of 4.5.[44]

THE DEVASTATING EFFECT OF WITNESS INTIMIDATION ON EFFECTIVE PROSECUTION

If one has any doubt about the utterly tragic consequences of witness intimidation, consider two cases.

The Murder of a Heroic Witness

Dennis Brown is sitting on a park bench with a few friends: three eighteen-year-old girls and Bobby Gibson. At around 8:00 p.m. the group notices two young men on bikes quickly approaching. One of them is Wesley Sykes, a known member of a notoriously violent street gang called the Bloods.[45]

"You disrespected my family," Sykes says. He opens fire, killing Dennis.[46]

The others flee and tell the authorities what they know: a man with a "messed-up eye" shot at them, killing Dennis.[47] They arrest Sykes and prepare for a trial.

The Bloods, however, decide that Sykes will not be convicted. Shortly after prosecutors give the defense attorney the list of potential witnesses, Turf, a relative of Sykes and a member of the Bloods, finds Gibson and the three girls—and gives them each a simple proposition: "lie or die."[48] "Take my money and lie," Turf said, "or take a bullet."[49]

The girls are terrified. They do not want their friend's murderer to go unpunished, but they are also afraid that they will be killed before the trial if they do not agree to lie.

The three girls take Turf's $2,000, and he takes them to Sykes's attorney's office. Turf watches as each girl signs new statements fingering someone else in the murder. Bobby Gibson, however, refuses to change his story. He knows what the girls have been forced to do, and he understands that they will be in danger if they refuse. But he is determined to do justice by his friend.[50]

Thirty-six hours after the defense receives the prosecution's trial witness list, Turf discovers Bobby's name and address. The gang member walks to Bobby's home, sees him on the porch, and shoots him dead in broad daylight.[51]

The Killing of a Witness to the Killing of a Witness

On September 15, 2004, Shareef "Sug" Thomas and Louis Bey, two other members of the Bloods, are walking the streets of Newark, New Jersey.[52] The two men, with nothing better to do, decide to rob someone. They walk to a parking lot, where they find Edwin Reyes-Cruz and Carmen Estronza. Thomas and Bey immediately draw their guns and order Reyes-Cruz to hand over all of his money. Reyes-Cruz does, and then Thomas shoots him in the head, killing him instantly. Estronza is the only witness to the crime.

Thomas and Bey are worried about Estronza, so using their Bloods connections they arrange to have her killed. Michael Melvin, a twenty-year-old gang member, is given the assignment.

Two months later on Thanksgiving Day of 2004, Estronza is enjoying an evening with friends Camilo Reyes, Kyhron Ward, and Jermeil Ward at a local bar. At about 2:30 a.m., Estronza and her friends leave the bar, where they meet Melvin. Melvin, with the help of two other men, marches the four victims to a vacant lot next to St. Thomas Aquinas Roman Catholic Church. Melvin orders his four victims to lie down on the ground, then fires one shot into each of their heads.

Without their witness, the prosecutors are compelled to drop Bey's murder charge. Melvin now decides to eliminate the men who helped him with the murders in case they decide to turn on him.

Melvin takes care of his first accomplice about a year later, on November 8, 2005, when he approaches him and fires multiple shots at his friend, killing him quickly. However, the victim's girlfriend witnesses the shooting and begins to scream. Melvin approaches the woman and begins to pistol-whip her. The commotion causes a neighbor to call the police.[53] They arrive and take Melvin into custody.

While he is in custody, several local residents tell police that Melvin is also responsible for the quadruple homicide from the prior year, which he committed in order to silence Estronza. Melvin is charged with the five murders. But while awaiting trial, Melvin uses his connections to the Bloods to organize the death of the other witness to the Estronza killing, which he figures will clear him of the charges of the quadruple murder. The hit succeeds, and Melvin's murder charges for the killing of Estronza and her three friends are dismissed due to a lack of evidence.[54]

It does not take much imagination to see the destructive consequences of the downward spiral of witness intimidation. The more easily criminals can get away with witness intimidation, the more powerful the criminals become. This leaves them freer to victimize others and intimidate more witnesses, all with impunity. Increased witness intimidation begets increased power and control over the community, which makes the threat of witness intimidation even more real and therefore more effective.

Yet, one of the primary blowback effects of shadow vigilantism is a loss of credibility in the system that encourages and legitimizes the noncooperation of witnesses and the intimidation of those who do cooperate. In a culture in which "snitching" has come to be seen as condemnable, the gangs' use of witness intimidation benefits from a cloak of moral ambiguity.

OTHER DOWNWARD SPIRAL DYNAMICS

The discussion so far has focused on an example of one particular downward spiral: (1) legal "technicalities" and lenient sentencing (doctrines of disillusionment) lead to (2) testilying and mandatory minimums, respectively (shadow vigilantism), which lead to (3) blowback (e.g., the "Stop Snitching" campaign), which inexorably leads to (4) less justice and more crime. But this is something of an oversimplification.

In the full picture, step 1 includes not just legal "technicalities" and lenient sentencing but essentially all of the doctrines of disillusionment illustrated in chapter 4. This includes the exclusionary rule that prevents the introduction of reliable evidence, which released Larry Eyler to kill more young men. The use of technical defenses for the guilty, as occurred with Ignatow, who escaped from torture-murder-rape liability by perjuring his way to an acquittal. A commitment to obscure rules rather than promote fairness, as in the release of the murderer Charles Devol Mapps because a thirteenth juror voted guilty. As well as a legal culture that treats the criminal justice process as a game in which the best tricks win, as when Kevin Healy escaped prosecution for murder when his counsel tricked the judge and prosecutor into delaying the case past the speedy trial deadline.

And in step 2, the resulting frustration of the shadow vigilantes expresses itself not only in testilying and mandatory minimums, discussed in the illustration above, but in a wide range of conduct by citizens and officials: refusing to indict or to convict a vigilante or person using excessive force against a criminal, supporting all manner of unjust and Draconian criminal law reforms, or any other of the shadow vigilante conduct discussed in part III.

The effect of these many forms of shadow vigilantism produces, in step 3, alienation and blowback. Recall, for example, the 1992 Los Angeles riots, triggered by the prosecution's reluctance to charge the officers in the beating of Rodney King and the ultimate jury nullification that led to their acquittal.[55]

Add to the Stop Snitching movement other similar movements, which may reduce people's willingness to cooperate with police and, as we have seen in other instances, unintentionally inspire extremists, for example, snipers who gunned down police officers in Dallas and Baton Rouge. Again, these developments produce their own reactions, such as the so-called Ferguson effect, in which police are less likely to engage in proactive policing both because they fear sparking criticism and because they see little reason to put themselves at risk for an unappreciative community. But, as with the Stop Snitching movement, this dynamic can only end up hurting the community—especially when African Americans already have grossly disproportionate victimization rates.[56] The downward spiral deepens, producing less cooperation, more crime, less justice, more disillusionment, and so on.

This is the destructive result of the *vigilante echo*, in which the distortions created by shadow vigilantism reverberate back in a blowback reaction that further degrades the criminal justice system. And that degradation—less justice and more crime—only feeds the discontent of the shadow vigilantes and inspires them to distort the system further, which only feeds the injustice and distrust that trigger blowback. Is there no means of stopping this vigilante echo?

12

THE DAMAGES AND DANGERS OF THE COMMUNITY PERCEIVING THE SYSTEM AS BEING INDIFFERENT TO DOING JUSTICE

As parts I and III document, ordinary people are commonly disillusioned about the criminal justice system's apparent indifference to the importance of doing justice. Both citizens and officials in the criminal justice process are inclined to manipulate and distort the system in order to force the justice that they see the system as reluctant to pursue. Certainly these are not desirable results. But perhaps they can be effectively dealt with simply through the criminal prosecution of vigilantes, both the classic and the shadow type? Perhaps that will stop the vigilantes and end the problem?

PROSECUTING VIGILANTES

If the perceived egregious failures of justice incline people toward classic vigilantism, presumably the system can simply deal directly with the legal violations by prosecuting the vigilantes. But this may not be an ideal solution. The prosecution of vigilantes may only increase, exaggerate, or expand the community's disillusionment with a system that is apparently unable to effectively punish serious wrongdoers yet is somehow able to punish those who step in to do the government's job. That is hardly good advertising for the system. The prosecution of vigilantes, especially those seen by the community as having some moral justification for their conduct, could change a community's view from a feeling that the system is simply indifferent to the failure-of-justice problem to a feeling that the system is openly hostile to solving it.

The prosecution of shadow vigilantes, in contrast, is not only unwise for the same reasons but also essentially impossible (as discussed at the end of chapter 10). Much of what shadow vigilantes do is not criminal, such as refusing to report a crime or to help investigators, refusing to indict or voting to acquit classic vigilantes or those who use excessive or unnecessary force to defend against criminals, exercising discretion to not prosecute or to sentence overly leniently in such vigilante or excessive force cases, or to vote for unjust and Draconian criminal law legislation. Where shadow vigilantes do break the law—such as with testilying—it is generally impossible to prove the offense beyond a reasonable doubt, which is why shadow vigilante officers are willing to engage in such conduct.

But even if prosecution of classic and shadow vigilantes was possible, it would not solve the problem, for the disillusionment and alienation provoked by systematic and avoidable failures of justice carry their own costs: even without vigilantism, they undermine the criminal justice system's moral credibility with the community, and thereby undermines its social and normative influences.

The point has been made in greater detail elsewhere, in particular in the scholarly monograph *Intuitions of Justice and the Utility of Desert.*[1] But we sketch the main points here.

SHOULD THE CRIMINAL LAW CARE WHAT THE LAYPERSON THINKS IS JUST?

In our 2015 book, *Pirates, Prisoners, and Lepers: Lessons from Life outside the Law*, using modern behavioral science studies and case studies from many periods in history, we document and illustrate how fundamental and deep-seated the desire for justice is by people across demographics and cultures. The case studies make clear that doing justice is not just another mild preference that people have. And failures of justice are not just another item on a list of disappointments that people have about their lives.

For laypersons, failures of justice can cause deep disappointment and even dramatic upset. The woman outraged by the light sentence for her husband's killer reported that it made her physically "sick to my stomach." People shocked by a justice failure have complained that it is "absolutely unconscionable," that it "keeps me up at night," that "it's a travesty," that "it's unbelievable and I am devastated," and that "it's insanity." The upset over a justice failure may be even more exaggerated for a victim; as one stated, "I will forever live with this shadow." Another said, "There's a sea of emotions I've had since this happened. . . . I find [the lenient sentence] very insulting." A rape victim explained she will "be forever marked" by the crime and the case's "embittering conclusion." To laypeople, justice is not just one more policy preference but rather a necessary prerequisite for having their world be right.[2]

What people want, and demand, is criminal liability and punishment based on notions of moral desert: doing justice, giving an offender the punishment he or she deserves, no more, no less.

Should criminal law track these community views of justice? It can be argued that there is democratic legitimacy in having criminal law reflect community views. After all, much of criminal law reflects our value judgments about what is and is not condemnable, about what is and is not harmful, and about the relative seriousness of different sorts of harms. Many of these choices are subject to a society's shared value judgments rather than being a product of strict logical analysis. Certainly, many moral philosophers and political scientists will argue that these value judgments ought to be guided by community views rather than by purely logical assessment. There is nothing new about these sorts of arguments.

What is new is evidence to suggest that there is not just democratic legitimacy in tracking a community's views but also crime-control effectiveness in doing so. That is, a criminal law that is perceived by the community as being a reliable moral authority in assessing criminal liability and punishment is a criminal law that will gain cooperation, compliance, and normative influence. In contrast, a criminal law that is seen by the community as regularly doing injustice and failing to do justice is one that is likely to provoke resistance and subversion and to lose the power to harness social and normative influence.

These conclusions are probably apparent from a variety of historical examples. No doubt we can all think of a number of examples of notoriously arbitrary or corrupt criminal justice systems with little or no moral credibility with the population they govern. Think of the former Soviet Union. The only means by which these systems maintain order is often through brutal and extensive reliance upon coercive police power. And when that source of control weakens, the crime rate dramatically increases. On the other hand, where a criminal justice system has earned a reputation for being fair and just, people are inclined to defer to it and to comply with its demands even when there is no coercive police power looking over their shoulders.

What social scientists have done in the last two decades is to show that this dynamic relationship—a criminal justice system's reduced moral credibility reduces people's willingness to defer to it and comply with it—not only exists in cases of extreme loss of moral credibility but also defines a continuous relationship; that is, a *marginal* decrease in moral credibility of the criminal justice system produces a *marginal* decrease in people's willingness to defer to it and comply with it.

Why should it be the case that undermining the system's moral credibility undermines its crime-control effectiveness? Here's why: The forces of social influence and internalized norms are potentially enormous. A criminal law that has earned moral credibility with the people can harness these powerful normative forces through a variety of mechanisms. A criminal law that has damaged its moral credibility cannot.

First, a criminal law with moral credibility can harness the power of stigmatization. Many people will avoid breaking the law if doing so will stigmatize them, socially brand them as lawbreakers, and thereby endanger their personal and social relationships. A criminal law that regularly punishes conduct that is seen as blameless or at least not deserving the condemnation of criminal liability, or that regularly chooses not to punish conduct that is clearly condemnable and blameworthy, will be unable to harness the power of stigmatization. Feelings of shame and embarrassment can have a role in shaping behavior, and a criminal law that is seen as morally on track can harness this force. People do not wish to be viewed as outcasts because of their immoral behavior. The criminal law's ability to stigmatize depends upon the reputation it earns for itself in matching criminal liability with the amount of blame the person deserves. Conduct that is deemed criminal is that which the community considers so unacceptable that punishment is warranted.

Second, a system that has earned moral credibility with the people can help avoid vigilantism. People will be less likely to take matters into their own hands if they are confident that the system is trying hard to do justice.

Third, a reputation for moral credibility can avoid inspiring the kind of resistance and subversion that we see in criminal justice systems with poor reputations. Such resistance and subversion can appear among any of the participants in the system. Do victims report offenses? Do potential witnesses come forward to help police and investigators? Do prosecutors and judges follow the legal rules, or do they feel free to make up their own? Do jurors follow their legal instructions, or do they make up their own rules? Do offenders acquiesce in their liability and punishment, or do they focus instead on thinking an injustice has been done to them? Is the system swamped with technical appeals because the guilty view the system as a game that can be beaten?

Finally, the most powerful force that comes from a criminal justice system with moral credibility is its power to shape societal norms and to cause people to internalize those norms. If criminal law has earned a reputation for doing justice, then when the law criminalizes some new form of conduct or makes some conduct a more serious offense than it had previously been, the community assumes from this legal action that the conduct really is more condemnable.

Consider the results of just one study about this dynamic between the system's moral credibility and people's deference to it. Subjects were tested to determine their willingness to defer in the variety of ways just described: whether they would help investigators, or report an offense, or take criminalization to mean that the conduct really was morally condemnable, and so on. With this baseline established, the subjects were then told of a variety of real cases in which the criminal justice system had done serious injustice or failed to do justice. The testing confirmed that this information tended to disillusion the subjects about the criminal justice system. After some other activities to distract them, the subjects were tested again on their views on deference and compliance, and their willingness to defer and comply had in each instance weakened.[3]

The results of these studies are actually quite surprising, if you think about them. When adult subjects are being tested in a study like this, they come to the study with already formed opinions about the moral credibility of the criminal justice system. There is a limited amount that a researcher can do to shift this preexisting view. But despite the fact that we can only slightly shift subjects' views, we nonetheless see some change in the willingness of subjects to defer to and comply with the criminal justice system.

The conclusions of the empirical studies can be summarized this way: criminal law rules that deviate from the community's notions of justice are not cost-free, as has generally been assumed in the past. Rather, when criminal law adopts rules or practices that produce criminal liability or punishment that is seen as a failure of justice or as unjust, the system suffers a loss of effectiveness. To be most effective, the criminal justice system should try to distribute liability and punishment in accord with the shared judgments of justice of the community it governs. In that way, it can build moral credibility and, in turn, gain effectiveness by harnessing the power of social and normative influence.

THE SYSTEM'S MORAL CREDIBILITY WITH THE COMMUNITY IT GOVERNS

There is reason to worry that the doctrines of disillusionment like those sketched in chapter 4 and in the appendix may have a detrimental effect in undermining the criminal justice system's moral credibility with the community it governs.

As the social psychology studies tell us, reputation is primarily a function of perceived motivation.[4] It is not the failures of justice themselves that do the damage. Many failures are easily forgiven by a community that understands the practical limits of reliably reconstructing past events and that abhors wrongful convictions and injustice. Doctrines like the beyond a reasonable doubt standard of proof and excluding coerced confessions make sense to people even if some guilty offenders may go free as a result.

What is damaging to a system's reputation are those instances, like the doctrines of disillusionment, that suggest rightly or wrongly that the system is indifferent to the importance of doing justice: letting clearly guilty offenders who committed serious offenses go free for what seem to many ordinary people to be trivial technicalities, or undermining justice to promote an interest that could be promoted in some other way.

The doctrines of disillusionment have had their effect. No doubt the US criminal justice system has a better reputation than that of many countries in the world,[5] but it still has a quite mixed reputation that could be substantially improved. In a 2013 Gallup poll, only 28 percent of those surveyed said they had a "great deal" or "quite a lot" of confidence in the US criminal justice system.[6] It ranked far below the ratings of many other institutions, including organized religion, the military, and small businesses.[7] Even the police ranked dramatically higher. At 57 percent, they have more than twice the percentage of people expressing a "great deal" or "quite a lot" of confidence in them. And that reduced confidence in the criminal justice system has been consistent over the past two decades during which the polling has been done.[8]

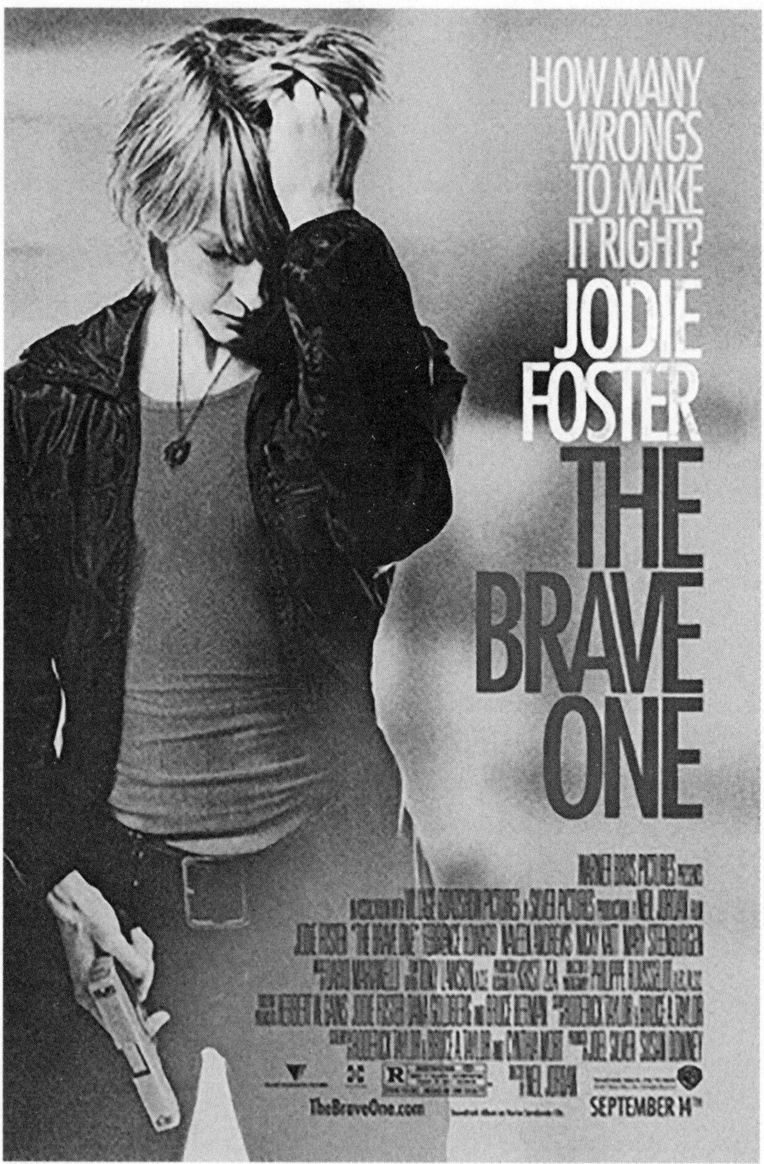

Fig. 12.1. Poster for Jodie Foster's famous revenge movie, *The Brave One*, as it appeared displayed outside movie theaters, 2007. (Courtesy of Warner Brothers)

Part of the disillusionment arises from a common view that the courts do not take seriously enough the importance of doing justice. An earlier nationwide survey sponsored by the American Bar Association found that when people were asked whether "the courts let too many criminals go free on technicalities," 74 percent of people agreed or strongly agreed (only 16 percent disagreed or strongly disagreed).[9]

One can understand how the decisions of the Warren Supreme Court in the 1960s could have produced this view, including decisions that applied the exclusionary rule in a variety of contexts and introduced the "fruit of the poisonous tree" doctrine.[10] (That doctrine excludes from use at trial not only evidence obtained illegally but also evidence later obtained *legally* but helped by an earlier illegal seizure. Thus, for example, in a case where evidence is obtained in violation of the rules and is later used as part of the evidence presented to a court to obtain a search warrant, even reliable and compelling evidence *obtained under that search warrant* is to be excluded as fruit of the poisonous tree.)

One Texas police chief captured the mood of many at the time of the Warren court's creation of the exclusionary rule: "It's the damnedest thing I ever heard."[11] President Dwight Eisenhower, who appointed Chief Justice Earl Warren, later concluded that doing so had been a mistake in light of Warren's decisions in criminal cases that some described as "handcuffing the police."[12] Many in Congress called for Warren's impeachment following the *Miranda* decision, making a similar argument that the decision was handcuffing the police rather than the criminals.[13] Truman Capote, testifying before a US Senate committee, said, "It seems almost unbelievable to me that the police force of one of our major cities is literally frightened to death to ask the prime suspect a single question for fear that their case against him might be jeopardized."[14] It may be no surprise, then, that from 1965 to 1994 the percentage of Americans saying the courts were too lenient on criminals rose from 47 percent to 85 percent.[15]

Another sign of the criminal justice system's reputational difficulties is found in popular culture. Many of the worst failure-of-justice rules were introduced in the 1960s and 1970s, and since that time an entire movie genre has blossomed. The doing-justice-where-the-system-has-failed movie has become a fantasy favorite for Hollywood. Starting with the wildly successful 1970s franchises of Charles Bronson's *Death Wish* and its sequels, and Clint Eastwood's Dirty Harry movies, it now seems as if most big names have done their vigilante flick, including Jodie Foster (*The Brave One*), Gerard Butler (*Law Abiding Citizen*), Kevin Bacon (*Death Sentence*), Jeremy Irons (*Fourth Angel*), Liam Neeson (Taken series), Denzel Washington (*Man on Fire*), Christopher Nolan (the Dark Knight series), Robert De Niro (*Righteous Kill*), and Michael Douglas (*Star Chamber*), among many others.[16]

It is probably not a healthy thing for a society to have an entire entertainment genre built around protagonists who are seen as heroes because they break the law, and audiences thrilled by it. Indeed, many of the movie protagonists come nowhere near making the claim that their conduct is morally justified, yet many people seem to view these protagonists as champions of justice. Screenwriters must keep close tabs on their audience's sensibilities, given that the success of their movies often depends upon those emotions. That is heroic protagonists must stay within a range of conduct not too far from admirable. What does it say about current popular views that so many movies and so many heroic leading actors and actresses feel comfortable having their characters engage in such gross violations of existing law yet retain their admirable status?

If the criminal law is to gain the community's support and deference, if it is to have any chance of earning a reputation as a moral authority whose values should be respected and internalized by citizens, it must improve its reputation for caring about the importance of doing justice.

13

WHAT IT TAKES TO STOP THE VIGILANTE ECHO

Stopping the vigilante echo and its downward spiral can be a difficult business. Consider each step in the dynamic that creates the downward spiral, starting with the last step. Can we stop the downward spiral by simply preventing the blowback?

One good example of blowback is the "Stop Snitching" campaign. Is it a surprise that a community faced with testilying by police, seriously unjust sentences under mandatory minimum statutes, and the wide range of other injustices produced by shadow vigilantism would be sufficiently skeptical of the system so as to urge noncooperation or, even more aggressively, to promote social stigmatization and even intimidation of cooperators? We do not think so. Where "Stop Snitching" takes root, its believers probably think they are morally justified.

Can we effectively discourage the subversive or manipulative misconduct of citizens and officials, be it testilying or supporting reforms that produce injustices such as mandatory minimums, or any of the other forms of civilian or official shadow vigilantism? We do not think we can. The shadow vigilantes consider themselves and their conduct to be morally and practically justified. They are acting to correct a criminal justice system that has shown itself to be indifferent to the importance of doing justice and is in breach of the social contract in which it swore to protect the citizens' persons and possessions and justly to punish wrongdoers.

Thus, the only effective means of stopping the vigilante echo and its downward spiral is to avoid starting the action and reaction dynamic in the first place—namely by avoiding those rules and practices that regularly and predictably produce the serious failures of justice that provoke shadow vigilantism.

PERFECTION IS NOT REQUIRED

This does not mean that the criminal justice system must be perfect. Perfection is obviously impossible, and, more importantly, nobody expects it. People understand that many offenders simply cannot be caught. Even when a suspect is identified, in many cases it is simply impossible with the available facts to reliably reconstruct what happened. And there is a strong consensus that avoiding wrongful convictions ought to be a high priority.

What is important to potential shadow vigilantes is the system's reputation for *wanting* to do justice. As social psychologists have made clear, its perceived *motivation*, rather than its actual performance, is what establishes its reputation.[1] The key question is, has the criminal justice system earned a reputation for giving justice the importance it deserves? Or has it instead shown itself willing to sacrifice justice in order to promote other, less important interests or for official convenience?

It would be hard for shadow vigilantes to morally justify their conduct if the criminal justice system had publicly committed itself to doing justice and avoiding injustice as its top priority and had earned such a reputation that people really believed in this commitment. This is not the system's current reputation, of course, as previous chapters make clear.

Certainly there are important societal interests beyond doing justice, and sometimes compromises will have to be made. But the system nonetheless could establish its commitment to doing justice by upholding certain principles by which such compromises are struck.

PREFER NON-JUSTICE-FRUSTRATING ALTERNATIVES

First, rules and practices producing failures of justice ought not to be tolerated if the interest being promoted could be as effectively promoted through non-justice-frustrating means. Producing a failure of justice ought to be the last option on the list of solutions, not the first, as it too often is seen to be today. Consider, for example, the many alternative—and potentially more effective—means of controlling police conduct other than the exclusionary rule that excludes reliable evidence that is obtained improperly. Automatic administrative sanctions, even criminal prosecution of officers in egregious cases, and easy and automatic civil compensation of all citizens whose rights are infringed (not just criminals) are just two of the alternatives that have been offered.[2] (Nothing in the Constitution requires the exclusionary rule, as the Supreme Court has made clear: the Constitution only requires some effective process for deterring "unreasonable" searches and seizures. Many have argued that personal liability of officers would be dramatically more effective than the exclusionary rule, which can allow criminals to go free and has little personal effect on the offending officer.[3])

IN BALANCING COMPETING INTEREST, DON'T IGNORE THE MORAL AND CRIME-CONTROL COSTS OF FAILURES OF JUSTICE

A second general principle is to publicly acknowledge that every failure of justice has a cost, both a moral cost and a practical crime-control cost, because of the system's reduced credibility and the accompanying reduced deference to it. It follows from this that when doing justice is being traded off against some other interest, there ought to be a clear assessment of the relative societal value of the competing interests.

Is the societal cost of letting a rapist-torturer-murderer like Melvin Ignatow walk free greater than the societal benefit that comes with extending double jeopardy protection even to defendants who gain acquittal by perjuring themselves at trial? It is not hard to argue that the acquittal does more damage than would the slightly narrower interpretation of the Double Jeopardy Clause that would deny Ignatow the defense.

Is the societal cost in allowing serial rapist-torturer-murderer Larry Eyler to be held at the police station for questioning several hours too long a greater societal cost than letting him rape, torture, and murder all of those young men with impunity? It is not hard to argue that the balance struck here is out of whack. The acquittal does more societal damage than allowing some flexibility in assessing the extent of prejudice and inconvenience to murder suspects or in using non-exclusionary methods of controlling such police conduct.

The Europeans take a different perspective on these issues, one that avoids the US problem. The European Charter for Human Rights rejects the fixed-rule approach used in the United States and looks instead to the actual extent of prejudice to the defendant, the seriousness of the offense, and *the effect of the decision on the system's reputation for fairness and justice.*[4] Allowing this kind of assessment of competing societal interests is an enormous step forward that the American criminal justice system has failed to take—a step forward that could avoid many of the most egregious failures of justice that fuel the current shadow vigilante impulse. There is nothing in the US Constitution that prevents this approach; it only requires the judicial imagination to see it as the better path.

CONCLUSION

The current system's apparent insensitivity to the importance of doing justice may not produce large numbers of classic vigilantes in the streets, but it has contributed to a disillusionment about the criminal justice system's interest in doing justice. And that disillusionment may well help people increasingly justify subverting the system as shadow vigilantes. In the spirit of the 1851 Vigilance Committee and the 1973 Lavender Panthers, the system's intentional and systemic failures of justice provide the shadow vigilantes with moral justification to take the law into their own hands, not by taking to the streets—typically only Hollywood fantasy does that now—but by manipulating the system to their own ends as they see others doing in order to squeeze justice from it.

Such shadow vigilantism may be less dramatic than taking to the streets, but it can be pervasive and ultimately more damaging to the integrity of the process. Members of the 1851 Vigilance Committee announced themselves and their doings so people would know their effect. Shadow vigilantism provides an unseen and unaccountable corrupting force that contaminates the entire process because one can never know when it is at work.

Yet the current approach of the criminal justice system seems to be that it considers itself free to create as much hostility with the community over failures of justice as it sees fit because there is nothing a disillusioned community can do about it. But this seems an arrogant and dangerous short game. There is much that a disillusioned or cynical people can do, beyond distracting themselves by spending billions of dollars going to vigilante hero movies. They can, through many avenues, manipulate the system to force from it what the system often seems reluctant to do. And that subversion can provoke a further disillusioning crime-inducing response.

We would all—both offenders and the community—be better off if the criminal justice system earned a reputation for doing justice without an outside force pushing it to do so.[1] The tragedy of this dirty war is twofold. First, it could have been avoided if the system simply was more sensitive to the importance of doing justice—giving offenders the punishment they deserve, no more and no less. Today's system could be saved by avoiding rules and practices that will predictably frustrate justice, unless there is some truly compelling reason to do so and there is no other, less justice-damaging alternative. (One of us has explored these alternative mechanisms at length, in *Law without Justice: Why Criminal Law Doesn't Give People What They Deserve.*) Second, forcing the disillusioned into shadow vigilantism often produces results that, in the larger perspective, even the shadow vigilantes would find objectionable. Mandatory minimums avoid the problem of unchecked lenient sentencing, but they also produce a stream of cases of predictable injustice.

No criminal justice system can have a perfect reputation for doing justice. Someone may always think it has improperly allowed a clearly guilty offender to go free, even if the belief is mistaken. But just as the system ought not to give up trying to avoid injustice simply because someone will always claim there is more injustice to be avoided, neither should the system give up trying to avoid failures of justice simply because someone will always claim there are more failures of justice to be avoided. The system can incrementally improve its moral credibility, and thereby its crime-control effectiveness, by reducing its current level of failures of justice.

Ironically, it is shadow vigilantism that in some ways may be saving some of the justice-frustrating doctrines from themselves, by taking the edge off the credibility loss that the system would otherwise suffer if it were not subverted. That is, if shadow vigilante citizens and officials one day magically stopped all shadow vigilante subversions, the criminal justice system might well essentially collapse under its own justice-frustrating rules and practices. If people actually suffered the full justice-frustrating cost of the doctrines of disillusionment, they might instantly abandon those doctrines because no society could live with the crime-producing results. In other words, it is very possible that the only thing that keeps the doctrines of disillusionment in place is the work of shadow vigilantes who blunt their actual effect.

The cure for vigilantism, whether classic or shadow, is a clear public commitment to giving offenders the punishment they deserve, nothing more and nothing less. That will require significant reforms to current rules and practices, but these reforms can bring not only greater justice but also greater stability, respect, and deference to criminal law in all its work.

Postscript

WHERE ARE THEY NOW?

We have recounted many stories in this volume, and it is easy to take a special interest in the people involved. In this postscript we give readers who might be interested a brief report on what has happened to the people in our stories since the events that made their stories relevant to this book.

EMMETT TILL

The murderers of Emmett Till, discussed in chapter 2, were never convicted, despite their confessions and the undeniable physical evidence. In the years following Till's death, his story became an important element in the civil rights movement, helped along by the actions of his mother, Mamie Till. In a poignant act that found the heart of the nation, Mamie insisted that her son's casket be kept open at his funeral in Chicago, claiming that she "just wanted the world to see" the brutality of her son's murder. With the encouragement of the NAACP, Till's mother toured the country, becoming a powerful fundraising force for the organization. Till's murder—and the shocking injustice of the judicial system's response—sparked outrage and a cry for change across the nation.

Till's murderers, Roy Bryant and J. W. Milam, faced the brunt of the outrage. They were shunned both by those who had once supported them and by the nation as a whole. When blacks in the area refused to work for them or buy their goods, their businesses collapsed. No longer able to make a life in Mississippi, the men moved to Texas. The move did little to improve their lives. Notoriety kept them marginally employed and fearful of vigilante reprisals.

Years later, Bryant remained remorseless. In a 1992 interview, an ill Bryant complained to his interviewer, "Emmett Till is dead. I don't know why he can't just stay dead."[1]

THE 1851 VIGILANCE COMMITTEE

The Vigilance Committee of 1851 was short-lived. When a new round of elections brought true leaders into office, the overseeing influence of the committee was no longer needed, and the group chose to disband. Many of the leaders of the committee became elected officials in San Francisco.

In 1856 a new group formed in San Francisco and attempted to take on the extra-governmental role of justice that had been so successful just five years earlier. The men of this new committee, however, were not motivated by the lack of law and order but rather by a quest for personal power. This group never gained popular support, and the transparency of its motives made it easy for the legitimate government to have the usurpers convicted in open court.[2]

THE LAVENDER PANTHERS

The authorities in San Francisco were forced by the Lavender Panthers' actions to take notice of the gay-bashing problem. When the gay community no longer felt they were without recourse, the Lavender Panthers disbanded.

Reverend Ray Broshears, in the years before his activism in San Francisco, had been interviewed about information he had concerning the assassination of President Kennedy. He was deposed by District Attorney Jim Garrison in New Orleans. In his deposition, Broshears—a roommate of David Ferrie—testified that Ferrie, along with Lee Harvey Oswald, and others were all part of a homicidal-homosexual clique that had conspired to kill Kennedy.[3]

After the Lavender Panthers faded away, Broshears remained a lightning rod for controversy. It is likely that he was the first ordained minister in the United States to perform marriage ceremonies for same-sex couples.[4] He was one of the founders of what grew to become the Gay Pride Parade, which is still an annual occurrence in San Francisco. He also worked as a journalist and was repeatedly sued for his writings. Many felt that he unfairly used his influence as the owner of his own newspaper, the *Gay Crusader*, to criticize individuals and organizations that disagreed with him.

Broshears died at home of a cerebral hemorrhage on January 10, 1982.

GULABI GANG

Recall the Gulabi Gang from chapter 2, the group founded in 2006 by Sampat Pal Devi in Banda, India, whose members used physical force to enforce women's rights in communities across the country. Several members of the activist group found their way into politics and now work through the system to bring about change for women. The group continues to grow, gaining members and attracting international attention. In 2014 a documentary about the Gulabi Gang was released, and in 2016 work was moving forward on a dance drama in the United Kingdom depicting the Gulabi Gang's story.[5]

DEANNA COOK

As you will recall from chapter 1, Deanna Cook was killed by her ex-husband, Delvecchio Patrick, while a 911 operator listened helplessly. The city of Dallas understood that it had failed Cook and that it needed to better address the problem of domestic violence. Prosecutors asked the jury to send a powerful message that "domestic violence will not be tolerated."[6] Patrick was convicted.

During the sentencing hearing, Cook's family gave victim impact statements. While eighteen-year-old N'Eycea Williams, one of Patrick's stepdaughters, was delivering hers, Patrick laughed and showed her his middle finger. Her younger sister, Aniya Williams, appeared unafraid when she took the stand, even telling Patrick, "I hope you get raped. You laugh, but it is not funny."[7]

The defense, noting that Patrick was the father of two children, asked for a five-year sentence, but the jury settled on eighty-five years of prison time and a $10,000 fine. Cook's family also filed a lawsuit against the city of Dallas because of the officers' slow response to the attack on Cook.[8] As of July 2017, the legal action is still ongoing.

DANNY PALM

Between 1992 and 1995 John Harper, a resident of Dictionary Hill, California, repeatedly threatened his neighbors, and the police did not stop him, as chapter 1 described. Neighbors documented more than 150 incidents affecting forty-two victims before Danny Palm killed Harper.

Palm was convicted of second-degree murder, but Judge William Mudd reduced the conviction to involuntary manslaughter. While in prison, Palm was an exemplary inmate. He held several jobs, including assisting one of the guard captains and helping the prison chaplain. In a letter to Judge Mudd, Palm wrote, "I thought you would be interested to know that I am making my time here in prison as positive and productive as possible. I assure you that my overwhelming emotion at the time I shot John Harper Jr. was stark fear for the safety of my family. Self-preservation is a primal instinct and not something within the 'control' of the person who experiences it."[9]

Palm was released after serving eight and a half years in prison. Neighbors welcomed him home by tying yellow ribbons to his mailbox, trees, and telephone poles. "I would say thank you," said Barbra Bunderson. "I'm glad he was willing to put himself on the line for the neighbors. I know he was worried about us, our family, and we're grateful to him."[10] Palm and his wife returned to their quiet life in Dictionary Hill.

LARRY EYLER

Larry Eyler, who authorities knew had been killing young men in the Midwest for years, was detained in 1983, but officers were forced to release him, and all the incriminating evidence against him was excluded from use during the trial (see chapter 4). At the time of his release, one deputy said that Eyler had been "freed to kill" again—and he did.[11] Eyler killed at least two more young men before authorities could collect enough additional evidence to convict him.

On October 3, 1986, Judge Joseph Urso sentenced Eyler to death. "If there ever was a person or a situation for which the death penalty was appropriate, it is you," Judge Urso said. "You are an evil person. You truly deserve to die for your acts." Eyler tried to negotiate a plea deal—he'd give a body count of his victims in exchange for a lesser sentence. The prosecution declined. Before the appeals had run their course, Eyler died from AIDS in prison in 1994.[12]

RONALD EBENS AND MICHAEL NITZ

In the summer of 1982, Ronald Ebens and Michael Nitz—two automotive workers—killed Chinese American Vincent Chin, as described in chapter 4. When Ebens and Nitz received only a few years of probation and a fine, the Asian American community was outraged, and a civil suit against Ebens and Nitz was launched. The suit—settled in 1987—

required that Nitz pay $50,000 and Ebens pay $1.5 million. Nitz paid his debt in weekly installments over ten years, but Ebens did not. Despite being able to buy a new motorcycle, he said he could pay nothing toward his judgment. The Chin family placed a lien on Ebens's property; he is not permitted to sell or refinance his home, and he now owes in excess of $8 million. In 2015 Ebens filed a motion to have the lien lifted, but it was not removed. The lien, says Helen Zia, executor of the Chin estate, will remind Ebens "of the crime he committed as he continues to thumb his nose at Asian Americans and the value of human life."[13]

FALN

The Fuerzas Armadas de Liberación Nacional (FALN), a Puerto Rican Communist terrorist organization, launched 120 terrorist attacks on American soil between 1974 and 1983, as described in chapter 4. Regardless, in 1999 President Bill Clinton—keen, many argued, to win over Hispanic voters before an upcoming election—granted clemency to sixteen of the convicted members.

Clinton's decision was condemned by the US Attorney's Office, the FBI, the Federal Bureau of Prisons, the former victims of FALN terrorism, and the majority of members of Congress. "It is a tragic day that these terrorists may soon again be walking America's streets," said Representative Vito J. Fossella.[14] When the prisoners returned to Puerto Rico, they were greeted with an exuberant welcome and cheers of "Bienvenidos a casa!"[15]

MANUEL AYREE

In 1981 Manuel Ayree, son of former Ghanaian diplomat Seth Ayree, raped a number of women in their homes in Manhattan. As mentioned in chapter 4, when he was identified and caught that same year, officials were unable to prosecute him because of his diplomatic immunity. He was sent back to Ghana but never investigated.

In 1982, however, a federal judge ordered Ayree to pay over $1 million in damages to two of his rape victims—$35,000 to each woman annually for the following three years and $5,000 a year for the remainder of their lives.[16] No money was ever actually paid. The trauma of his crimes still lingers with his victims. "I'm 41 years old," said Carol Holmes, "and I can't sleep with the lights out."[17]

THE LEGION OF DOOM

Chapter 5 told the story of the students at Paschal High School in Fort Worth, Texas, who formed a group called the Legion of Doom. Begun as a means to combat petty theft and drug pushing, the group morphed into violent action.

Of the eight members of the Legion who were indicted, seven pleaded guilty to felony charges, received a week in jail, and were placed on probation under an agreement that their records would be expunged upon completion of their probationary period. The eighth student pleaded guilty to misdemeanor charges and paid a fine. The sentencing decision was influenced in part by a lack of prior criminal records, as well as the general perception that the Legion's members were "good kids" who'd reacted badly to a difficult situation.[18] Black leaders in the community believed that the issue of race was involved, with investigators hesitant to crack down on white, upper-class students. "If this had been in a less affluent neighborhood," said Clyde Tillman, a school district employee, "[justice] would have been served much sooner."[19]

Within several years of the incidents, the vast majority of the group's members had moved on to college or employment, and no convicted student violated his probation.

STEVE UTASH

In April 2014 Steve Utash was driving through a Detroit neighborhood when a little boy stepped into the road, causing an accidental collision. Utash tried to help the boy, but a group of bystanders attacked and severely beat him, critically injuring him (see chapter 5).

Three days after the beating, authorities arrested and took into custody five suspects. During a pretrial hearing on June 16, Bruce Wimbush made a plea deal in exchange for testifying at the trial against the other assailants. "We saw Mr. Utash hit the kid," he testified. "I striked him once. I hit him in the jaw. I let my anger get to me."[20] Two days later, Utash's other four attackers pleaded guilty to assault with the intent to do bodily harm, but charges of assault with intent to murder, as well as a charge of ethnic intimidation, were dropped in exchange for the guilty pleas.

The prosecutor was pleased with the plea deals: "We thought that this was a just resolution of the cases against the defendant. It was also discussed with the representatives from Mr. Utash's family. They thought it was an acceptable solution. And hopefully it will allow Mr. Utash to continue healing."[21]

James Deontae Davis, twenty-four, was sentenced to five years of probation, with the first year to be served in jail; Latrez Cummings, nineteen, was sentenced to three years of probation with the first six months to be served in jail; Bruce Wimbush Jr., eighteen, was given three years of probation under the Holmes Youthful Trainee Act and must submit to periodic drug screenings; and Wonzey Saffold, thirty, who had multiple previous felony convictions, received a prison sentence of six years and four months.[22]

After four months in the hospital, Utash was able to post a letter online to thank those who had helped him:

> I'll always remember all of you loving people. Thank you to Debbie Hughes who threw her body over mine to stop the crowd from killing me, she sure is a brave woman. Also, thank you to all the medical people

> that surrounded me. I notice people in the medical field are all angels here to make other people's life continue. Without them, where would we go? Thank you to the people at St. John Hospital, thank you to the people at DMC Rehab facility. Everything about what happened to me was worth it to feel the pure love of mankind in its purist [sic] form. People are love, and I love you all.[23]

THE PITTSBURGH PRISON GUARDS

In a Pittsburgh correctional facility in 2009, a group of officers—led by Harry Nicoletti—began physically and sexually abusing convicted sex offenders in the prison, as described in chapter 5. In April 2011—long after the alleged abuse—accusations were made against the guards, and an investigation began. The eight guards were suspended without benefits from their posts while officials looked into the allegations. During the process, Nicoletti was indicted by a grand jury and arrested for his role in the abuse of the inmates. Though he was charged with ninety-four counts, Nicoletti defended himself. "They're false allegations," he told a reporter. "Simple as that. They're false allegations."[24]

In November 2011, only a month before Nicoletti's preliminary hearing was set to begin, six of the other guards turned themselves over to police. During the pretrial hearing, thirty-one witnesses testified against the former corrections officer, including current and former inmates who were abused by Nicoletti.[25]

In the 2013 trial, Nicoletti was found guilty of twenty-seven of the counts against him, resulting in a sentence of five years' probation and six years' house arrest. Judge David Cashman decided against prison time in the facility in which Nicoletti abused the inmates; as Cashman explained, "You were painted as an ogre; you were painted as a sex fiend; you were painted as a villain who likes to torture and seek out sex offenders. I'm sparing you from the danger you imposed on the individuals you were in charge of. I hope you understand that."[26]

One of the other guards was given twelve years' probation, and another was found not guilty. For the remaining guards, all charges were dropped.

HERMAN WRICE

Philadelphia resident Herman Wrice, whose story was told in chapter 6, founded Mantua Against Drugs (MAD), a community-oriented program that sought to fight community drug use with direct confrontation. Wrice transformed his piece of Philadelphia with his strong community activism, but he didn't stop there. He trained what he christened "street warriors" in over 350 communities across the United States. Using methods he developed in West Philadelphia, organizers have incorporated chants, marches, and vigils into community activist programs throughout the country.

Wrice's homegrown message attracted the attention of many, including the president. In the summer of 1990, Wrice and over three hundred children welcomed President George H. W. Bush to the West Philadelphia Community Center in Mantua, chanting, "No more drugs! No more pain! We don't want your crack cocaine!" The president, flanked by celebrity athletes, community leaders, and other hard-hat-donning MAD members, had come to salute Wrice. Bush praised the work of MAD and the Mantua community, announcing that they had demonstrated that "individual neighborhoods can indeed work together to restore hope and self-respect" and that "community commitment can extinguish the destructive blaze of crack burning up our streets and our kids." He praised Wrice in particular, calling him the "John Wayne of Philadelphia," wearing the traditional white hat of the good guys.[27]

Wrice's advocacy continued for years until March 10, 2000, when he died of a heart attack at the age of sixty-one. It is a final testament to his dedication that he was in Fort Lauderdale, Florida, on the day of his death, preparing for a community drug march.[28]

RANCH RESCUE

American ranchers living near the Mexican border felt personally and economically threatened by immigrants crossing illegally into the United States, as discussed in chapter 7.

In 2005 one of the organization's members, Texas resident Casey Nethercott, lost his ranch after two undocumented immigrants sued him for abuses suffered during their capture. He was also convicted of unlawful possession of a firearm by a felon and sentenced to several years in prison.

In 2006 Arizona passed Proposition 102, or the Standing in Civil Actions Act, which prohibits undocumented immigrants who have won a civil lawsuit "from receiving punitive damages."[29] In 2011 the law was made retroactive in an effort to help Nethercott, but a judge ruled that the judgment would stay, since there was no evidence that the immigrants had been to Arizona, the incident occurred before the new law's retroactive effective date, and the damages awarded were not punitive. Nethercott stayed optimistic. "I didn't get my ranch back . . . but at least the law's in effect," he said. "Nobody else will lose their home."[30] Volunteer-based border patrol organizations remain controversial today.

THE CROWN HEIGHTS MACCABEES

Recall, in chapter 7, that the Hasidic Jewish community of Crown Heights, New York, facing the growing menace of local crime, formed a neighborhood watch group. The group, called the Maccabees, had an enormous impact in reducing crime rates in the area; however, crime was controversially displaced to neighboring communities, sparking ethnic unrest.

Over the next several years, the number of Maccabees volunteers grew, but by the late 1960s, political pressure forced the group to dissolve. Rabbi Samuel Schrage, the group's founder, died in 1976 at the age of forty-three.

Still, the Maccabees remained in some form or another for several more decades, cropping up in neighboring New York communities under various names. They remain active today, with offshoots across the city, along the East Coast, and in the United States as a whole. Back in Crown Heights, two groups, the Shmira and the Shomrim, keep separate dispatch centers on opposite sides of the area and are still active protectors of their communities.[31]

THE ANIMAL LIBERATION FRONT

The ALF, discussed in chapter 7, used violent means to damage property associated with animal exploitation, and they remain active today, even maintaining a website.

While some members are occasionally caught for ALF-affiliated activities, many attacks are left unsolved because they're launched by small cells or lone actors. There is no centralized leadership that law enforcement can target.[32] Federal authorities have designated the group as a domestic ecoterrorism group, and one of its affiliated individuals has been listed on the FBI's Most Wanted Terrorist list.[33] As a response to the ALF's increasingly controversial actions of the 1990s, federal legislators passed the 1992 Animal Enterprise Protection Act, lobbying by affected animal-utilizing organizations. The act criminalizes stealing from and causing damage or property loss to an "animal enterprise."[34]

Beyond the organization's illicit projects, the ALF website has become a resource for information on numerous animal-related issues; among other things, the website provides suggestions for ways to help fund vet care for pets, information about shelters that are known for good animal care and animal-oriented nonprofits looking for support, and medical theories that argue for the health benefits of giving up meat. The website is also explicit about the organization's ideology and mission: "Animal rights is the freedom for all sentient beings to live a natural life, free from human exploitation, and free from unnecessary pain and suffering." For ALF supporters, "speciesism"—or "discrimination solely on the basis of species"—"is as illegitimate as discrimination on the basis of sex, or race, or the ability to cha-cha."[35]

OPERATION RESCUE

Founded in Texas in the mid-1980s, Operation Rescue is a militant pro-life organization that protests abortion clinics and trains pro-life advocates to be effective fighters for the pro-life movement. While Operation Rescue doesn't explicitly support violence, some of its followers do: in 1993, Scott Roeder, a supporter of Operation Rescue, murdered abortion doctor George Tiller as Tiller left his church (see chapter 7).

After the assassination, Scott Roeder fled but was soon arrested and charged with first-degree murder.[36] While awaiting trial, Roeder expressed his frustration at Operation Rescue for denying any support or knowledge of him. He noted that he'd donated to their group in the past and that the group "better get its story straight, because my lawyer said it'd be good for me to show that I was supporting a pro-life organization." Roeder also stated that he possessed "probably a thousand dollars' worth of receipts" from donations.[37] In March 2010 a jury convicted Roeder of first-degree murder after deliberating for thirty-seven minutes, and Roeder was sentenced to life in prison without the possibility of parole for fifty-two years.[38]

More than five years after the killing, Operation Rescue still distances itself from the assassination, claiming that there was no need to kill Dr. Tiller because "in spite of the delays and a government laced with corruption, the system was working."[39] Roeder, they claim, simply did not know enough about the legal situation and thus felt compelled to act on his own.

Today, the original Operation Rescue and its derivative organizations continue to advocate against abortion and providers of the procedure; one of those derivative organizations, Operation Save America, has expanded its agenda to include a variety of fundamentalist Christian, conservative goals.[40]

OPERATION PERVERTED JUSTICE

Xavier von Erck formed Project Perverted Justice, an organization that used online chat rooms to identify and humiliate pedophiles by publicizing their personal information or filming them. As discussed in chapter 7, the organization, as well as the *Dateline NBC* show *To Catch a Predator* with which it was affiliated, received outpourings of both criticism and support.

Child safety advocate Marc Klaas and *America's Most Wanted* host John Walsh—both fathers of children murdered by predators—condone the organization's work, as do a variety of other advocates and law enforcement officials. Criticism of the organization is aimed at its anonymity, its potential to unfairly entrap an accused predator, and what are deemed its unethical tactics. "There's no way to hold them accountable if they do go over the line," says Scott Morrow, liaison for an anti–Perverted Justice organization. Others claim that the organization's public accusations, whether real or unfounded, can irreparably ruin the lives of those accused.[41]

Criticism also stems from intermittent violence that occurred in the years following the organization's founding. In 2005 Michael Anthony Mullen—outraged after hearing about Joseph Duncan III, a sexual predator in another state—murdered two convicted sex offenders in Whatcom County, Washington.[42] While not associated with Project Perverted Justice, the murders fanned fears surrounding vigilante action taken against pedophiles. The following year, another incident attracted criticism. In November 2006 Louis Conradt, an assistant district attorney living in Texas, became a target of *To Catch a Predator*. When police officers—filmed by an NBC camera crew—forced their way into his home, Conradt killed himself with a gunshot to the head.[43] A flurry of criticism followed, and in 2007 Conradt's sister, Patricia Conradt, sued NBC for its interference with police and failure to protect her brother. The $105 million lawsuit was "amicably resolved," and the show *To Catch a Predator* aired for the last time in December 2007.[44]

KEN McELROY

Skidmore, Missouri, was tormented by Ken McElroy, a violent town bully, pedophile, and thief who intimidated or attacked anyone who challenged him (see chapter 8). In 1981 McElroy was shot to death in plain view of forty-some townspeople outside a bar. McElroy's killer went undiscovered.

Three years after the shooting, attorney Richard McFadin, on behalf of McElroy's wife, filed a wrongful death suit against the county sheriff, the town mayor, and one of the accused (but unproved) killers; they settled for $17,000, but nobody admitted guilt. Thirty-five years later, the Bowenkamps—the victims of McElroy's most brazen violence—are dead, and Skidmore has gotten smaller. Nevertheless, the town has maintained its secret; McElroy's killers are still unknown.[45]

BERNHARD GOETZ

In 1984 four teenagers on a New York subway surrounded thirty-seven-year-old Bernhard Goetz, demanding money. Goetz, carrying an unlicensed gun, shot all four of them, paralyzing and mentally disabling nineteen-year-old Darrell Cabey. Despite his deliberate and unapologetic violence, Goetz was convicted only of criminal weapons possession, as discussed in chapter 3.

The court sentenced Goetz for the single weapons count to a year in prison, with a possible release time of just sixty days.[46] He ultimately served eight months in prison.[47] In a civil suit brought on behalf of Cabey, the jury found Goetz guilty and awarded Cabey $43 million in damages.[48] Goetz went on to become an animal rights activist and an outspoken vegetarian.

JOE HORN

Joe Horn of Pasadena, Texas, shot and killed two burglars he'd seen robbing his neighbor's home (chapter 9). He was cleared by a grand jury the following year, but the decision was highly controversial. The New Black Panther Nation, a controversial black political organization, was vocally outspoken about Horn's actions, but the counterprotest staged by Horn's neighbors and supporters was enormous. "It's really simple," said one supporter, waving an American flag. "Don't break into people's houses and you won't get shot."[49] The case drew widespread scrutiny of the Castle Doctrine, which permits Texas residents to use deadly force to protect themselves and their homes. Horn, for his part, was unapologetic. "I did what I thought was the right thing to do, and I did it," he said at a Tea Party rally in 2009. "It's unfortunate that it turned out the way that it did, but that's just the way it is."[50]

RODNEY KING

In March 1991 four LAPD officers beat city resident Rodney King after a high-speed car chase. A predominately white jury later acquitted the officers (chapter 9).

The Rodney King beating sparked outrage across the nation, fueling racial tensions and anger about the treatment of minorities. The acquittal of the officers triggered the 1992 Los Angeles riots. Over the subsequent days, fifty-five people were killed, almost two thousand were injured, seven thousand people were arrested, and $1 billion was lost in property damage. The riots were eventually put down by the California Army National Guard.[51]

In 1994 King, who filed a lawsuit against the city of Los Angeles, was awarded $3.8 million in damages and compensation for the beating.[52] Regardless, King continued to have run-ins with the law. He went on to write a book and make a movie about his life; he also made appearances on several TV shows. In 2012 he died from drowning while on drugs.[53]

POLLY KLAAS

Richard Allen Davis—previously convicted for a variety of violent crimes—abducted twelve-year-old Polly Klaas from her home in Petaluma, California, and murdered her (chapter 9). On June 18, 1996, a jury in San Jose, California, Superior Court found Davis guilty on all counts and convicted him of first-degree murder with four special circumstances (robbery, burglary, kidnapping, and a lewd act on a child) supporting imposition of the death penalty. On August 5, 1996, Judge Thomas Hastings agreed with the jury's recommendation and sentenced Davis to death. At the sentencing hearing, Davis shocked the courtroom with his antagonistic behavior. He denied attempting any lewd acts with Polly because, he claimed, the girl had told him her father, Marc Klaas, had sexually abused her. An enraged Marc Klaas lunged and shouted at Davis and was forcibly removed from the court. Judge Hastings concluded the sentencing by imposing the death penalty. "Mr. Davis, this is always a traumatic and emotional decision for a judge," Hastings said. "You made it very easy today by your conduct."[54] Since Polly's abduction, Mark Klaas has become a strong advocate for improving child safety and increasing penalties for criminals who target children, and Polly Klaas's death prompted passage of California's three strikes law.

Davis remains alive today, as challenges to the method of execution used by the state have prevented any executions in California since 2006. A new protocol has been approved but is still being contested in the courts.[55]

SHANE TAYLOR

In 1988 Shane Taylor was convicted for two nonviolent burglaries related to a drug addiction (chapter 9). In 1996 Taylor was convicted for possessing less than ten dollars' worth of meth and got a twenty-five-year sentence.

Taylor served over fifteen years of the sentence before a nonprofit organization, the Three Strikes Project, worked to secure his freedom. His case was referred to the nonprofit by the very judge who delivered the sentence. In the spring of 2013 Taylor was released, thanks to the hard work of the project's students and staff. "When the day came when I packed up my stuff and walked out that gate—wow," recalled Taylor. Today, Taylor—reunited with his family—has a stable job on a farm in Bakersfield, California, but even now, his twenty-five-to-life sentence still haunts him. "I couldn't talk anymore," he says. "I figured it'd be one or two years. My third strike was for $5 [sic] worth of meth."[56]

WILLIE BOSKET

In 1978 fifteen-year-old Willie Bosket killed two people and committed other serious crimes (chapter 9). His five-year sentence sparked statewide outrage and prompted the passage of the Juvenile Offender Act.

Bosket was released from prison but was quickly rearrested. He later bragged that between the ages of nine and fifteen he had committed over two thousand crimes. While in prison, Bosket earned a reputation as a dangerous inmate. He assaulted several guards and now serves his life sentences in a specially made cell with bars and Plexiglas. As one of New York's most dangerous inmates, he is under surveillance at all times, and the guards assigned to monitor him are forbidden to speak with him.[57]

WESLEY SYKES

Chapter 11 tells the story of Wesley Sykes—a member of the LA-based gang the Bloods—who murdered Dennis Brown and then murdered Bobby Gibson, one of the witnesses who was to testify against Sykes for the Brown murder. Recall that three of Gibson's friends had also witnessed the killing but were too scared to testify. After hearing about Gibson's assassination, the friends decided to overcome their fear. The trio went to the police and told them everything they knew.

The courage of the witnesses to stand up against the threats worked. A jury convicted Sykes of second-degree murder, and he received a sentence of twenty-five years to life. Today, the women still maintain quiet presences in their communities. "There's no more walking around the block like they used to," says prosecutor Stephen Murphy.[58]

MICHAEL MELVIN

After two members of the Bloods gang robbed and killed Edwin Reyes-Cruz in Newark in 2004, another gang member, Michael Melvin, was assigned to kill the witness to the killing (chapter 11). He killed the witness and three of her friends who happened to be with her at the time. There was a witness to this quadruple murder, but Melvin hunted him down and killed him too. While on the scene, Melvin also tried to kill the man's girlfriend, but before he killed her the police arrived.

In a plea deal, Melvin pleaded guilty to first-degree aggravated manslaughter, second-degree aggravated assault, and two weapons charges. He was sentenced to sixteen years in prison, but he was never punished for the quadruple homicide.[59]

Appendix

ILLUSTRATIVE CASES UNDERMINING THE CRIMINAL JUSTICE SYSTEM'S MORAL CREDIBILITY

Chapter 4 gives a number of examples of the kinds of cases that produce perceived failures of justice that undermine the criminal justice system's moral credibility with the community, any one of which reported in the news media can spark the shadow vigilante impulse. But a reader might be concerned that the chapter 4 cases illustrating the doctrines of disillusionment might be unique outliers. Unfortunately, such gross failures of justice are all too common. In this appendix we give dozens more examples of the kinds of cases that we use as illustrations in chapter 4.

CRIMINAL JUSTICE, THE GAME

Vitiating Attempted Murder because There Are Not Enough Jury Oaths

Timothy Becktel runs into an acquaintance, Stephen Kozmiuk, on February 25, 2009.[1] The two men go back to Becktel's home and spend the evening drinking. At some point they begin to argue. Becktel grabs a large serrated knife from the kitchen and stabs Kozmiuk repeatedly. Kozmiuk escapes out the front door, and Becktel follows him out into the alley.

Becktel tells responding officers that he killed Kozmiuk, but in fact he is still alive. A jury convicts him of assault with attempt to murder, and the judge sentences him to fifteen to forty years in prison. Becktel appeals. During the jury selection process, the trial court had required that all prospective jurors swear to answer "truthfully, fully and honestly."[2] However, after the jury was selected, the trial court never administered the additional oath that is usually given. Based on this omission, the court of appeals reverses the conviction, even though the appellate judge does not dispute that Becktel is guilty as charged.

Releasing Murderers because of a Magistrate's Employment History

In 1999 David Hughes, Charles Freeman, and Joseph Metz are running an illegal drug-dealing operation in West Virginia. They record all of the transactions in a notebook.[3] Mary Friend, Metz's mother, accidentally acquires the notebook. The three men are concerned that Friend and Metz's grandmother Maxine Stalnaker, who also knows of her grandson's illegal drug ventures, might tell police, so they decide to kill the two women and retrieve the incriminating evidence.

After the killings Metz and Freeman dump the women's bodies. Family and friends are concerned about the mysterious disappearance of the two women and on December 3 file a missing person report.

Years later, in May 2013, police officers get a lead that allows them to restart the investigation, which this time produces good evidence of the crimes committed by the three men.

However, the law requires the charges against the three men to be dropped, because it is noted that the deputy who filled out the missing person report in 1999, a man named John Coffman, is the same man who, fourteen years later and now a magistrate, was tasked to issue the arrest warrants. Despite their guilt, the three murderers walk away free.[4]

Court Helps Offender Hide His Complicity in Murder

In 1979, Jean Packwood and Donald Desbiens are on a bank robbery spree, hitting at least three San Francisco area banks within a few months.[5] They are worried, however, that Desbiens's girlfriend, Janette Pimentel, knows too much about their escapades. The two men shoot her to death and dump her body in the Golden Gate National Recreation Area. The police are suspicious of the two men but do not have sufficient evidence to arrest them.

The FBI builds up evidence to arrest Packwood for the bank robberies, and he eventually confesses his involvement in three of the San Francisco robberies. Packwood describes the robberies in detail, including Desbiens's involvement in them and Desbiens's relationship with Pimentel. Packwood insists that Desbiens killed his girlfriend on his own. As part of a plea deal, Packwood pleads guilty to the bank robberies and agrees to cooperate in the investigation of the robberies and Pimentel's murder. In exchange, Packwood will serve only six years in prison.

The plea agreement includes many provisions, including the following: "Should it be determined by the United States Attorney's Office that Mr. Packwood has willfully given materially incomplete or false testimony he shall be subject to prosecution for any appropriate federal criminal violation, including but not limited to perjury, and false statements."[6] After Packwood begins serving his six-year sentence, evidence surfaces that he did indeed take part in the murder of Desbiens's girlfriend. He is put on trial for the killing, but the court concludes that the perjury (saying he had nothing to do with the murder) was not a substantial enough breach to remove his immunity. Despite the overwhelming evidence of Packwood's participation in the killing and his clear attempts to deceive the United States Attorney's Office, the court holds Packwood immune from prosecution for the murder.

Giving the Defendant the Benefit of His Deception in Entering a Guilty Plea

In 2004 Stacy Hunt concocts a plan to import cocaine that he is having shipped to the airport in Anchorage, Alaska.[7] Unfortunately for Hunt, police become aware of this scheme, obtain a warrant to search the package when it arrives at the airport, allow the package to be delivered as planned, and arrest Hunt as he is driving away after picking up the package. After he is indicted for cocaine distribution, he flees the state. He is arrested three years later in California and sent back to Alaska to face the federal drug charges.

Hunt, who has faced many criminal drug charges in the past, acts as his own counsel. In a plea deal, Hunt confesses to possessing a controlled substance with the intent to distribute. During the negotiations, he uses words like "substance" and "illegal drug" and never the word "cocaine."[8] As a result of his guilty plea and his prior criminal history, the judge sentences him to fifteen years in prison. Hunt appeals, claiming that he never actually pleaded guilty to possessing cocaine. The appellate court buys Hunt's argument. Because he never used the word "cocaine," the court concludes that he can only be held liable for the minor offense of distributing a controlled substance, for which the maximum sentence is a year in prison.[9]

Homicide Reversal because of a Verdict Sheet Format Reviewed by the Defense Counsel

In 1991, Jeffrey Damiano, Eric Birdsall, and Jaime Rullan blast Pink Floyd songs in their car as they spend the evening bar hopping in New Paltz, New York.[10] They drive to Ohioville Bridge, which runs above the New York State Thruway, and turn off their headlights. From the height of the bridge they begin dropping stones onto cars. Damiano heaves up the largest boulder he can find, a fifty-two-pound piece of granite. At that moment, Karen Zentner is driving under the bridge, Damiano heaves the huge boulder over the edge, and the men watch as it crashes through Zentner's windshield. The force of the impact cracks her ribs and splits open her heart.

Zentner is left dead. Two years later, Rullan pleads guilty to criminal facilitation and agrees to testify against the other two men. The jury finds Damiano guilty of second-degree murder and two counts of reckless endangerment (for dropping rocks on other drivers earlier in the evening).

Damiano appeals his conviction. On the verdict sheet given to the jury, the alternative legal name of the offense was included in parentheses after the official statutory name of the offense. For example, next to "murder in the second degree" on the verdict sheet is the parenthetical phrase "depraved mind murder"; next to "manslaughter in the second degree" there appears "reckless endangerment" in parentheses. The trial judge had shown the verdict sheet to both parties, and neither had objected to it. The appellate court concludes that the parenthetical language might have confused the jury. The court does not dispute that Damiano murdered the young woman and put other lives in grave danger but nonetheless sets aside Damiano's conviction.

Excluding Black Jurors and then Complaining of an Improper Jury

Arthur Huey and a partner sell marijuana in Louisiana, and the law catches up with them.[11] During the jury-screening phase prior to trial, Huey's counsel asks to exclude six prospective jurors from the pool because they are African American or Hispanic and Huey fears these jurors may be prejudiced against him when they hear the racial slurs he uses on some tape-recorded phone calls that will be used as evidence. When the prospective jurors in question are asked about the issue, all respond that they will not be influenced by the racial epithets. Therefore, they are not excluded from the pool of prospective jurors. When the jurors are actually selected, Huey and his counsel use their juror challenges to remove five of the jurors they had sought to exclude.

At the conclusion of the trial, Huey and his partner are found guilty on all counts. Huey appeals, claiming that the jury selection process was improper because African American jurors were excluded because of their race. The United States Court of Appeals for the Fifth Circuit overturns all convictions against the defendants.

Thirteen-Year-Old Daughter with Muscular Dystrophy Was Not "Physically Helpless" because She Tried to Push Away Her Rapist Father

Jane Doe, a thirteen-year-old who is wheelchair-bound, is at home alone with her father, Curtis Davis, when he sexually assaults her.[12] Davis takes his daughter into the bedroom, picks her up from her wheelchair, and places her on the bed. She resists, strikes her father, and screams for help. Davis sexually assaults her multiple times. Doe reports the incident to the police, and Davis is arrested and charged with the rape of a person who is "physically helpless."[13] At trial, the jury finds Davis guilty. Davis appeals his conviction, claiming that he was accused under the wrong law, since his victim is not "physically helpless."[14] While Doe, a thirteen-year-old girl with muscular dystrophy, may be "physically helpless" in one sense, she is not in the narrow sense that the court gives the statutory language. Davis's conviction is overturned.

SUPPRESSING RELIABLE EVIDENCE

Rape and Robbery Confessions Suppressed after Miranda Warning because Defendants Have Been Appointed Counsel for a Previous Offense

In 1987, four men—Raphael James, Mark Denny, Eddie Viera, and Mark Smith—burst through the front door of a Brooklyn Burger King with guns drawn. They demand that the two employees empty the register and hand over the money.[15] After pocketing the cash, the four men force the employees to disrobe at gunpoint. The four men take turns sodomizing the female employee and then force other sexual tortures on the employees. Once the robbers leave, the two employees frantically call the police. Raphael James is arrested for the Burger King rape and robbery. James responds by saying he wants to talk and blurts out, "I did the robbery but I didn't do no rape."[16] A few hours later, Denny is also arrested. When he arrives at the station, Denny, like James, makes a statement and says, "I didn't do that one [rape]—I heard Mark Smith raped her."[17]

Before their joint trial, James and Denny ask for a hearing to suppress the incriminating statements they made when they were arrested. The court agrees that because James and Denny were under investigation for a previous robbery and had hired attorneys to represent them in that case, they should not have been allowed to say anything without their counsel present. Moreover, while the defendants' statements may have been spontaneous—neither defendant had been questioned by police—the court concludes that the statements were not "spontaneous enough" and must be suppressed.

Murder Confession Suppressed because Multiple Miranda Warnings Were Not Enough

In the early hours of a February morning in 1971, Julius Wideman brutally beats and then shoots to death James Allen on a Philadelphia street.[18] As he flees the scene, Wideman dumps his gun into a sewer gutter and returns to his home and wife. The police go to Wideman's home, and, accompanied by his wife, he is brought into the station. When Wideman admits that he owns the car seen by witnesses, he is given his Miranda warnings. When detectives question him again, they give Wideman additional Miranda warnings. While at the station he takes a nap. Although Wideman has denied his guilt throughout the morning hours, after resting, talking to his wife, and being administered a polygraph, he finally admits that he did beat, shoot, and kill James Allen. The officer gives Wideman Miranda warnings yet again and takes a formal written statement of what had happened earlier that day.

Based on the statement, the police find the gun in the sewer a few blocks away from where he shot Allen. The officers continue to Wideman's house and find Allen's blood on Wideman's car. The evidence of

Wideman's guilt is overwhelming, and the jury convicts him of second-degree murder. On appeal, however, Wideman claims that his confession should be suppressed because while he had been advised of his Miranda rights several times, he claims that those warnings were too far removed from the time when he actually confessed. Further, all the evidence found as a result of his confession, such as the gun and the blood-spattered car, should also be suppressed because the police would not have found that evidence but for his confession. The court grants his claim.

Spontaneous Incriminating Statements Suppressed When Made to Officers Serving a Court Order to Appear in a Lineup

On June 21, 1975, twenty-year-old Diane Snell meets and chats with Harry Skinner, age forty-five, at a local bar in Amherst, New York.[19] Hours later, after they leave the bar together, Skinner makes sexual advances toward Snell, who refuses each time. The rejections send Skinner into a rage. He savagely beats Snell to death and dumps her body in a nearby ditch.

Police talk to Skinner several times, so Skinner hires a lawyer. The lawyer calls the police department to tell the authorities that he now represents Skinner. A court order is issued for Skinner to appear in a lineup, and his attorney consents to his appearance. Skinner becomes distressed about appearing in a lineup. The officers try to calm him by explaining that he can contact his attorney. Seeing that Skinner remains anxious, an officer tells him he can get the whole story off his chest once and for all. Skinner agrees to talk to the detectives. They give him his Miranda warnings again, after which Skinner begins describing incriminating details of the murder. Skinner says he wants to make a formal statement. But he then changes his mind and refuses to give the statement because he wants to talk to his attorney first. The officers do not pursue the matter further, and Skinner leaves the station. Eventually the police get enough evidence to move forward to trial. At trial, a jury finds him guilty of first-degree manslaughter, and the judge sentences him to twenty-five years in prison.

On appeal, there is no question about his guilt, but he seeks to suppress the incriminating statements that he made when the police had come to serve him with the lineup order. He argues that, even though he was not in custody and had not yet been arrested, and even though he had been given his Miranda warnings and had chosen to make statements anyway, those statements should be suppressed because his lawyer was not present. The court grants his claim.[20] Because he cannot be effectively prosecuted without his incriminating statements, Skinner walks.

Incriminating Statements Tape-Recorded by Coconspirator Are Suppressed because Counsel Is Not Present

In 1980 Perley Moulton Jr. and Gary Colson are stealing vehicles and stripping them for parts.[21] The police receive a tip that the crimes are being committed at a particular auto shop. A police officer goes to the garage and asks the owner if he can search the service bays and is told no, so he leaves. Moulton and Colson then take the stripped frame of their latest theft to nearby woods and light it on fire. They walk back to the auto shop leaving a trail in the snow. After discovering the fire, the police follow the trail back to the shop. The police get a warrant and then seize the stolen property. Moulton and Colson are arrested and indicted on four counts of theft. Both plead not guilty and are released on bail pending trial. While out on bail, Colson receives anonymous threatening phone calls. On November 4, 1982, he calls the police to report the calls and to inform them that he wants to discuss his case. The police tell him to talk to his lawyer before he calls again.

On November 6, Moulton and Colson meet at a restaurant in Belfast, Maine, to discuss their plans for the trial. Moulton suggests that they murder the state's primary witness. They discuss various ways to kill him. Three days later, Colson and his lawyer meet at the police station. During this meeting, Colson confesses to the thefts and describes the conversation in which Moulton suggests killing the witness. Colson is granted immunity from any additional charges beyond the ones for which he has already been indicted in exchange for testifying against Moulton. Colson allows the police to record his phone calls. Recordings are made of Moulton discussing his plans to murder the witness and about his past thefts with Colson. Moulton is convicted of burglary and theft of the Ford pickup truck, the dump truck, and the auto parts. On appeal, Moulton claims that his recorded statements to Colson should have been suppressed because his counsel was not present during his discussions with Colson. The appellate courts grant his claim.[22] Moulton walks free.[23]

Drug Producer's Incriminating Statements during Takedown Suppressed because Officers Hadn't Given Miranda Warnings Quickly Enough during the Action

In 1991 the Kansas Bureau of Investigation obtains information that a metal building on a rural area is being used for the large-scale production and distribution of drugs.[24] The bureau obtains a warrant to search the property and to seize any drug-related material or firearms. The warrant team uses two helicopters and about twenty officers during their raid. Upon entering the building, officers discover numerous marijuana plants, drug paraphernalia, and firearms. Two officers assigned to the perimeter notice a car entering the dirt road leading toward the property. The car turns toward the building, but as soon as the driver notices the police, he throws the car into reverse and tries to flee. The two perimeter officers draw their weapons and force Vincent Perdue, the owner of the facility, and his fiancée to exit the car.

An officer asks Perdue what he is doing on the property, and Perdue responds that "he is there to check on his stuff."[25] When the officer asks, "What stuff?" Perdue answers, "The marijuana that I know that you guys have found in the shed."[26] Perdue then tells the officers that the marijuana belongs to him and his fiancée. The officers then read Perdue his Miranda rights and place him under arrest.

Prosecutors charge Perdue with possession of marijuana with the intent to distribute and the use of a firearm in relation to drug trafficking. After hearing Perdue's statements during his arrest, the jury finds Perdue guilty of both counts. On appeal, Perdue claims that he should have been given his Miranda rights before he made his incriminating statements. The court agrees with him and holds those statements inadmissible.[27] The conviction is reversed.

Murder Weapon Suppressed because Cops Should Not Have Made an Arrest with Guns Drawn

In New York City in 1990 an outbreak of robberies of cabs has resulted in the death of several drivers.[28] City cab drivers agree with the NYPD to submit to routine periodic stops, especially if officers note suspicious behavior. As police watch, an erratically driven cab with three male passengers leaves the Major Deegan Highway at Fordham Road. Two officers on patrol notice the behavior and follow the cab for several blocks. When it pulls to the side of the road, the officers pull up a short distance behind the cab. Gregory Hampton steps out of the cab carrying a "thin, white plastic bag that appeared to be 'weighted' down by a heavy object."[29] Upon seeing this bag, the officers exit their squad car and approach him with their guns drawn. They order him to stop, and Hampton complies. Once the officers are close enough, they see the outline of an Uzi machine gun in the bag. They order Hampton to carefully place the bag on the ground. Hampton drops the bag to the ground, where it rips open. The machine gun is now in plain view. The other men in the cab flee.

Hampton is arrested and searched. The search produces narcotics, two more guns, jewelry, and nearly five thousand dollars in cash. Police also find insurance and vehicle registration cards that link Hampton to a young woman. Hampton claims the woman is his girlfriend, but a brief investigation reveals that she is a murder victim. Hampton is taken in for questioning. He waives his Miranda rights and ultimately admits to murdering the woman during a robbery and also another woman during a different robbery. Officers use two lineups to connect him to both homicides. The state charges Hampton with two counts of murder, in addition to machine-gun and drug possession charges.

He is convicted, and the defense appeals. The court concludes that the officers should not have drawn their weapons when they did because by doing so they were essentially forcibly detaining the defendant without reasonable cause. The appellate court reverses the conviction and suppresses the weapons and other evidence collected after the arrest. Hampton's robbery and murder of the two women go unpunished.

Four-Million-Dollar Drug Deal in Public Place Suppressed because the Court Concludes That Police Did Not Have "Reasonable Suspicion" to Investigate

At 5:00 a.m., Carol Bayless drives slowly down 176th Street in a New York City neighborhood notorious for its drug activity.[30] When the car stops, four men appear and they walk to her car. Bayless unlocks the trunk, and the men place two large black duffle bags inside. A pair of police officers watch the suspicious activity unfold. When Bayless's car begins to move away, the officers pull up directly behind to follow her. Seeing this, the four men on the street run off. The officers call in, requesting a license plate check, but before this comes back they see that Bayless is approaching a highway on-ramp, so they turn on their sirens and pull her over. The officers pop open the trunk, discover the thirty-four kilograms of cocaine and two kilos of heroin, with a value of nearly four million dollars, and promptly arrest her. The state charges Bayless with conspiracy and possession of cocaine and heroin with intent to distribute. Bayless files a motion to suppress the evidence taken from the car.[31] The judge reasons that even though Bayless engaged in suspicious activity in an area known for its drug dealing, the officers had no reason to pull her over and conduct a search. Bayless is never tried.

Key Evidence Suppressed because Child Molester Was Denied the Opportunity for His Roommate to Destroy or Hide It

In the middle of a rainy night in Arizona, Gary Ault walks the quarter mile from his residence and slips into the home of a six-year-old girl—Jane Doe—who is sleeping in her bedroom.[32] As Ault creeps silently toward Doe's room, he leaves large, muddy footprints behind. He enters the little girl's room, approaches the bed, unzips her pajamas, and begins fondling her genitals as she sleeps. Doe awakens and begins screaming, which brings her family running and sends Ault scrambling out of the house. Doe's parents immediately call the police to report the intrusion. The police arrive and discover distinctive muddy footprints on the floor. After Doe gives them a physical description of her assailant, two of the officers who know Ault suspect that he is the assailant. Doe selects Ault from a photographic lineup as her attacker.

Police are let into Ault's home by his roommate. The roommate gives the police permission to search the premises at 5:00 a.m. The police leave, and Ault returns to his house at 6:45 a.m. When the officers return to Ault's home, Ault answers the door, wearing only a pair of shorts. The deputies ask him to accompany them to the station for questioning, and after his initial refusal, Ault agrees to go with them after he gets dressed. While they are waiting for him to dress, an officer observes a pair of large, muddy tennis shoes and connects them to the footprints in Doe's home. The officer asks Ault if they are his, and he says they are not. To ensure the safety of the potential evidence, the shoes are brought to the police station. Ault is arrested. Later that afternoon, the officers obtain a search warrant to inspect Ault's clothing in his home and find a pile of damp clothes that match Doe's description. Ault is convicted for child molestation and second-degree burglary.

Ault appeals, contending that the tennis shoes found at the house should be suppressed because the officers did not have permission to enter. The state counters that the officers had probable cause to search the house. In any case, they inevitably would have found the shoes during that search under the warrant at the same time they found the incriminating damp clothes.[33] The court reverses Ault's conviction. The convicted child molester thus gets a free pass on his sexual assault of the child.

Gun Suppressed because Police Should Have Waited for the Suspect to Reach for His Gun before Drawing Their Own

Calvin Moore gets into a heated dispute in public involving a handgun.[34] The police station receives an anonymous phone tip about the disturbance. The caller describes how the handgun is clearly visible and expresses concern for the safety of the people in the area. The man's possession of the handgun is illegal. The station radios the information to two nearby officers on patrol. When the two officers arrive at the scene, they find Moore standing on the street corner described by the caller and wearing clothing matching the caller's description. When they step out of their vehicle and walk toward Moore, he starts to walk away from them. Given the accuracy of the caller's description, they approach Moore, draw their guns, and call out, "Police, don't move."[35] Moore continues to walk away, but as the officers follow, he finally comes to a halt. Moore is the right man; he is carrying a gun. He is arrested and charged with criminal possession of a weapon. He is convicted of illegal gun possession. On appeal, however, a majority of the appellate panel grants his claim and suppresses the gun.[36] The court reasons that because the officers stopped Moore with their weapons drawn, they no longer had any justification for searching Moore's jacket for a weapon.[37]

Gun Suppressed because a Murder Suspect Put the Gun in His Car Just before Being Arrested

Miguel Torres, known by his alias Poppo, is living in New York City. For some time, the police have been closely watching Torres because they have linked him to several homicides.[38] The police receive an anonymous phone tip that Poppo is getting his hair cut at a barber shop at 116th Street and

Third Avenue in Manhattan. He is wearing a white sweater and carrying a gun in a shoulder bag.[39] Two plainclothes officers see Torres, who is wearing a white sweater and carrying a green nylon shoulder bag, leave the barber shop accompanied by another man. Before the officers can reach the suspects, Torres and his friend enter Torres's black Cadillac Eldorado. Given that the caller was correct about Torres's location, the officers assume the caller may also be right about Torres having an illegal handgun in his shoulder bag. Knowing this, the detectives move toward the vehicle with their guns drawn and identify themselves as police officers. They order the two men out of the Eldorado. The men get out of the car, but they leave the shoulder bag behind on the front seat. The officers frisk the two suspects. One officer reaches into the front seat and pulls out Torres's green nylon bag, which the officer finds to be unusually heavy. The detective feels around the outside of the bag and notices the outline of a gun, which turns out to be a Rossi revolver loaded with five rounds of ammunition. The detectives arrest Torres and charge him with criminal possession of a firearm.

Torres pleads guilty to third-degree criminal possession of a weapon. In jail, however, he changes his mind and appeals his case to the higher court of appeals. The court grants Torres's request to suppress the gun, with a majority of the panel concluding that entering into a suspect's vehicle is a "significant encroachment" upon that person's rights.

DECISION MAKERS WHO ARE BLIND TO JUSTICE

Murderer—"King" of Prison—Paroled to Reduce Capacity Kills Ten More

In 1966, Kenneth Allen McDuff, a convicted burglar, and his friend Roy Green finish a job pouring concrete at a construction site in Temple, Texas, and decide to drive to Fort Worth.[40] While driving, McDuff spots a teenage girl, Edna Sullivan, talking with two boys, Robert Brand and

Mark Dunman, at a baseball diamond. As McDuff and Green approach them, McDuff pulls out his .38 pistol and forces the teenagers to hand over their wallets, and ends up sexually assaulting Sullivan and killing the three teens.[41] Green, riddled with guilt, turns himself in and describes the entire episode to police. McDuff is arrested and convicted and receives a death sentence for the murders, in part because the jury concludes that McDuff is likely to kill again. McDuff is twice scheduled to go to the electric chair, but both times he receives a stay of execution a few days before.[42]

In 1989 there is overcrowding in Texas prisons. The parole board knows of McDuff's criminal history and is aware of the trial jury's opinion that he is likely to murder again. The board selects McDuff for release on parole, even though other less serious and less dangerous offenders could have been released instead. When US Marshal Parnell McNamara in Waco, Texas, learns of McDuff's parole he asks, "Have they gone crazy?"[43]

Three days after McDuff's release, police discover the body of Sarafia Parker. A witness had seen her together with McDuff in his pickup truck before she was murdered. It is possible that she is his first post-parole victim.[44] In 1991 McDuff kidnaps Brenda Thompson and ties her up in his vehicle. When McDuff comes upon a Waco Police Department checkpoint, Thompson kicks at the windshield to get the attention of the officers, but McDuff speeds away. McDuff later physically and sexually tortures Thompson, putting out cigarettes on her skin and raping her before killing her. He then continues in this pattern, killing at least nine other people.

Sexual Predator Sent for Treatment Judged No Longer a Danger and Released to Murder Twenty People

In 1968 William Bonin begins sexually assaulting young men.[45] Bonin continues to prey on vulnerable kids as he kidnaps and sodomizes several youngsters. In 1969 the police catch him in the act and arrest him. Bonin tells authorities when they capture him that "they were lucky they had caught him because he felt that he might have killed the boy" this time.[46] He pleads guilty to molestation, forced oral copulation, and kidnapping. Believing Bonin is very sick and dangerous, the court sends him to Atascadero State Hospital for treatment. In 1971 doctors determine that treatment is ineffective for Bonin, so they ship him to the nearby prison.[47] But in 1974 doctors at the prison decide that Bonin is no longer a danger, so they release him.

Within a year of his release, he rapes a young man and is arrested for the attack. While in police custody, Bonin tells authorities he will kill his future victims to ensure that they can never testify against him. The court again convicts him for forcible oral copulation, but just a few years later a parole board releases him a second time.[48]

Again, within a year, police arrest Bonin for molesting another teenage boy. In 1979 Bonin begins a killing spree around southern California. His first victim is seventeen-year-old Markus Grabs. Bonin binds him in ignition wire and drives him to his house, where he proceeds to sodomize and beat him, finally stabbing him seventy-seven times. Bonin leaves Grabs's body on the side of a Malibu freeway. Three weeks later, the body of fifteen-year-old Donald Hyden is found in a trash bin off the Ventura Freeway. It is determined that Hyden has been raped and strangled with a ligature. His murderer also cut his throat and made an attempt to castrate the young man. Over the next year, Bonin murders at least twenty-one victims using similar methods. Most of his victims are young male hitchhikers or schoolboys.[49] After abusing and murdering them, he usually dumps their bodies along one of the freeways in southern California, which earns him the moniker the Freeway Killer. In the spring of 1980 the Los Angeles Police Department arrest him in a parking lot, where they catch him sodomizing a fifteen-year-old boy.

Teacher Who Raped Fourteen-Year-Old Who Kills Herself Gets Thirty Days as Judge Blames Victim for the Rape

In 2007 Cherice Moralez is a fourteen-year-old freshman at Billings Senior High School in Montana.[50] Moralez takes a business class taught by Stacey Rambold, a forty-nine-year-old who would like to have sex with Moralez.[51] Between October and December 2007, Rambold rapes Moralez on three separate occasions. Moralez's attitude and behavior begin to change. Her liveliness diminishes, and she begins to get into trouble at school. The problem is finally revealed during a meeting of Moralez's church group, where she tells the group leader about the rapes. Moralez's mother is notified, and she calls the police. On October 31, 2008, Rambold is arrested and charged with three felony counts of sexual intercourse without consent with a minor.

As the case is pending, Moralez has trouble dealing with her classmates at school: "It was all dark looks."[52] Moralez falls into a depression and kills herself.[53] Judge G. Todd Baugh presides over the case in December 2010. Rambold is told to complete a Sexual Offender Treatment Program, in lieu of punishment, but Rambold is kicked out of the program for having an affair. Now forced back into court, Rambold pleads guilty to one of the three counts of rape, and the prosecution recommends that he receive a twenty-year prison sentence with ten years suspended. However, Judge Baugh has sympathy for Rambold because he believes that the rapist has "suffered enough" already.[54] Further, the judge concludes that Moralez "was older than her chronological age," that she was "as much in control of the situation" as Rambold, and that the rape "wasn't this forcible beat-up thing."[55] Baugh gives Rambold a sentence of thirty days in jail. The mandatory minimum for the offense is two years.

Probation for Aggressor Who Kills Another in a Fight the Aggressor Started

On June 6, 2006, two brothers, Isaiah and Evan Eskew, attend Wirt High School's graduation ceremony in Gary, Indiana.[56] Evan, there to see a friend graduate, once dated Deanna Edwards, who is also at the ceremony with her current boyfriend, Tywon Newsome. Although Evan Eskew and Newsome have not seen each other in several years, tensions linger over insults Eskew made three years earlier. When the ceremony is almost over, the Eskew brothers head to their car and retrieve a handgun. A physical brawl ensues between the Eskew brothers and Newsome. When Evan accidentally drops the gun during the struggle, Isaiah picks it up, aims at Newsome's head, and fires twice, grazing Newsom's lip and left ear. Isaiah then fires again at Newsome. This time the bullet rips through Newsome's chest and punctures his lung. Evan flees from the parking lot, and Isaiah, after beating Newsome up a bit more, also leaves. Isaiah goes to the emergency room for medical attention. During questioning by police, he tells officers what transpired and is immediately taken into custody. Newsome dies from the gunshot wound. Isaiah, who did the shooting, pleads not guilty to murder and unlawful possession of a firearm. He faces a potential sentence of forty-five to sixty-five years in prison.

At trial, the jury finds Isaiah guilty of reckless homicide and illegal possession of a firearm on school property. While the judge could give a sentence of eleven years, he gives a sentence of probation instead. For killing Newsome, Isaiah is required to speak once a year to groups of young people.

Mississippi Governor Pardons Murderers Who Worked for His Family

Joseph Ozment and three other individuals rob a convenience store in Hernado, Mississippi, and kill the lone employee.[57] An anonymous tipster later informs police that he saw the robbers flee in a getaway car, and ten days later, Ozment and his accomplices are arrested and charged with armed robbery and murder. During his confession to police, Ozment states, "I pulled out my pistol because the man was still moving on the floor. I didn't want him to be able to identify me or the other guy so I shot him twice. . . . I shot him in the head."[58] Ozment makes a deal with the state and testifies against his accomplices to avoid getting the death penalty. He pleads guilty to murder, armed robbery, and conspiracy to commit armed robbery and is given a life sentence.

In 2001 Anthony McCray and his wife have been arguing while dining in a café in McComb, Mississippi.[59] McCray leaves the café, then returns with a gun. He shoots his wife in the back, killing her. After his arrest, McCray insists that his shooting of his wife was accidental, but multiple witnesses make it clear that this is not true. McCray pleads guilty and is sentenced to life in prison.

Ozment and McCray, along with more than two hundred other offenders in prison, are assigned to work at the Mississippi governor's mansion, and because of that service, Governor Haley Barbour gives the men full pardons when he leaves the governor's office in 2012.

DEFENSES FOR THE GUILTY

By the Time a Rape Victim Recovers from the Trauma Enough to Cooperate with Police to Identify her Rapist, the Statute of Limitations Has Run Out

On the evening of March 16, 1978, teenager Lori Kustudick makes plans to meet her friends for an early St. Patrick's Day party at a dance club known as the Some Other Place Lounge.[60] Kustudick waits for her friends, passing the time by having a few drinks and talking to a few familiar faces, but her friends never appear. Around 2:30 a.m. a young man (later identified as Herbert Howard) approaches Kustudick's table. He offers her a ride home. While his friend drives, Howard rapes and savagely beats Kustudick. Among other injuries he cracks her skull and tortures her with a burning cigarette. Despite the serious injuries she escapes the car and runs to freedom. At 4:04 a.m. Officer Hartmann of the Cook County Sheriff's Department spots Kustudick running diagonally across an intersection, completely naked. Kustudick, in a state of shock, tells the officer, "I want to go home; I just want to go home." He wraps her in a blanket and rushes her to Lutheran General Hospital. The police build a case against Howard, but his victim is both mentally and physically compromised and is unable to help them.[61] Without sufficient evidence against Howard, the authorities must release him.

After years of therapy, Kustudick comes to understand that only by facing what happened to her can she move past it. She is now ready and able to do what she can to bring about justice. The police provide Kustudick a book of mug shots as "a big thick, thick book . . . like a couple of the yellow pages from Chicago together."[62] She is easily able to identify Howard, who happened to be the same person who was the prime suspect of police back at the time of the offense. However, the prosecutors soon determine that Howard cannot be tried. In Illinois, all rape prosecutions have a five-year statute of limitations. Because the statute of limitations has expired, the state is powerless to pursue Howard for his vicious rape and beating.

When a Killer Gets a Manslaughter Verdict, He Walks Free under the Statute of Limitations

In 1974, Claude Nix, a trucker from South Carolina and father of six, drives a truck headed north on US Highway 13.[63] He is just south of Harrington, Delaware, en route to Albany, New York. At the time, the United States is in the throes of the 1970s energy crisis, and independent truckers are on strike protesting the increase in diesel fuel prices. As a result of the truckers' strike, industries along the East Coast, including Pennsylvania, Delaware, New York, and New Jersey, have been forced to lay off workers because materials are not being delivered. The strike is affecting thousands of people, and many are upset with the striking truckers.

Many of the striking truckers are upset with those who are still driving. In Pennsylvania, a bridge along the turnpike is dynamited, and hotels frequented by truckers receive bomb threats. In West Virginia, National Guard troops ride with truckers to protect them. As Nix drives along US 13, a shot is fired from a passing car. The bullet penetrates the driver's side window and kills Nix. Police commence a massive investigation into Nix's murder. The investigation progresses but slowly. In 1987 the police finally have enough evidence and witnesses to arrest Lester Cane, a thirty-eight-year-old house painter living south of Dover, Delaware. The police charge Cane with second-degree murder on March 2, 1987. At trial, the jury is instructed that they can convict Cane either of second-degree murder or of the lesser offense of manslaughter, or they can acquit him. The jury convicts Cane of manslaughter. While there is no statute of limitations for murder, there is a five-year statute of limitations for manslaughter. Thus, when the jury convicts Cane of the lesser offense, the defense counsel files a motion to have the conviction completely invalidated.

Cane is released. His killing of Claude Nix goes unpunished.

Retrial of a Meth Addict Who Murdered a Crying Baby Barred Despite His Subsequent Confession

In 1991 Michael Lane is dating single mother Jennifer Watts.[64] The couple live together in Utah with Watts's two-year-old child, PJ. While watching the baby, Land gets high on meth and kills the child. He places the dead baby back in his crib. When Watts arrives home, she is overcome with grief and immediately calls the police. Lane tells Watts that he has no idea what happened to PJ, and she believes his story. However, the police consider him the primary suspect. Lane is arrested and put on trial for the murder. During the trial, Watts, believing Lane's claims of innocence, supports Lane in court. Lane keeps denying any involvement, and his story is not contradicted by the medical testimony because the doctors disagree about some aspects of the injuries. The jury deliberates for four hours because a lone juror does not believe Lane's story, but eventually she changes her vote. Lane is acquitted of the murder charge and allowed to walk free.

Nearly fifteen years later, in August 2005, Lane arranges a meeting with his local bishop during which he confesses that he did indeed kill PJ Watts. The bishop urges Lane to turn himself in to the authorities and to face the consequences for his actions. Following the bishop's advice, Lane says good-bye to his friends and family and leaves his central Utah home to turn himself in to authorities. When he arrives at the police station, Lane asks to speak to homicide detectives about PJ's murder and confesses everything.[65] The police officers tell him that he cannot plead guilty and be convicted of the murder because of double jeopardy. This comes as a shock to Lane, who is unaware of that legal doctrine. Moreover, since Lane never testified at his trial in 1991, the detectives know that he cannot even be charged with perjury. Lane walks free without even a token punishment.

Murderer-Rapist Acquitted on Perjured Alibi Cannot Be Prosecuted Despite Subsequent Confession

In 1987, Irvin Bolden and his girlfriend, Joel Tillis, are both students at Northeast Louisiana University.[66] Bolden feels Tillis's friendship with her former roommate Brenda Spicer intrudes on his time with his girlfriend. Bolden and Spicer have argued about the issue. Bolden seethes with resentment. He lures Spicer to an empty storage warehouse, rapes her, and then strangles her to death. Spicer's body is found the next day. Bolden is charged and brought to trial. He testifies that he had nothing to do with Spicer's death. The jury acquits him based on his perjured testimony. Bolden and Tillis move to Memphis, Tennessee, where a year later, Bolden strangles Tillis to death, wraps her body in red sheets, and dumps her along a highway in Arkansas. Investigators find her body in May 1989 but have no evidence to proceed with the case.

In 1991 Bolden moves from Tennessee to New Jersey and begins a relationship with Jennifer Spurlock. The relationship ends, and Spurlock moves back home with her mother. When she returns to the residence that she and Bolden had recently shared and retrieves some belongings,

Bolden files a complaint with New Jersey police, who arrest Spurlock the next day on burglary charges. Bolden is granted a restraining order against Spurlock. Facing burglary charges for her unauthorized entry into Bolden's apartment, Spurlock decides to tell police what Bolden had previously confessed to her: that he had killed Joel Tillis and Brenda Spicer. Bolden is called in to be interviewed by investigators. Believing he is cornered and out of options, he confesses to murdering both women. But while Bolden now admits that he killed Spicer, he cannot be retried for her murder because he was previously acquitted. Double jeopardy precludes bringing new charges, even though Bolden's perjury tainted the original trial.

NOTES

CHAPTER 1. FEAR, MEET INDIFFERENCE: BREACHING THE SOCIAL CONTRACT

1. The facts of the narrative are drawn from the following sources: Rebecca Lopez, "Stalking Victim Heard Issuing Final 911 Plea before Her Death," WFAA-TV Channel 8, March 6, 2013, http://www.wfaa.com/story/news/crime/2013/03/07/stalking-victim-heard-issuing-final-911-plea-before-her-death/14048898/ (accessed May 24, 2017); Scott Goldstein, "Dallas Woman Found Murdered 2 Days after Calling 911 for Help," *Dallas Morning News*, August 20, 2013; Tanya Eiserer and Scott Goldstein, "Woman Murdered While on Phone with Dallas 911 Was Victim of Domestic Violence for Years," *Dallas Morning News—Crime Blog*, March 8, 2013, http://crimeblog.dallasnews.com/2013/03/woman-murdered-while-on-phone-with-dallas-911-was-victim-of-domestic-violence-for-years.html (accessed May 24, 2017); Tonyita Hopkins, interview by Brian Williams, *Rock Center*, NBC, May 17, 2013, http://www.nbcnews.com/video/rock center/51922996 (accessed May 24, 2017); Tanya Eiserer, "911 Tape Reveals Horrific Last Minutes for Murdered Dallas Woman," *Dallas Morning News*, March 6, 2013; Victoria Cavalier, "Woman Murdered While on 911 Call Not Found for Two Days," *New York Daily News*, August 22, 2012.
2. Goldstein, "Dallas Woman Found Murdered."
3. Lopez, "Stalking Victim."
4. Ibid.
5. Ibid.
6. Ibid.
7. Eiserer, "911 Tape."
8. Thomas Hobbes, *Leviathan* (New York: Oxford University Press, 1996); John Locke, *Second Treatise of Government* (Indianapolis, IN: Hackett, 1980); Jean-Jacques Rousseau, *Du contrat social* (Mineola, NY: Dover, 1967).
9. Lopez, "Stalking Victim."
10. Eiserer, "911 Tape."
11. Hopkins, interview by Williams.
12. Cavalier, "Woman Murdered."
13. For an account of subsequent events, see this book's postscript.

14. The facts of the narrative are drawn from the following sources: J. Harry Jones, "Judge Revisits Day He Overruled Jury Verdict," *San Diego Union Tribune*, November 21, 2004; Ernie Grimm, "Bullets for the Bully," *San Diego Reader*, May 20, 2004; *Fatal Encounters*, "Road Kill," first broadcast May 30, 2013, on Investigation Discovery Channel; Ron Donoho, "Law and Disorder," *San Diego Magazine*, March 1997; Carey Goldberg, "Support Builds for Killer Who Broke Cycle of Fear," *New York Times*, June 18, 1996.

15. Donoho, "Law and Disorder."

16. Grimm, "Bullets for the Bully."

17. Ibid.

18. Ibid.

19. Ibid.

20. Donoho, "Law and Disorder."

21. Grimm, "Bullets for the Bully."

22. See, for example, American Law Institute, Model Penal Code, §§ 3.06(1)(a) and (3)(d), 3.11(2) (Philadelphia, 1962).

23. Ibid., § 3.04(2)(b)(ii); authorities collected in Paul H. Robinson, Matthew Kussmaul, Camber Stoddard, Ilya Rudyak, and Andreas Kuersten, "The American Criminal Code: General Defenses," *Journal of Legal Analysis* 7, no. 1 (2015): 37–150.

24. Under the common law formulation, the use of defensive force until the threat is imminent or the use of such force is "immediately necessary," under the formulation of the Model Penal Code, § 3.40(1). Paul H. Robinson and Michael Cahill, *Criminal Law*, 2nd ed. (Fredrick, MD: Wolters Kluwer Law and Business, 2012), 306–307.

25. The growing popularity of the "stand your ground" rule, which creates an exception in some situations to the Model Penal Code rule requiring retreat before use of deadly force, probably reflects such unhappiness. Robinson and Cahill, *Criminal Law*, pp. 331–32.

26. Donoho, "Law and Disorder."

27. Ibid.

28. Goldberg, "Support Builds for Killer."

29. Scott R. Drury and Dan Polsby, "Joint Stipulation," Palm v. State.

30. Ibid.

31. Grimm, "Bullets for the Bully." For an account of subsequent events, see this book's postscript.

CHAPTER 2. THE MORAL VIGILANTE

1. Clallam County (Washington State) prosecutor Deborah Kelly upon her 2012 prosecution of Patrick Drum for his murder of two previously convicted sex offenders. Lexi Pandell, "The Vigilante of Clallam County," *Atlantic*, December 4, 2013, https://www.theatlantic.com/national/archive/2013/12/the-vigilante-of-clallam-county/281968/ (accessed May 15, 2017); Laura L. Myers, "Patrick Drum Allegedly Killed Gary Blanton and Jerry Ray, Washington Sex Offenders," *Huffington Post*, June 5, 2012, http://www.huffingtonpost.com/2012/06/05/patrick-drum-gary-blanton-jerry-ray-sex-offenders-washington_n_1572196.html (accessed May 15, 2017).

2. Robert Kennedy, in remarks before the Joint Defense Appeal of the American Jewish Committee and the Anti-Defamation League of B'nai B'rith (Chicago, IL, June 21, 1961).

3. The facts of the narrative are drawn from the following sources: *Freedom Never Dies: The Legacy of Harry T. Moore*, directed by Sandra Dickson and Churchill Roberts (Gainesville, FL: Documentary Institute, 2000), DVD; "Biographical Sketch of Harry Moore," PBS, 2001, http://www.pbs.org/harrymoore/harry/mbio.html (accessed May 15, 2017); Monica Davey and Gretchen Ruethling, "After 50 Years, Emmett Till's Body Is Exhumed," *New York Times*, June 2, 2005, https://nyti.ms/2jKO5Hv (accessed May 15, 2017); Charles M. Payne, *I've Got the Light of Freedom: The Organizing Tradition and the Mississippi Freedom Struggle* (Berkeley: University of California Press, 1996); "George Lee," Northeastern University of Law, Civil Rights and Restorative Justice, 2014, http://nuweb9.neu.edu/civilrights/george lee/ (accessed May 15, 2017); Hugh Stephen Whitaker, "A Case Study in Southern Justice: The Emmett Till Case" (unpublished master's thesis, Florida State University, 2004), 7071, http://diginole.lib.fsu.edu/etd/7071 (accessed May 15, 2017); Gerhard Peters and John T. Woolley, "Lyndon B. Johnson: Televised Remarks Announcing the Arrest of Members of the Ku Klux Klan," American Presidency Project, March 26, 1965, http://www.presidency.ucsb.edu/ws/?pid=26836 (accessed May 15, 2017); "Emmett Till Biography," Biography.com, http://www.biography.com/people/emmett-till-507515 (accessed May 15, 2017); "Civil Rights Martyrs," Southern Poverty Law Center, 2014, https://www.splcenter.org/what-we-do/civil-rights-memorial/civil-rights-martyrs (accessed May 15, 2017).

4. *Freedom Never Dies.*

5. Davey and Ruethling, "After 50 Years."

6. "George Lee."

7. Ibid.

8. Davey and Ruethling, "After 50 Years."
9. Payne, *I've Got the Light of Freedom*, p. 39.
10. "Civil Rights Martyrs."
11. Whitaker, "Case Study in Southern Justice," p. 102.
12. Ibid., p. 103.
13. Ibid., p. 102.
14. "Emmett Till Biography."
15. Ibid.
16. Ibid.
17. Whitaker, "Case Study in Southern Justice," p. viii.
18. Ibid., p. 136.
19. Ibid., p. 125.
20. Ibid., p. 154.
21. Ibid., p. 155.
22. Ibid.
23. Peters and Woolley, "Lyndon B. Johnson."
24. Ibid.
25. The facts of the narrative are drawn from the following sources: Lance Hill, *The Deacons for Defense: Armed Resistance and the Civil Rights Movement* (Chapel Hill: University of North Carolina Press, 2004); Mike Marqusee, "By Any Means Necessary," *Nation*, July 5, 2004; Douglas Martin, "Robert Hicks, Leader in Armed Rights Group, Dies at 81," *New York Times*, April 24, 2010, p. A30; Ben Garett, "Profile: Deacons for Defense and Justice: The Use of Guns in the Civil Rights Movement," About.com, http://civilliberty.about.com/od/guncontrol/a/Deacons-for-Defense.htm (accessed May 17, 2017); George E. Hardin, "Deacons Largely Uncredited for Defense of Civil Rights," *Tri-State Defender* (Memphis, TN), May 20, 2010; Elwood Watson, "Deacons for Defense and Justice," BlackPast.org, http://www.blackpast.org/?q=aah/deacons-defense-and-justice (accessed May 17, 2017).
26. Marqusee, "By Any Means Necessary," p. 1.
27. Ibid., p. 2.
28. Hardin, "Deacons Largely Uncredited."
29. Ibid.
30. Ibid.
31. Hill, *Deacons for Defense*, p. 162.
32. Ibid., p. 231.
33. The facts of the narrative are drawn from the following sources: Bernard DeVoto, *The Year of Decision: 1846* (New York: Little, Brown, 1943); Mary Floyd

Williams, *History of the San Francisco Committee of Vigilance of 1851: A Study of Social Control on the California Frontier in the Days of the Gold Rush* (Berkeley: University of California Press, 1921); Howard Shinn, *Mining Camps: A Study in American Frontier Government* (New York: Harper Torchbooks, 1965); James Delavan, *Notes on California and the Placers: How to Get There, and What to Do Afterwards; By One Who Has Been There* (New York: H. Long & Bros., 1850); Robert M. Senkewicz, *Vigilantes and the Gold Rush* (Palo Alto, CA: Stanford University Press, 1985).

34. DeVoto, *Year of Decision*, pp. 218–24.
35. Senkewicz, *Vigilantes and the Gold Rush*, p. 14.
36. Williams, *History of the San Francisco Committee*, p. 105.
37. Ibid., p. 107.
38. Ibid., p. 119.
39. Ibid., p. 143.
40. Ibid., p. 144.
41. Williams, *History of the San Francisco Committee*.
42. Ibid., p. 292.
43. Ibid., p. 293.
44. The facts of the narrative are drawn from the following sources: Ivan Sharpe, "Lavender Panthers: Homosexuals Rally in Self-Defense," *Calgary Herald*, July 10, 1973, p. 14; "The Sexes: The Lavender Panthers," *Time*, October 8, 1973; "Lavender Panthers Essay," PSA, https://sites.google.com/site/psabrittanybrock/ (accessed May 17, 2017).
45. Sharpe, "Lavender Panthers."
46. Ibid.
47. Ibid.
48. "The Sexes."
49. The facts of the narrative are drawn from the following sources: Soutik Biswas, "India's 'Pink' Vigilante Women," BBC News, November 26, 2007, http://news.bbc.co.uk/2/hi/south_asia/7068875.stm; Amrit Dhillon, "Pretty in Pink, Female Vigilantes Also Handy with an Axe," *Age*, December 15, 2007; Amana Fontanella-Khan, "India's Pink Vigilantes," *Daily Beast*, February 26, 2011, http://www.thedailybeast.com/galleries/2011/02/25/india-s-pink-vigilantes (accessed May 17, 2017); G. M. B. Akash, "Quest for Justice—Vigilantes in Pink," *GMB Akash: A Photojournalist's Blog*, http://gmbakash.wordpress.com/2012/09/22/quest-for-justice-vigilantes-in-pink/ (accessed May 17, 2017); Smriti Gopal, "Women's Gang in 'Pink Saris,'" *Desi Blitz*, December 25, 2010, http://www.desiblitz.com/content/womens-gang-in-pink-saris (accessed May 17, 2017); "India's Pink Posse," *Asia Sentinel*, January

18, 2008, http://www.asiasentinel.com/society/indias-pink-posse/ (accessed May 17, 2017); Tracy Clark-Flory, "Beware the Pink Posse: Hundreds of Women in Pink Saris Roam the Streets Carrying Sticks and Axes," *Salon*, November 27, 2007, http://www.salon.com/2007/11/26/pink_posse/ (accessed May 17, 2017).

50. Fontanella-Khan, "India's Pink Vigilantes"; Gopal, "Women's Gang in 'Pink Saris'"; "India's Pink Posse."

51. Clark-Flory, "Beware the Pink Posse."

52. Dhillon, "Pretty in Pink."

53. Biswas, "India's 'Pink' Vigilante Women"; Akash, "Quest for Justice."

54. Dhillon, "Pretty in Pink."

55. Fontanella-Khan, "India's Pink Vigilantes."

CHAPTER 3: THE SHADOW VIGILANTES

1. The facts of this story are derived from the following sources: "New York Crime Rates 1960–2012," Disaster Center, http://www.disastercenter.com/crime/nycrime.htm (accessed June 7, 2017); George P. Fletcher, *A Crime of Self Defense: Bernhard Goetz and the Law on Trial* (Chicago: University of Chicago Press, 1988); "65 Cent Fare Considered in Talks on Coping with Subway Crime," *New York Times*, September 27, 1980, p. A1; Charles Hanley, "In Subway Crime, N.Y. Still Leads the World," *Los Angeles Times*, March 17, 1985, http://articles.latimes.com/1985-03-17/news/mn-35322_1_subway-crime (accessed June 7, 2017); *Downtown Safety Security and Economic Development* (New York: Citizens Crime Commission of New York City, 1986), p. 148; "The Fear Hits Home: Ravitch Kin Are Not Night Riders," *New York Daily News*, January 21, 1982, p. 4; Mark S. Feinman, "The New York Transit Authority in the 1980s," NYCSubway.org, December 8, 2004, http://www.nycsubway.org/wiki/The_New_York_Transit_Authority_in_the_1980s#Crime_is_Still_High (accessed June 7, 2017); Otto Friedrich, "Not Guilty," *Time*, June 29, 1987, p. 10; David E. Pitt, "Goetz Is Cleared in Subway Attack; Gun Count Upheld; Goetz Jurors Found Both Sides' Evidence Difficult to Accept," *New York Times*, June 17, 1987, p. A1; Esther B. Fein, "Angry Citizens in Many Cities Supporting Goetz," *New York Times*, January 7, 1985, p. B1; Kirk Johnson, "Goetz Is Cleared in Subway Attack; Gun Count Upheld; Acquittal Won in Shooting of 4 Youths but Prison Term Possible on Weapon Charge," *New York Times*, June 17, 1987, p. A1; Joseph Berger, "Goetz Case: Commentary on Nature of Urban Life," *New York Times*, June 18, 1987, p. B6; Dave Caldwell, "Jury Decides Minot Man's Actions Were Self-Defense," *Minot* (ND) *Daily*

News, May 25, 2011; People v. Goetz, 68 N.Y.2d 96, 497 N.E.2d 41, 506 N.Y.S.2d 18 (N.Y. 1986), http://www.casebriefs.com/blog/law/criminal-law/criminal-law-keyed-to-dressler/general-defenses-to-crimes/people-v-goetz/ (accessed June 7, 2017).

2. "New York Crime Rates 1960–2012."
3. Fletcher, Crime of Self Defense.
4. "65 Cent Fare Considered."
5. Hanley, "In Subway Crime."
6. "The Fear Hits Home."
7. Feinman, "New York Transit Authority."
8. *Downtown Safety Security*, p. 148.
9. *Goetz*, 68 N.Y.2d at100–102.
10. Fletcher, Crime of Self Defense, p. 17.
11. Ibid.
12. *Goetz*, 68 N.Y.2d at 101, 102.
13. Fein, "Angry Citizens."
14. *Goetz*, 68 N.Y.2d at 96.
15. Friedrich, "Not Guilty."
16. Johnson, "Goetz Is Cleared."
17. Berger, "Goetz Case."
18. Fletcher, *Crime of Self Defense*, p. 199.
19. This narrative was compiled from People v. Bradford, 939 P.2d 259 (S. Ct. Calif. 1997).
20. *Bradford*, 939 P.2d, "Cheryl V., Section E."
21. *Bradford*, 939 P.2d, "3. Disappearance of Tracey Campbell."
22. Bradford, 939 P.2d, "6. Defendant's Second Arrest."
23. Ibid.
24. *Bradford*, 939 P.2d, "2. Defense Case."
25. For more details, see the postscript.

CHAPTER 4: SPARKING THE SHADOW VIGILANTE IMPULSE

1. This narrative is drawn primarily from the following sources: Jennifer Leahy, "Homicide: Roseann Siddell, 34," *Houston Chronicle*, October 13, 2007, http://blog.chron.com/homicide/2007/10/roseann-siddell-34/ (accessed June 8, 2017); Christine Dobbyn, "The Case of the 13th Juror," *ABC 13 Eyewitness News* (Houston), February 11, 2009, http://abc13.com/archive/6652170/ (accessed June 8, 2017);

Brian Rogers, "Houston Murder Trial Tossed Out after Bailiff's Huge Mistake," *Houston Chronicle*, February 10, 2009, http://www.chron.com/news/houston-texas/article/Houston-murder-trial-tossed-out-after-bailiff-s-1744805.php (accessed June 8, 2017).

2. Dobbyn, "Case of the 13th Juror."

3. This narrative is drawn primarily from the following sources: People v. Thomas, 463 N.E.2d 832 (Ill. App. Ct. 1984); Bill Boyce and Linnet Myers, "Experts Defend Law That Freed Man in Killing," *Chicago Tribune*, May 4, 1985, http://articles.chicagotribune.com/1985-05-04/news/8501270562_1_new-trial-juvenile-court-prosecutors (accessed June 8, 2017); Linnet Myers, "Clerk's Error Frees Man Held in Killing," *Chicago Tribune*, May 3, 1985, p. A1.

4. *Thomas,* 463 N.E.2d at 832.

5. Myers, "Clerk's Error Frees Man."

6. This narrative is drawn primarily from the following sources: People v. Healy, 688 N.E.2d 786 (1997); State v. Healy, 1992 WL 12580086 (Ill. Cir.); People v. Healy, Post Conviction Motion, 1992 WL 12580087 (Ill. Cir.); 725 ICLS 5/103-5.

7. *Healy*, 688 N.E.2d at 787.

8. Ibid. at 788.

9. Ibid.

10. Ibid. at 789.

11. For a discussion of the justifications that have been offered in support of justice-frustrating legal rules and practices, see Paul H. Robinson and Michael T. Cahill, *Law without Justice: Why Criminal Law Doesn't Give People What They Deserve* (New York: Oxford University Press, 2006), part 2.

12. Miranda v. Arizona, 384 U.S. 436 (1966).

13. This narrative is drawn from the following sources: People v. Ferro, 63 N.Y.2d 316 (N.Y. 1984); People v. Ferro, 92 A.D.2d 298 (1983) rev'd, 63 N.Y.2d 316 (N.Y. 1984); Scott Christianson, *Innocent: Inside Wrongful Conviction Cases* (New York: New York University Press, 2006).

14. *Ferro*, 92 A.D.2d at 300.

15. Ibid.

16. The dissenting judge argues that placing the furs in front of Ferro does not constitute an interrogation, so his statements to the detective should be admissible. The judge reasons that the police never questioned Ferro or subjected him to any physical coercion to get him to talk. Additionally, the judge thinks that the majority applies the law "too literally and mechanically"; therefore, Ferro's conviction should be upheld. *Ferro*, 63 N.Y.2d at 324.

17. The narrative is based on the following sources: People of the State of Illinois v. Larry W. Eyler, Case No. 83 CF 1585, "Report of Proceedings," February 3, 1984; People of the State of Illinois v. Larry W. Eyler, Case No. 83 CF 1585, "Supplemental Memorandum in Support of Defendant's Motions to Suppress," February 1, 1984; People of the State of Illinois v. Larry W. Eyler, Case No. 83 CF 1585, "Supplemental Memorandum in Opposition to Defendant's Motion to Suppress," February 1, 1984; People of the State of Illinois v. Larry W. Eyler, No. 84-126 (North Eastern Reporter, 2nd Series, October 25, 1989), 268-92; John O'Brien, "The Eyler Legacy: 21 Deaths," *Chicago Tribune*, March 9, 1994, http://articles.chicagotribune.com/1994-03-09/news/9403090089_1_larry-eyler-murders-notorious-serial-killers (accessed June, 8 2017); Sarah Talalay, "Eyler Dies in Prison," *Chicago Tribune*, March 7, 1994, http://articles.chicagotribune.com/1994-03-07/news/9403070026_1_larry-eyler-daniel-bridges-steven-agan (accessed June 8, 2017); John O'Brien, "Call Helped Link Eyler to Slayings," *Chicago Tribune*, December 16, 1990, http://articles.chicagotribune.com/1990-12-16/news/9004140228_1_larry-eyler-steven-agan-illinois-prison (accessed June 8, 2017); Jon O'Brien, "Professor Who Lived with Eyler Charged in '82 Torture Killing," *Chicago Tribune*, December 19, 1990, p. S1; George Papajohn, "Eyler Sentenced to 60 Years for '82 Indiana Killing," *Chicago Tribune*, December 29, 1990, p. S5; Gera-Lind Kolarik and Wayne Klatt, *Freed to Kill: The True Story of Larry Eyler* (New York: Avon Books, 1992); Eyler v. Babcox, 582 F. Supp. 981 (N.D. Ill. 1983); People v. Eyler, 477 N.E.2d 774 (Ill. App. 1985); Eyler v. Illinois, 498 U.S. 881 (1990); George Anastaplo, "Lawyers, First Principles, and Contemporary Challenges: Explorations," *Northern Illinois University Law Review* 19 (1999): 353.

18. Kolarik and Klatt, *Freed to Kill*, p. 258.

19. For the aftermath of this story, see the postscript.

20. The narrative is drawn from the following sources: Ferguson v. State, 642 A.2d 772, 787 (1994); Ferguson v. Com., Pennsylvania Bd. of Prob. & Parole, 111 Pa. Cmwlth. 562, 563-65, 534 A.2d 579, 580-81 (1987); Commw. v. Ferguson, 1987 Pa. Super. LEXIS 8078 (Pa. Super. Ct. May 27, 1987).

21. For the aftermath, see the postscript.

22. The narrative is drawn from the following sources: Ravi Venkataraman, "The Murder of Vincent Chin—30 Years Later," New America Media, June 17, 2012, http://newamericamedia.org/2012/06/the-murder-of-vincent-chin---30-years-later.php (accessed November 8, 2017); United States v. Ebens, 800 F. 2d 1422 (6th Cir. 1986); Ross Parker, "'It's Not Fair . . .,' Vincent Chin's Last Words," *Court Legacy* 14, no. 4, November 2007.

23. Venkataraman, "Murder of Vincent Chin."

24. Parker, "'It's Not Fair . . .,'" p. 1.

25. Ibid., p. 2.

26. Ibid., p. 3.

27. Ibid., p. 4.

28. This narrative is derived from the following sources: Kristine Guerra, "Wife Who Was Raped Says Husband's Sentence Unjust," *IndyStar* (Indianapolis, IN), May 21, 2014, http://www.indystar.com/story/news/crime/2014/05/19/wife-raped-says-husbands-sentence-unjust/9299531/ (accessed June 8, 2017); Matt Pearce, "Indiana Judge Assailed for Light Sentence in Husband-Wife Rape Case," *Los Angeles Times*, May 20, 2014, http://www.latimes.com/nation/nationnow/la-na-nn-indiana-rape-judge-20140520-story.html (accessed June 8, 2017); Meg Wagner, "Wife Outraged When Husband Who Drugged, Raped Her Avoids Jail Time: 'I Was Told That I Needed to Forgive My Attacker,'" *New York Daily News*, May 20, 2014, http://www.nydailynews.com/news/national/man-guilty-drugging-raping-wife-avoids-jail-time-article-1.1798871 (accessed June 8, 2017); Elizabeth Chuck, "Indiana Judge under Fire after Giving No Jail Time to Rapist," NBC News, May 27, 2014, http://www.nbcnews.com/news/us-news/indiana-judge-under-fire-after-giving-no-jail-time-rapist-n115216 (accessed June 8, 2017).

29. Guerra, "Wife Who Was Raped."

30. Pearce, "Indiana Judge Assailed."

31. Ibid.

32. Chuck, "Indiana Judge under Fire."

33. This narrative is drawn primarily from the following sources: Mara Bovsun, "Justice Story: FALN Bomb Kills 4 at Fraunces Tavern, Where George Washington Said Farewell to Troops," *New York Daily News*, January 21, 2012, http://www.nydailynews.com/new-york/faln-bomb-kills-4-fraunces-tavern-article-1.1008711 (accessed June 8, 2017); *Justice Undone: Clemency Decisions in the Clinton White House* (Washington, DC: House Committee on Government Reform, March 14, 2002), http://news.findlaw.com/hdocs/docs/clinton/pardonrpt/ (accessed June 8, 2017); *Encyclopedia of Chicago History*, s.v. "Fuerzas Armadas de Liberación Nacional (FALN)," by Gina M. Perez, http://www.encyclopedia.chicagohistory.org/pages/489.html (accessed June 8, 2017); *Wikipedia*, s.v. "Fuerzas Armadas de Liberación Nacional Puertorrique," last edited October 13, 2017, http://en.wikipedia.org/wiki/Fuerzas_Armadas_de_Liberaci%C3%B3n_Nacional_Puertorrique%C3%B1a; David M. Bresnahan, "FALN Victim's Son Chastises Clinton," *World Net Daily*, February 4, 2000, http://www.wnd.com/2000/02/412/ (accessed June 8, 2017).

34. Bovsun, "Justice Story."

35. *Encyclopedia of Chicago History*, s.v. "Fuerzas Armadas de Liberación Nacional."

36. Ibid.

37. *Justice Undone.*

38. Dieter Nohlen, *Elections in the Americas: A Data Handbook, Volume I* (New York: Oxford University Press, 2005), p. 552.

39. Debra Burlingame, "The Clintons' Terror Pardons," *Wall Street Journal*, February 12, 2008.

40. *Encyclopedia of Chicago History*, s.v. "Fuerzas Armadas de Liberación."

41. Committee on Government Reform, *The FALN and Macheteros Clemency: Misleading Explanations, a Reckless Decision, a Dangerous Message* (Washington, DC: US Government Printing Office, 1999), https://www.congress.gov/106/crpt/hrpt488/CRPT-106hrpt488.pdf (accessed November 13, 2017).

42. Committee on Government Reform, "Findings of the Committee on Government Reform," 1999, http://fas.org/irp/world/para/docs/final_faln_rpt2.htm (accessed June 8, 2017).

43. Bresnahan, "FALN Victim's Son Chastises."

44. The narrative is drawn from the following sources: Bob Hill, *Double Jeopardy: Obsession, Murder, and Justice Denied* (New York: William Morrow, 1995); Elinor J. Brecher, "Brenda Schaefer: 'That Woman Who Disappeared'; How Could This Ordinary Person with No Apparent Enemies—a Doctor's Office Assistant Who Lived with Her Parents—Just Simply Vanish?" *Courier-Journal* (Louisville, KY), March 5, 1989, p. A4; Susan Craighead, "Attorney's Slip of the Tongue Led to Break in Schaefer Case," *Courier-Journal* (Louisville, KY), March 1, 1990, p. A1; Susan Craighead, "Family Urge Bond Be Set at Affordable Level," *Courier-Journal* (Louisville, KY), February 1, 1990; Susan Craighead, "Police Focused Investigation on Ignatow from Start, Files Show," *Courier-Journal* (Louisville, KY), February 13, 1990, p. B1; Todd Murphy, "Ignatow Witness Pleads Guilty to Evidence Tampering," *Courier-Journal* (Louisville, KY), December 3, 1991, p. B1; Mary O'Doherty, "Threatening-Letter Trial Begins for Missing Woman's Boss," *Courier-Journal* (Louisville, KY), August 9, 1989, p. B1; Clay Ryce, "Schaefer's Boss Is Charged in Threat against Her Fiancée," *Courier-Journal* (Louisville, KY), March 26, 1989, p. B1; Leslie Scanlon, "Bizarre Murder Case Enters New Stage with Jury Selection," *Courier-Journal* (Louisville, KY), December 4, 1991, p. B3; Leslie Scanlon, "Schaefer Wasn't Going to Wed Ignatow," *Courier-Journal* (Louisville, KY), December 14, 1991, p. A5; Leslie Scanlon, "Shore-Ignatow to Tell Jury Her Side of Schaefer Case," *Courier-Journal* (Louisville, KY), December 17, 1991, B1; Leslie Scanlon, "I Did Not Kill Her; Ignatow's Ex-Lover

Admits Helping Dig Hole for Victim," *Courier-Journal* (Louisville, KY), December 18, 1991, p. A1; Leslie Scanlon, "Ignatow Confesses to Killing Schaefer," *Courier-Journal* (Louisville, KY), October 3, 1992, p. A1; Leslie Scanlon, "Ignatow's Defense Rests without His Testimony in Murder Trial," *Courier-Journal* (Louisville, KY), December 21, 1991, p. A11; Leslie Scanlon, "Ignatow's Lawyer Blames Shore-Inlow; Former Girlfriend Described as Jealous," *Courier-Journal* (Louisville, KY), December 10, 1991, p. A1; Leslie Scanlon, "Kenton Jury Acquits Ignatow in Death of Fiancé[e] Schaefer," *Courier-Journal* (Louisville, KY), December 22, 1991, p. A1; Leslie Scanlon, "No Evidence Links Ignatow with Murder, Jurors Say," *Courier-Journal* (Louisville, KY), December 23, 1991, p. A1; Cary B. Willis, "FBI Recorded Murder Suspect in Brenda Schaefer Case," *Courier-Journal* (Louisville, KY), February 6, 1990, p. A1; Cary B. Willis, "Ignatow Lawyer Says Release of Tape Should Rule Out Death," *Courier-Journal* (Louisville, KY), February 7, 1990, p. A1; Cary B. Willis, "Top Schaefer-Case Suspect Talks to Federal Grand Jury," *Courier-Journal* (Louisville, KY), October 17, 1989, p. B3; Andrew Wolfson, "Court Won't Hear Ignatow Perjury Appeal; 2001 Conviction for Lying about Schaefer Stands," *Courier-Journal* (Louisville, KY), April 21, 2004, p. B5; Andrew Wolfson, "Finding Evidence in Home a Fluke," *Courier-Journal* (Louisville, KY), October 3, 1992, p. A1; Deborah Yetter, "Federal Grand Jury Indicts Ignatow on Perjury Charge," *Courier-Journal* (Louisville, KY), January 9, 1992, p. A1; Deborah Yetter, "Textbook Example; Ignatow Fits Profile of Sexual Sadist," *Courier-Journal* (Louisville, KY), October 11, 1992, p. A1; Paul Robinson and Michael Cahill, *Law without Justice* (New York: Oxford University Press, 2005), chap. 6; Associated Press, "After Nearly Two Years in Prison, Ignatow, Cleared in Slaying, Free," *Daily News* (Bowling Green, KY), December 24, 1991, p. 9A; Associated Press, "Man, Acquitted Once, Gets 8 Years in Death of Tortured Girlfriend," *Seattle Times,* November 14, 1992, http://community.seattletimes.nwsource.com/archive/?date=19921114&slug=1524598 (accessed June 8, 2017).

45. Robinson and Cahill, *Law without Justice*, p. 161.

46. Ibid., p. 162.

47. Ibid., p. 164.

48. Associated Press, "After Nearly Two Years in Prison."

49. Associated Press, "Man, Acquitted Once."

50. The facts of the narrative are derived from the following sources: Chuck Ashman and Pamela Trescott, *Diplomatic Crime* (New York: Knightsbridge Publishing, 1987); Robert Ferrigno, "There's Also a Short Arm of the Law," *Chicago Tribune*, September 27, 1987, p. C1; Jo Ann Moriarty, States News Service, June 25, 1987; Eric Pianin, "Bounds of Diplomatic Immunity; Victims to Testify in Support of Helms Bill

Limiting Exemptions," *Washington Post*, August 5, 1987, https://www.washingtonpost.com/archive/local/1987/08/05/bounds-of-diplomatic-immunity/5d050b31-cb14-43b4-b28e-eb5634e8faed/?utm_term=.e92a697cb797 (accessed June 9, 2017).

51. Pianin, "Bounds of Diplomatic Immunity."

52. Ferrigno, "There's Also a Short Arm of the Law."

53. Ferrigno, "There's Also a Short Arm of the Law."

54. Pianin, "Bounds of Diplomatic Immunity."

55. This narrative is drawn primarily from the following sources: Frank Fernandez, "Deltona Sex Sting Raises Entrapment Issue," *Daytona Beach News-Journal*, January 12, 2014, http://www.news-journalonline.com/article/20140112/NEWS/140119803?p=1&tc=pg (accessed June 9, 2017); Frank Fernandez, "Jury Finds Longwood Man Arrested in Deltona Sex Sting Not Guilty," *Daytona Beach News-Journal*, December 17, 2013, http://www.news-journalonline.com/article/20131217/news/131219504?p=1&tc=pg (accessed June 9, 2017); Gary Taylor, "Former Cop, High School Worker among 15 Arrested in Volusia Cyber Sting," *Orlando Sentinel*, September 6, 2011, http://articles.orlandosentinel.com/2011-09-06/news/os-volusia-sex-arrests-20110906_1_cyber-sting-high-school-worker-undercover-investigators (accessed June 9, 2017); "15 Arrested in Florida for Attempting to Hook Up with Minors for Sex," *My Death Space*, December 26, 2011, http://mydeathspace.com/vb/showthread.php?23968-15-arrested-in-Forida-for-attempting-to-hook-up-with-minors-for-sex (accessed June 9, 2017).

56. Fernandez, "Deltona Sex Sting."

57. Fernandez, "Jury Finds Longwood Man."

58. Fernandez, "Deltona Sex Sting."

59. Ibid. For the aftermath, see the postscript.

60. This narrative is drawn primarily from the following sources: People v. Tomaski, 985 N.Y.S.2d 824 (Sup. Ct. 2012); "How to Get Away with Murder, Part Two," *Prosecutor's Discretion* (blog), July 20, 2012, http://prosecutorsdiscretion.blogspot.com/2012/07/how-to-get-away-with-murder-part-two.html (accessed June 8, 2017); "How to Get Away with Murder, Part One," *Prosecutor's Discretion* (blog), July 18, 2012, http://prosecutorsdiscretion.blogspot.com/2012/07/how-to-get-away-with-murder-part-one.html (accessed June 8, 2017); Samuel Newhouse, "Guilty Killer May Escape Prison through Legal Loophole," *Brooklyn Daily Eagle*, December 8, 2011, http://50.56.218.160/archive/category.php?category_id=4&id=47914 (accessed June 8, 2017).

61. For a discussion, see Robinson and Cahill, *Law without Justice*, chaps. 9, 10.

62. Philosopher John Rawls would have us consider the problem from the

Original Position under the Veil of Ignorance. That is, consider the decision one would make in setting a legal rule or practice if one was deciding the issue before the society began and therefore before one knows one's place in that society would be. For example, one would not know whether one would become a serial killer or his next victim. From this perspective, how would one formulate the rules to properly balance the interests of controlling police and prosecutors or promoting the integrity of the criminal justice process, on the one hand, with our interest in punishing serious wrongdoing and maintaining the moral credibility of the criminal law, on the other hand? For many of the rules and practices illustrated in this chapter, it seems possible that the current US position would not survive the test of the Rawlsian Original Position. Who would support a rule that prohibits the detention of a serial killer and instead lets him torture and murder people with impunity? Who would support a rule that values Ignatow's peace of mind in being free from another prosecution after his perjury-induced acquittal as more important than his being punished for his torture, rape, and murder of Brenda Schaefer? And this is true even when one throws onto the scales the interests of other guilty offenders in positions similar to these perpetrators. A Rawlsian analysis might well support narrowing the doctrines of disillusionment to minimize cases like these.

CHAPTER 5. TEN RULES FOR THE MORAL VIGILANTE

1. The narrative is drawn from the following sources: Dan Malone, "How the Legion Got Its Start: Group Began by Harassing Gays, Member Recalls," *Dallas Morning News*, March 31, 1985, p. 1A; Joe McQuade, "Legion of Doom: Good Gone Bad," *Houston Chronicle*, March 30, 1985; J. Michael Kennedy, "Legion of Doom Accused of Bombings, Threats: Gang of Top Students Puzzles Fort Worth," *Los Angeles Times*, April 20, 1985, p. A6; Storer Rowley, "Best and Brightest Sow Fear, Call It Law," *Chicago Tribune*, April 1, 1985, pp. 1–2; Selwyn Crawford, "Straight and Narrow: Ex-FW Student Vigilantes Have Left Trouble Behind," *Dallas Morning News*, December 19, 1988, p. 15A.

2. Malone, "How the Legion Got Its Start."

3. Kennedy, "Legion of Doom Accused."

4. The aftermaths of most of the stories in this book are provided in the postscript.

5. The narrative is drawn from the following sources: Brian McGinty, "Shadows in St. James Park," *California History* 57, no. 4, Winter (1978–79): 57; Carl Nolte, "A

Lynching Remembered—Bay Area's Dark Day," *San Francisco Chronicle*, November 23, 2008, p. A1; Anita Venezia, "The Hart Kidnapping and Midnight Lynching," *Alive Magazine*, June 7, 2011, http://aliveeastbay.com/archives/the-hart-kidnapping-and-midnight-lynching/ (accessed June 13, 2017); *San Francisco Chronicle*, November 18, 1933, p. 1.

6. *San Francisco Chronicle*, November 18, 1933, p. 1.

7. Ibid.

8. Ibid.

9. This narrative is drawn primarily from the following sources: Tresa Baldas, "Steve Utash Mob Beating Victim out of Hospital," *Detroit Free Press*, May 17, 2014; Monica Davey, "Five Plead Guilty to Beating a Motorist in Detroit," *New York Times*, June 19, 2014, p. A15; "Bruce Wimbush Pleaded Guilty," Click on Detroit, June 16, 2014, http://www.clickondetroit.com/news/suspect-in-steve-utash-beating-takes-plea-deal/26508856 (accessed June 13, 2017); Tara Edwards, "First Look at Steve Utash since Beating in Detroit," WXYZ Detroit, May 13, 2014; Simon Shaykhet, "Additional Arrests Made in Brutal Detroit Beating of Driver Steve Utash," WXYZ Detroit, April 8, 2014, http://www.wxyz.com/news/additional-arrest-made-in-brutal-detroit-beating-of-driver-steve-utash (accessed June 13, 2017); Tara Edwards, "Suspect in Steve Utash Beating Takes Plea Deal," WXYZ Detroit, June 16, 2014, http://www.wxyz.com/news/first-look-at-steve-utash-since-beating-in-detroit (accessed June 13, 2017).

10. Jennifer Schwager, "Denounce Reckless Actions of Animal Rights Activists," *Animal Petitions: Humans Defending Animals from Other Humans*, July 2014, http://animalpetitions.org/5405/denounce-reckless-actions-of-animal-rights-activists/ (accessed June 13, 2017).

11. The narrative is drawn from the following sources: Adam Brandolph, "Former SCI Pittsburgh Prison Guard to Serve Five Years of Probation in Abuse of Sex Offenders," TribLive, March 28, 2013, http://triblive.com/news/admin page/3740580-74/guard-nicoletti-charges#axzz37Y0cqMSp (accessed June 13, 2017); Marty Griffin, "SCI Pittsburgh Guard Facing Inmate Abuse Charges," CBS Pittsburgh, September 27, 2011, http://pittsburgh.cbslocal.com/2011/09/27/sci-pittsburgh-guard-facing-inmate-abuse-charges/ (accessed June 13, 2017); "Sources: SCI Pittsburgh Guards Could Possibly Face Charges," CBS Pittsburgh, May 4, 2011, http://pittsburgh.cbslocal.com/2011/05/04/sources-sci-pittsburgh-guards-could-possibly-face-charges/ (accessed June 13, 2017); Marty Griffin, "Zappala: More Arrests of Corrections Officers Possible," CBS Pittsburgh, September 28, 2011, http://pittsburgh.cbslocal.com/2011/09/28/zappala-more-arrests-of-corrections-officers

-possible/ (accessed June 13, 2017); Robert Mangino, "Abuse Allegations Mount at SCI Pittsburgh," CBS Pittsburgh, September 28, 2011, http://pittsburgh.cbslocal.com/2011/09/28/abuse-allegations-mount-at-sci-pittsburgh/ (accessed June 13, 2017); Marty Griffin, "31 Witnesses Set to Testify during Hearing for Suspended Prison Guard," CBS Pittsburgh, December 7, 2011, http://pittsburgh.cbslocal.com/2011/12/07/31-witnesses-set-to-testify-during-hearing-for-suspended-prison-guard/ (accessed June 13, 2017); Harold Hayes, "Suspended SCI Pittsburgh Guard to Stand Trial on 101 Counts," CBS Pittsburgh, December 9, 2011, http://pittsburgh.cbslocal.com/2011/12/09/suspended-sci-pittsburgh-guard-to-stand-trial-on-101-counts/ (accessed June 13, 2017); Andy Sheehan, "Correction Officer Goes to Trial on Sadism Charges," CBS Pittsburgh, January 9, 2013, http://pittsburgh.cbslocal.com/2013/01/09/correction-officer-goes-to-trial-on-sadism-charges/ (accessed June 13, 2017); Richard Lord, "Lawsuit Alleges SCI Pittsburgh Guards Sexually Abused Inmates," *Pittsburgh Post-Gazette*, September 22, 2011, http://www.post-gazette.com/local/city/2011/09/22/Lawsuit-alleges-SCI-Pittsburgh-guards-sexually-abused-inmates/stories/201109220349(accessed June 13, 2017).

12. Lord, "Lawsuit Alleges."

13. Ibid.

14. Ibid.

15. "Abortion Opposition Stressed in Kidnapping Trial in Illinois," *New York Times*, January 26, 1983, http://www.nytimes.com/1983/01/26/us/abortion-opposition-stressed-in-kidnapping-trial-in-illinois.html (accessed November 10, 2017); Juli Cragg, "The FBI Says Three Men Held Dr. Hector Zevallos . . .," United Press International, August 31, 1982, https://www.upi.com/Archives/1982/08/31/The-FBI-says-three-men-held-Dr-Hector-Zevallos/6888399614400/ (accessed November 10, 2017).

CHAPTER 6. MORAL VIGILANTES BREAKING BAD: COMMUNITY DRUG WARS

1. The narrative is drawn from the following sources: William Raspberry, "Vigilantes Wage War on Junkies," *New Pittsburgh Courier*, February 19, 1972; Michael Javen Fortner, "'Must Jesus Bear the Cross Alone?': Reverend Oberia Dempsey and His Citizen's War on Drugs," *Journal of Policy History* 27, no. 1 (2015): 118–56; Malcolm W. Browne, "Pastor Organizes Militia to Combat Crime in Harlem," *New York Times*, October 21, 1967, p. 33; Natalie Shibley, "Squashing Superfly: A Harlem Minister Fights Dope," *Religions of Harlem*, April 7, 2011, http://

religionsofharlem.org/2011/04/07/squashing-superfly-a-harlem-minister-fights-dope/ (accessed June 20, 2017); "Claims Harlem Has 40,000 Dope Addicts," editorial, *Chicago Daily Defender*, October 10, 1962, p. 2; "Cop Slain, 2 Attack Lawlessness in Harlem," editorial, *New York Amsterdam News*, November 14, 1970, p. 16; "Harlem Vigilantes Move on Pushers," editorial, *Chicago Daily Defender*, June 23, 1965, p. 2; "Says Harlemites Arm Themselves Because of Crime Rise in Area," editorial, *New York Amsterdam News*, October 21, 1967, p. 7; "Churches in Harlem Hurt by Crime," editorial, *Washington Afro-American*, January 21, 1969, p. 3; Oberia Dempsey, "Dope Battle Lost: The War Goes On," *New York Amsterdam News*, November 2, 1968, p. 10; Brian Mann, "How the Rockefeller Drug Laws Changed America," North County Public Radio, January 24, 2013, http://www.northcountrypublicradio.org/news/story/21316/20130124/how-the-rockefeller-drug-laws-changed-america (accessed June 20, 2016).

2. Browne, "Pastor Organizes Militia."
3. Shibley, "Squashing Superfly."
4. Ibid.
5. "Harlem Vigilantes Move on Pushers."
6. Dempsey, "Dope Battle Lost."
7. "Churches in Harlem Hurt by Crime."
8. "Claims Harlem Has 40,000 Dope Addicts."
9. Raspberry, "Vigilantes Wage War on Junkies."
10. "Blacks Declare War on Dope," *Ebony* 25, no. 8 (June 1970): 31–40.
11. Mann, "How the Rockefeller Drug Laws."
12. Ibid.
13. For this narrative, the information is drawn from the following sources: Leon Dash, "Rosa Lee: A Mother and Her Family," interview by Brian Lamb, C-Span, September 18, 1996, video, 58:16, https://www.c-span.org/video/?75246-1/rosa-lee-mother-family (accessed June 20, 2017); Leon Dash, *Rosa Lee: A Mother and Her Family in Urban America* (Philadelphia: Basic Books, 1996); Leon Dash, "Rosa Lee's Story: The Series," *Washington Post*, September 18–25, 1994, http://www.washingtonpost.com/wp-srv/local/longterm/library/rosalee/part1.htm (accessed June 20, 2017).
14. Dash, *Rosa Lee: A Mother*, pp. 111, 112.
15. Dash, "Rosa Lee."
16. Ibid.
17. Dash, *Rosa Lee: A Mother*, pp. 96–98.
18. Dash, "Rosa Lee."

19. Richard Isralowitz, *Drug Use: A Reference Handbook* (Santa Barbara, CA: ABC-CLIO, 2004), p. 39.

20. Bruce D. Johnson et al., "Drug Abuse in the Inner City: Impact on Hard Drug Users and the Community," in "Drugs and Crime," eds., Michael Tonry and James Q. Wilson, *Crime and Justice* 13 (1990): 9–67, 11.

21. Ibid., p. 11; Brian C. Bennett, "Crime & Mayhem: Alcohol Leads the Pack in FBI Uniform Crime Reports," *Brian Bennett.com*, 2006, http://www.briancbennett.com/charts/fed-data/crime/arrest-overview.htm (accessed June 20, 2017).

22. US Department of Justice, *Pennsylvania Drug Threat Assessment* (Johnstown, PA: National Drug Intelligence Center, June 2001), p. 4, https://www.justice.gov/archive/ndic/pubs0/670/670p.pdf (accessed November 15, 2017).

23. Mario R. de la Rosa and Juan-Luis Recio Adrados, eds., *Drug Abuse among Minority Youth: Advances in Research and Methodology* (Rockville, MD: US Department of Health and Human Services, 1993), p. 130, http://archives.drugabuse.gov/pdf/monographs/130.pdf (accessed June 20, 2017).

24. John C. Ball et al., "Day-to-Day Criminality of Heroin Addicts in Baltimore: A Study in Continuity in Offense Rates," in *Contemporary Masters in Criminology*, eds., Joan McCord and John Laub (New York: Springer Science & Business Media, 2013), p. 116.

25. Isralowitz, *Drug Use*, p. 39.

26. "Drug Abuse and Addiction: One of America's Most Challenging Public Health Problems: Magnitude," National Institute on Drug Abuse, http://archives.drugabuse.gov/about/welcome/aboutdrugabuse/magnitude/ (accessed June 20, 2017).

27. *National Drug Control Strategy, Data Supplement 2014* (Washington, DC: Office of National Drug Control Policy, 2014), https://obamawhitehouse.archives.gov/sites/default/files/ondcp/policy-and-research/ndcs_data_supplement_2014.pdf (accessed June 20, 2017).

28. "Drug Facts: Drug-Related Hospital Emergency Room," National Institute on Drug Abuse, http://www.drugabuse.gov/publications/drugfacts/drug-related-hospital-emergency-room-visits (accessed June 20, 2017).

29. "Drug Facts: Nationwide Trends," National Institute on Drug Abuse, June 2015, http://www.drugabuse.gov/publications/drugfacts/nationwide-trends (accessed June 20, 2017).

30. "Drug Abuse and Addiction."

31. National Drug Control Strategy, p. 57.

32. The narrative is drawn from the following sources: Bill Gaither, "Herman

Wrice: 1939–2000," *Powelton Post* (Philadelphia, PA), May 2000, http://poweltonvillage.org/profiles/herman_wrice.html (accessed June 20, 2017); Yvonne Latty, "Mantua Drug Warrior Dies: Herman Wrice Stricken in Fla. before March," Philly.com, March 11, 2000, http://articles.philly.com/2000-03-11/news/25604360_1_herman-wrice-wrice-process-drug-dealers (accessed June 20, 2017); Amy S. Rosenberg and Maida Odom, "Bush: Mantua Example for U.S.," Philly.com, July 25, 1990, http://articles.philly.com/1990-07-25/news/25900197_1_anti-drug-rally-herman-wrice-anti-drug-movement (accessed June 20, 2017).

33. Gaither, "Herman Wrice."

34. Lori Roza, "Shout 'Em Out Nagging Gets Rid of Criminals and Their Customers," September 15, 1996, *Chicago Tribune*, http://articles.chicagotribune.com/1996-09-15/business/9609150353_1_wrice-process-herman-wrice-drug-dealers

35. Ibid.

36. Gaither, "Herman Wrice."

37. Ibid.

38. Bruce L. Benson, *To Serve and Protect: Privatization and Community in Criminal Justice* (New York University Press, 1998) https://archive.org/stream/tsapbb/tsapbb_djvu.txt.

39. The narrative is drawn from the following sources: Isabel Wilkerson, "'Crack House' Fire: Justice or Vigilantism?" *New York Times*, October 22, 1988, p. 6; "Crack: A Disaster of Historic Dimension, Still Growing," editorial, *New York Times,* May 28, 1989, p. 4; "Neighborhood Dilemma: Fight Crime with Crime?" Associated Press, February 13, 1988, http://www.apnewsarchive.com/1988/NeighborhoodDilemma-Fight-Crime-With-Crime-/id-bb0554af524430c9aea95d505045feb9 (accessed June 20, 2017); "2 Acquitted in Torching of Alleged Crack House," editorial, *Chicago Tribune*, October 7, 1988, p. 3.

40. "Neighborhood Dilemma."

41. Ibid.

42. Ibid.

43. Wilkerson, "'Crack House' Fire."

44. Ibid.

45. Ibid.

46. Karlyn Barker, "Dobson Guilty of Kidnapping, Robbery, Acquitted of Murder," *Washington Post*, December 12, 1973, p. B1; Edward Walsh, "Baltimore Jury Indicts Suspect, 20, in Slaying of Indicted Md. Delegate," *Washington Post*, July 21, 1972, p. D1; Walsh, "Del. Turk Scott Slain in Baltimore," *Washington Post*, July 14, 1973, p. A1; "Antidrug Group, Slaying Linked," *Milwaukee Sentinel*, July 19, 1972, p.

6; "Black October Defends Its Policy of Killing," editorial, *Washington Post*, August 27, 1973, p. C2; "Legislator, Indicted in Drug Case, Fatally Shot," editorial, *Los Angeles Times*, July 14, 1973, p. A4; "Minister's Son Charged with Murdering Legislator," *Herald-Journal* (Spartanburg, SC), July 20, 1973, p. 48; "Slain Legislator Shot Seven Times," editorial, *Philadelphia Tribune*, July 17, 1973, p. 1; "Black October's Letter to Paper," editorial, *Washington Post*, July 19, 1973, p. A7.

47. "Black October Defends its Policy of Killing," *Washington Post*, August 27, 1973, p. C2.

48. "Black October—the Killing of a Drug-Dealing State Delegate," *Voice of Baltimore*, May 21, 2012, http://voiceofbaltimore.org/archives/4910 (accessed June 20, 2017).

49. "Slain Legislator Shot Seven Times," p. 1.

50. "Antidrug Group, Slaying Linked," p. 6.

51. "Black October's Letter to Paper," p. A7.

52. Martin Waldron, "Black Group Says It Killed 2 Pushers in a War on Drugs: Victims Identified," *New York Times*, August 27, 1973, p. 26.

53. "Black October's Letter to Paper," p. A7.

54. William Raspberry, "Black Vigilantes May Start Killing Pushers of Heroin," *Tuscaloosa News*, February 13, 1972, http://news.google.com/newspapers?id=lgMdAAAAIBAJ&sjid=QJwEAAAAIBAJ&pg=5399,2306760&dq=heroin+vigilante+killed&hl=en (accessed November 16, 2017).

CHAPTER 7. HOW BEING RIGHT CAN RISK WRONGS

1. This narrative is derived from the following sources: Andrew Pollack, "2 Illegal Immigrants Win Arizona Ranch in Court," *New York Times*, August 19, 2005, p. A16; Jerry Seper, "16 Illegals Sue Arizona Rancher," *Washington Times*, February 9, 2009, p. A3; Craig Bannister, "After Finding 13 Illegal Aliens Sleeping in His Barn, AZ Rancher Now Armed 24/7," CNSNews.com, May 10, 2012, http://cnsnes.com/blog/craig-bannister/after-finding-13-illegal-aliens-sleeping-his-barn-az-rancher-now-armed-247 (accessed June 20, 2017); Mark Potok, "Anti Immigration Vigilante Loses Lawsuit," United Press International, November 23, 2006, http://www.upi.com/Top_News/2006/11/23/Anti-immigration-vigilante-loses-lawsuit/UPI-84731164343631/ (accessed June 20, 2017); Newmexican, "Border Security through the Eyes of Southern Arizona Ranger," Americans for Legal Immigration PAC, February 9, 2013, http://www.alipac.us/content/border-security-through-eyes-southern-arizona

-rancher-1367/ (accessed June 20, 2017).

2. Randal C. Archibold, "A Border Watcher Finds Himself under Scrutiny," *New York Times*, November 24, 2006, http://www.nytimes.com/2006/11/24/us/24border.html (accessed November 16, 2017).

3. Border Patrol agents on the southwestern border of the United States increased from 9,100 agents in 2001 to more than 18,500 in 2013. Department of Homeland Security, *Budget-in-Brief: Fiscal Year 2014* (Washington, DC: Department of Homeland Security, 2014), https://www.dhs.gov/sites/default/files/publications/FY%202014%20BIB%20-%20FINAL%20-508%20Formatted%20(4).pdf (accessed June 20, 2017); Department of Homeland Security, "Border Security Results," http://www.dhs.gov/border-security-results (accessed June 20, 2017).

4. This narrative is derived from the following source: Austin Scott, "Maccabees' Patrol Helps Reduce Crime," *Daytona Beach* (FL) *Morning Journal*, December 21, 1964, p. 3; Matthew Shaer, "Tough Jews," *Tablet Magazine*, December 14, 2011, http://www.tabletmag.com/jewish-news-and-politics/86067/tough-jews?all=1 (accessed June 20, 2017); Rabbi Michoel Seligson, "Rabbi Samuel Schrage: The Maccabee," *Crown Heights News*, December 18, 2010, http://crownheights.info/crown-heights-news/30851/rabbi-samuel-schrage-the-maccabee/ (accessed June 20, 2017).

5. Scott, "Maccabees' Patrol Helps Reduce Crime."

6. This narrative is derived from the following sources: Bill Maher, "Celebrating 20 Years of Free the Animals," *Huffington Post*, April 30, 2012, http://www.huffingtonpost.com/bill-maher/peta-ingrid-newkirk-free-the-animals_b_1464990.html (accessed June 20, 2017); David S. Hawtin, "Animal Liberation Front Tactics and Their Effects on Animal Research" (thesis, American Public University System, May 2014), http://www.academia.edu/7581288/ANIMAL_LIBERATION_FRONT_TACTICS_AND_THEIR_EFFECTS_ON_ANIMAL_RESEARCH (accessed June 20, 2017); Michael Janofsky, "Feds Accuse 11 of Ecoterrorism, Targeted Meatpacker, Ski Resort, Timber Firm," *Chicago Tribune*, January 21, 2006, http://articles.chicagotribune.com/2006-01-21/news/0601210075_1_elf-and-alf-indictment-federal-charges (accessed June 20, 2017); Richard C. Paddock, "UCLA to Take Activists to Court," *Los Angeles Times*, February 21, 2008, http://articles.latimes.com/2008/feb/21/local/me-animals21 (accessed June 20, 2017); Kirsten Scharnberg and Tim Jones, "Ground Zero of Labs vs. Animal-Rights Activists," *Chicago Tribune*, June 9, 2005, http://articles.chicagotribune.com/2005-06-09/news/0506090213_1_animal-rights-research-labs-animal-liberation-front (accessed June 20, 2017); Steven Best and Anthony J. Nocella II, introduction to *Terrorists or*

Freedom Fighters: Reflections on the Liberation of Animals (Herndon, VA: Lantern Books, 2004); "Ecoterrorism: Extremism in the Animal Rights and Environmentalist Movements," Anti-Defamation League, http://archive.adl.org/learn/ext_us/Ecoterrorism.asp (accessed June 20, 2017); Scott Stewart, "Escalating Violence from the Animal Liberation Front," *Stratfor Global Intelligence: Security Weekly*, July 29, 2010, http://www.stratfor.com/weekly/20100728_escalating_violence_animal_liberation_front#axzz38lnIozp (accessed June 20, 2017); "The Animal Liberation Primer," Animal Liberation Front, http://www.animalliberationfront.com/ALFront/ALFPrime.htm (accessed June 20, 2017); David Martosko, ed., "Animal Rights Terror Group Takes Credit for Torching Cattle Trucks," *Daily Caller*, January 12, 2012, http://dailycaller.com/2012/01/12/animal-rights-terror-group-takes-credit-for-torching-cattle-trucks (accessed June 20, 2017).

7. Maher, "Celebrating 20 Years."

8. Ibid.

9. Hawtin, "Animal Rights Extremists."

10. Janofsky, "Feds Accuse 11 of Ecoterrorism."

11. "Rodney Coronado," Activist Facts, https://www.activistfacts.com/person/3255-rodney-coronado/ (accessed November 15, 2017).

12. Paddock, "UCLA to Take Activists to Court."

13. Scharnberg and Jones, "Ground Zero of Labs."

14. Best and Nocella, *Terrorists or Freedom Fighters*, p. 13.

15. Stewart, "Escalating Violence."

16. Martosko, "Animal Rights Terror Group Takes Credit."

17. This narrative is derived from the following sources: Jason Trahan and Chris Colgin, "Campaign against Child Sex Predators Draws Critics," *Dallas Morning News*, September 11, 2006; Allen Salkin, "Web Pedophile Hunters Go Too Far, Some Critics Claim," *New York Times*, December 17, 2006, p. A1; Marisa Schultz, "Online Vigilantes Hunt Down Pedophiles," *USA Today*, March 16, 2004, https://usatoday30.usatoday.com/tech/news/internetprivacy/2004-03-16-online-vigilantes_x.htm (accessed June 20, 2017); Eric Zorn, "Did Vigilante Catch Pedophile, or Wreck a Life?" *Chicago Tribune*, May 9, 2004, p. C1; Donna Blankinship, "Man Turns Himself In for Killing 2 Child Rapists: Police Say They Believe Man's Claim That He Was Able to Locate the Victims through a County Sheriff's Website That Lists Addresses of Sex Offenders," *Vancouver* (BC) *Sun*, September 7, 2005, p. A3; Julia Scheeres, "Vigilantes Troll for Pedophiles," Wired.com, March 18, 2004, http://archive.wired.com/culture/lifestyle/news/2004/03/62650?currentPage=all (accessed June 20, 2017); "Mullen Gets 44 Years after Pleading Guilty to Two Killings," *AP Alert* (Washington, DC),

March 11, 2006.

18. Scheeres, "Vigilantes Troll for Pedophiles."

19. Ibid.

20. Ibid.

21. Operation Perverted Justice, http://www.perverted-justice.com/ (accessed June 20, 2017).

22. *Murderpedia*, s.v. "Michael Anthony Mullen," http://murderpedia.org/male.M/m/mullen-michael-anthony.htm (accessed November 15, 2017); Tomas Alex Tizon, "Man Admits to Killing 2 Sex Offenders, Cites Idaho Case," *Los Angeles Times*, September 07, 2005, http://articles.latimes.com/2005/sep/07/nation/na-vigilante7 (accessed June 14, 2017).

23. Michael Mullen's killing of the two sex offenders was similar in this respect to the killing by Scott Roeder of George Tiller, the abortion doctor. For sources on the facts of this case, see "911 Call Reveals Cold-Hearted Attitude toward MA Woman's Abortion Death," Operation Rescue, December 6, 2007, http://www.operationrescue.org/archives/911-call-reveals-cold-hearted-attitude-toward-ma-woman%E2%80%99s-abortion-death/ (accessed June 20, 2017); "Abortion Blockades on Decline Trend Was Established before Buffer Zone Ruling," *San Francisco Chronicle*, July 5, 1994, p. A3; Mary Mapes, "No Mercy," *Huffington Post*, July 25, 2009, www.huffingtonpost.com/mary-mapes/no-mercy_b_209529.html?view=print (accessed June 20, 2017); Sara Rimer, "Abortion Foes in Boot Camp Mull Doctor's Killing," *New York Times*, March 19, 1993, p. A12; Isabel Wilkerson, "Drive against Abortion Finds a Symbol: Wichita," *New York Times*, August 4, 1991, p. 20; Angela Williams and Fiona Morgan, "The Murder of Dr. George Tiller Recalls the Long History of Anti-Abortion Violence," *INDYWEEK*, June 3, 2009, www.indyweek.com/indyweek/the-murder-of-dr-george-tiller-recalls-the-long-history-of-anti-abortion-violence/Content?oid=1215895&mode=print (accessed June 20, 2017); Tara Murtha, "No End in Site: Operation Rescue Takes Its Terror Tactics to the Web," *Philadelphia Weekly*, January 25, 2012, p. 4; Georgia M. Sullivan, "Protection of Constitutional Guarantees under 42 U.S.C. Section 1985(3): Operation Rescue's 'Summer of Mercy,'" *Washington and Lee Law Review* 49, no. 1 (1992): 237, http://scholarlycommons.law.wlu.edu/wlulr/vol49/iss1/15://scholarlycommons.law.wlu.edu/wlulr/vol49/iss1/15 (accessed June 20, 2017); Monica Davey, "Closed Clinic Leaves Abortion Protestors at a Loss," *New York Times*, June 8, 2009, p. A10.

24. Wilkerson, "Drive against Abortion."

25. Murtha, "Anti-Abortion Group Operation Rescue."

26. Williams, "The Murder of Dr. George Tiller."

27. "Abortion Blockades on Decline Trend."

28. Rimer, "Abortion Foes in Boot Camp."

29. Operation Rescue published stories of abortions it claims Tiller botched, killing patients. "Christin Alysabeth Gilbert Died from a Third-Trimester Abortion," Justice for Christin, http://www.justiceforchristin.com/ (accessed June 20, 2017). One article on its website is titled "You Can Help Put George Tiller in Prison," which includes passages such as "You see, right now the infamous late-term baby-killer George Tiller is in the fight of his life!" See "You Can Help Put George Tiller in Prison!" Operation Rescue, http://www.operationrescue.org/noblog/you-can-help-put-george-tiller-in-prison/(accessed June 20, 2017).

30. Williams and Morgan, "Murder of Dr. George Tiller."

CHAPTER 8. COMMUNITY COMPLICITY WITH VIGILANTES

1. The information for this case came from the following sources: Nigel Cawthorne, *Underworld U.K. Vigilantes* (London: Quercus, 2010); Mark Gado, "The Slaughter of Innocence," *Crime Library: Criminal Minds & Methods*, http://www.trutv.com/library/crime/criminal_mind/psychology/pedophiles/2.html (accessed June 22, 2017); Gary Jones and James Fletcher, "We'll Shed No Tears; Murdered Sex Fiend Who Lived in Shadow of Hatred," *Daily Mirror* (London), February 19, 2000, http://www.thefreelibrary.com/WE'LL+SHED+NO+TEARS%3B+Murdered+sex+fiend+who+lived+in+shadow+of+hatred.-a060292519 (accessed June 22, 2017); Mary Braid, "Uproar in Court as Paedophile Case Is Dropped," *Independent* (London), November 29, 1994, http://www.highbeam.com/doc/1P2-4689402.html (accessed June 22, 2017); "Witness Plea after Paedophile Killing," BBC News, February 19, 2000, http://news.bbc.co.uk/2/hi/uk_news/648475.stm (accessed June 22, 2017).

2. Jones and Fletcher, "We'll Shed No Tears."

3. Ibid.

4. Cawthorne, *Underworld U.K. Vigilantes*, p. 88.

5. Jones and Fletcher, "We'll Shed No Tears."

6. Braid, "Uproar in Court."

7. Cawthorne, *Underworld U.K. Vigilantes*, p. 88.

8. Braid, "Uproar in Court."

9. Cawthorne, *Underworld U.K. Vigilantes*, p. 91.

10. "Witness Plea after Paedophile Killing."

11. Cawthorne, *Underworld U.K. Vigilantes,* pp. 91, 93.

12. The information for this case came from the following sources: Harry N. MacLean, *In Broad Daylight* (New York: St. Martin's Press, 1988); A. G. Sulzberger, "Town Mute for 30 Years about a Bully's Killing," *New York Times*, December 15, 2010, p. A22; David Kajicek, "Ken McElroy," Crime Library: Notorious Murderers, www.trutv.com/library/crime/notorious_murders/classics/ken_mcelroy/biblio.html (accessed June 22, 2017); Rod Mitchell, "Ken Rex McElroy: The Skidmore, MO Bully," Talkguest.com, http://www.talkguests.com/mcelroy.htm (accessed June 22, 2017).

13. Mitchell, "Ken Rex McElroy."

14. MacLean, *In Broad Daylight*, p. 68.

15. Sulzberger, "Town Mute for 30 Years."

16. For sources on the facts of this case, see Adrian Maher and Kathleen Kelleher, "Destruction of Tables in Venice Draws Criticism: Vandalism: Despite Charges of Vigilantism from Youths and Others, Many Residents Say the Action Was Justified to Curb Noise and Violence," *Los Angeles Times*, August 30, 1994, http://articles.latimes.com/1994-08-30/local/me-32826_1_venice-resident (accessed June 22, 2017); Lisa Richardson, "Breaking Up the Party on the Boardwalk: Venice: Hammer-Wielding Residents Allegedly Smash Picnic Tables They Say Are Used for Raucous Late-Night Meeting Sites," *Los Angeles Times*, August 29, 1994, http://articles.latimes.com/1994-08-29/local/me-32582_1_picnic-tables (accessed June 22, 2017).

17. Richardson, "Breaking Up the Party."

18. Maher and Kelleher, "Destruction of Tables in Venice."

19. Ibid.

CHAPTER 9. THE COMMUNITY AS SHADOW VIGILANTES

1. Dave Caldwell, "Jury Decides Minot Man's Actions Were Self-Defense," *Minot* (ND) *Daily News*, May 25, 2011.

2. "Our subjects may feel that the criminal justice system is not likely to apprehend criminals, convict them when it apprehends them, or justly punish them when it convicts them. They may feel that the criminal justice system is failing in its role of protecting citizens. Our present results may stem from a general sentiment that when the criminal justice system does a poor job in punishing offenders it is appropriate for individual citizens to do more in defense of self and property and in law enforcement. The more ineffective the system is seen to be, the more people may

be willing to let victims take matters into their own hands.... The strength of the differences between community standards and legal code results that we found would indicate, at a minimum, that large segments of the population are deeply dissatisfied with the criminal justice system. These observed discrepancies may illustrate one of the 'hidden costs' to policies that fail to provide adequately funded police forces, or to court systems that fail to punish blameworthy offenders." Paul Robinson and John Darley, *Justice, Liability, & Blame: Community Views and the Criminal Law* (Boulder, CO: Westview Press, 1995), p. 80.

3. Neil P. Cohen et al., "The Prevalence and Use of Criminal Defenses: A Preliminary Study," *Tennessee Law Review* 60 (1993): 967. "The data reveal that in fact, self-defense was raised more frequently than any other defense included in the study."

4. This narrative is drawn primarily from the following sources: Chris Bury and Howard L. Rosenberg, "Man Cleared for Killing Neighbor's Burglars," ABC News, June 30, 2008, http://abcnews.go.com/TheLaw/story?id=5278638 (accessed June 22, 2017); Brian Rogers, Ruth Rendon, and Dale Lezon, "Joe Horn Cleared by Grand Jury in Pasadena Shootings," *Star Chronicle* (Houston, TX), June 30, 2008, http://www.chron.com/neighborhood/pasadena-news/article/Joe-Horn-cleared-by-grand-jury-in-Pasadena-1587004.php (accessed June 22, 2017); Rucks Russell, "Horn Death Threat Caught on Tape," KHOU, December 10, 2007, http://web.archive.org/web/20071214014744/http://www.khou.com/topstories/stories/khou071210_tnt_joehorndeatht hreat.302e7df.html (accessed June 22, 2017).

5. Bury and Rosenberg, "Man Cleared."

6. Rogers, Rendon, and Lezon, "Joe Horn Cleared."

7. "Crack Epidemic?" South Central History, June 22, 2017, http://www.southcentralhistory.com/crack-epidemic.php (accessed November 29, 2017).

8. "Uniform Crime Reports and Index of Crime in Los Angeles in the State of California Enforced by Los Angeles from 1985 to 2005," Disaster Center, http://www.disastercenter.com/californ/crime/976.htm (accessed June 22, 2017).

9. Julia Dunn, "Los Angeles Crips and Bloods: Past and Present," EDGE, July 26, 1999, http://stanford.edu/class/e297c/poverty_prejudice/gangcolor/lacrips.htm (accessed June 22, 2017).

10. This narrative is based on the following sources: Douglas Linder, "The Rodney King Beating Trials," *Jurist*, December 2001, http://www.jurist.org/j20/famoustrials/the-rodney-king-beating-trials.php# (accessed June 22, 2017); Warren Christopher, *Report of the Independent Commission on the Los Angeles Police Department* (Collingdale, PA: Independent Commission on the Los Angeles Police Department, 1991), chap. 1: "The Rodney King Beating"; Lou Cannon, *Official*

Negligence: How Rodney King and the Riots Changed Los Angeles and the LAPD (Boulder, CO: Westview Press, 1999), p. 205; Sheryl Stolberg, "Juror Says Panel Felt King Actions Were to Blame," *Los Angeles Times*, April 30, 1992, p. A1.

11. Christopher, *Report of the Independent Commission*, p. 7.

12. Cannon, *Official Negligence*, p. 205.

13. Linder, "Rodney King Beating Trials."

14. Stolberg, "Juror Says Panel Felt."

15. "Jurors: King Verdict Was Not Racially Motivated," *News-Journal* (Daytona Beach, FL), May 1, 1992, 7A.

16. Stanford University, "Jury Gave Endorsement of Police Brutality, Law Faculty Say," news release, May 6, 1992, http://web.stanford.edu/dept/news/pr/92/920506Arc2233.html (accessed June 22, 2017).

17. D. M. Osborne, "Reaching for Doubt," *American Lawyer*, September 1992, p. 65. For an account of the aftermath of the acquittal in the Rodney King beating case, see the postscript.

18. The empirical studies similarly suggest great leniency toward citizens exercising law enforcement authority, even when they make mistakes in the use of force. Robinson and Darley, *Justice, Liability, & Blame*, pp. 72–81.

19. National Police Misconduct Reporting Project, *2010 Annual Report* (Washington, DC: Cato Institute 2010), http://www.policemisconduct.net/statistics/2010-annual-report/ (accessed June 22, 2017).

20. Thomas Clouse, "Jury Acquits Spokane Officer," *Spokesman-Review* (Spokane, WA), September 10, 2009, http://www.spokesman.com/stories/2009/sep/10/jury-finds-officer-not-guilty-assault/ (accessed June 22, 2017).

21. Scott Sunde, "No Third Trial for Ex-Deputy Accused of Jail Assault," *Seattle Post-Intelligencer*, July 8, 2010, http://www.seattlepi.com/local/article/No-third-trial-for-ex-deputy-accused-of-jail-886478.php (accessed June 22, 2017).

22. Haeyoun Park and Jasmine Lee, "Looking for Accountability in Police-Involved Deaths of African-Americans," *New York Times*, July 13, 2016.

23. Robinson and Darley, *Justice, Liability, & Blame*, p. 79. See also Carolyn Sung and Catherine E. Shoichet, "Freddie Gray Case," CNN, July 27, 2016, http://www.cnn.com/2016/07/27/us/freddie-gray-verdict-baltimore-officers/ (accessed June 22, 2017).

24. Katy Holloway, Trevor Bennett, and David P. Farrington, *Does Neighborhood Watch Reduce Crime?* no. 3, *Crime Prevention Research Review* (Washington, DC: US Department of Justice, 2008), p. 6; citing National Crime Prevention Council, *The 2000 National Crime Prevention Survey: Are We Safe?* (Washington, DC: National

Crime Prevention Council, 2001).

25. Ric Simmons, "Private Criminal Justice," *Wake Forest Law Review* 42 (2007): 911, 920–21.

26. This kind of community action, at least of the tamer neighborhood watch variety, is actually consistent with the commonly applauded trend in criminal justice toward greater community participation. At the trial and punishment phase, restorative justice has become extremely popular and has a broad political spectrum of supporters. Even community involvement in prosecution decisions and what has been called "community prosecution" have gained support. See Nicholas W. Klitzing, "Fixing the Unfixable: Community Prosecution as a Problem-Solving Strategy to Reduce Crime and Restore Order in East St. Louis," *Saint Louis University Public Law Review* 32 (2013): 157–99. Community involvement in most aspects of criminal justice is on the rise, and the underlying shadow vigilante impulse will have an increasing number of ways to express itself.

27. The narrative is drawn from the following sources: Douglas O. Linder, "The George Zimmerman Trial: An Account," Famous Trials, 2014, http://law2.umkc.edu/faculty/projects/ftrials/zimmerman1/zimmermanaccount.html (accessed June 22, 2017); Douglas O. Linder, "The George Zimmerman Trial: Chronology," Famous Trials, 2013, http://law2.umkc.edu/faculty/projects/ftrials/zimmerman1/zimmermanchrono.html (accessed June 22, 2017).

28. Warner Todd Huston, "Citizens Band Together to Form 'Glock Block' Saying 'We Don't Call the Police,'" *Mr. Conservative* (blog), June 18, 2013, http://www.mrconservative.com/2013/06/19406-citizens-band-together-to-form-glock-block-saying-we-don't-call-the-police/ (accessed June 22, 2017); Anna Sanders, "Welcome to the 'Glock Block': Vigilante Neighbors in Oregon Town Say They Are No Longer Calling the Police and Have Armed Themselves Instead," *Daily Mail* (London), June 17, 2013, http://www.dailymail.co.uk/news/article-2343491/Welcome-Glock-Block-Vigilante-neighbors-Oregon-town-say-longer-calling-police-armed-instead.html (accessed June 22, 2017).

29. The narrative is based on Denise Noe, "The Killing of Polly Klaas," TrueTV, http://archive.li/4TXuD#selection-695.0-695.26; Mike Reynolds, "Three Strikes and You're Out: Stop Repeat Offenders," Three Strikes, 2016, http://www.threestrikes.org/ (accessed June 22, 2017); Juan Ignacio Blanco, "Richard Allen Davis," *Murderpedia*, http://murderpedia.org/male.D/d/davis-richard-allen.htm (accessed June 22, 2017); John Borland, "#184 Sentence Enhancement: Repeat Offenders," *California Journal* (1994), http://www.calvoter.org/archive/94general/props/184.html (accessed June 22, 2017).

30. Noe, "Killing of Polly Klaas."

31. Marc Klaas, in memory of his daughter, started two foundations named after Polly. The first, the Polly Klaas Foundation, is a "national nonprofit dedicated to the safety of all children, the recovery of missing children, and public policies that keep children safe in their communities." ("Our Mission," Polly Klaas Foundation, http://www.pollyklaas.org/about/mission.html [accessed June 22, 2017]). Mr. Klaas later founded Klaas Kids, which works to prevent crimes against children and lobbies for stronger sentencing for violent offenders ("About the Foundation," Klaas Kids Foundation, http://klaaskids.org/about/ [accessed June 22, 2017]).

32. For the aftermath of this story, see the postscript.

33. Blanco, "Richard Allen Davis."

34. On June 29, 1992, Kimber Reynolds, Mike's daughter, had just finished dinner with her friend at a nice trendy restaurant in downtown Fresno and was heading to her car when she was attacked. Two men on motorcycles approached her from behind and tried to grab her purse. As she struggled, one of the men pulled out a gun and shot her point-blank in the head. When Mike found out that his daughter's shooter was a drug addict who had frequently been arrested and charged with gun, drug, robbery, and assault crimes, he promised he would do all he could to stop these types of repeat offenders from murdering someone else's daughter. See Dan Morain, "A Father's Bittersweet Crusade," *Los Angeles Times*, March 7, 1994, http://articles.latimes.com/1994-03-07/news/mn-31132_1_mike-reynolds (accessed June 22, 2017).

35. *Encyclopedia of American Politics*, s.v. "California Proposition 184, the Three Strikes Initiative," 1994, http://ballotpedia.org/California_Proposition_184,_the_Three_Strikes_Initiative_(1994) (accessed June 22, 2017).

36. Borland, "#184 Sentence Enhancement."

37. Nicole Shoener, "Three Strikes Laws in Different States," Legal Match: Find the Right Lawyer, last updated October 10, 2017, http://www.legalmatch.com/law-library/article/three-strikes-laws-in-different-states.html (accessed November 30, 2017).

38. Ibid.

39. Kieran Riley, "Trial by Legislature: Why Statutory Mandatory Minimum Sentences Violate the Separation of Powers Doctrine," *Boston University Public Interest Law Journal* 19 (2010): 285, 289–90.

40. Patrick Leahy, "Bipartisan Legislation to Give Judges More Flexibility for Federal Sentences Introduced," press release, March 20, 2013, http://www.leahy.senate.gov/press/bipartisan-legislation-to-give-judges-more-flexibility-for-federal-sentences-introduced (accessed June 22, 2017).

41. Ellen Perlman, "Terms of Imprisonment," *Governing: The State and*

Localities, April 2000, http://www.governing.com/topics/public-justice-safety/Terms-Imprisonment.html (accessed June 22, 2017).

42. Riley, "Trial by Legislature," pp. 308–309.

43. Paul H. Robinson, Geoffrey P. Goodwin, and Michael Reisig, "The Disutility of Injustice," *New York University Law Review* 85 (2010): 1940, 1973, fig. 1.

44. For a discussion of how this conflict could have come about in a democratic society, see ibid., pt. 3.

45. This factual account is based on Kelly Duane de la Vega and Katie Galloway, "Three Strikes of Injustice," *New York Times*, October 8, 2012, http://www.nytimes.com/2012/10/09/opinion/three-strikes-of-injustice.html?mcubz=1 (accessed June 22, 2017); Matt Taibbi, "Cruel and Unusual Punishment: The Shame of Three Strikes Laws," *Rolling Stone*, March 27, 2013, http://www.rollingstone.com/politics/news/cruel-and-unusual-punishment-the-shame-of-three-strikes-laws-20130327 (accessed June 22, 2017); Brooke Donald, "Stanford Law's Three Strikes Project Works for Fair Implementation of New Statute," *Stanford News*, June 6, 2013, http://news.stanford.edu/news/2013/june/three-strikes-project-060613.html (accessed June 22, 2017).

46. de la Vega and Galloway, "Three Strikes of Injustice," 2:02.

47. Taibbi, "Cruel and Unusual Punishment."

48. The Stanford Law School Three Strikes Program helped get Shane Taylor's sentence revised, and he was released after serving fifteen years in prison. See Donald, "Stanford Law's Three Strikes Project."

49. Taibbi, "Cruel and Unusual Punishment."

50. California amended the three strikes law in 2012. Now only serious or violent felonies qualify. *Encyclopedia of American Politics*, s.v. "California Proposition 36, Changes in the 'Three Strikes' Law," 2012, https://ballotpedia.org/California_Proposition_36,_Changes_in_the_%22Three_Strikes%22_Law_(2012) (accessed June 22, 2017).

51. To be fair to the judges of that period, some of the improperly lenient sentencing was a product of theories of rehabilitation or other punishment theories that were not based on what an offender deserved or did not deserve but rather on other goals that were influential at the time. The sentencing policy landscape has changed. In the only amendment to the Model Penal Code since its enactment in 1962 (the code is the basis for criminal codes in three-quarters of the states), the American Law Institute in 2007 dramatically altered the sentencing purposes provision of the Model Code to set desert as the dominant purpose, which can never be violated. That new clarity of purpose, together with the use of carefully constructed sentencing guidelines, can avoid the problem of improperly lenient sentences and thereby

eliminate the need for mandatory minimum sentences.

52. This factual account is based on Katherine Ramsland, "Willie Bosket," Crime Library, http://www.crimelibrary.com/notorious_murders/young/bosket/1.html; Fox Butterfield, "A Boy Who Killed Coldly Is Now a Prison 'Monster,'" *New York Times*, March 22, 1989, http://www.nytimes.com/1989/03/22/nyregion/a-boy-who-killed-coldly-is-now-a-prison-monster.html?pagewanted=all&mcubz=1 (accessed June 22, 2017); John P. Woods, "New York's Juvenile Offender Law: An Overview and Analysis," *Fordham Urban Law Journal* 9 (1980): 1.

53. Butterfield, "Boy Who Killed Coldly."

54. Fox Butterfield, *All God's Children: The Bosket Family and the American Tradition of Violence* (New York: Vintage, 1995), p. 213.

55. "Outrage to Keep Teen-Aged Killer in Pen," *Spokane* (WA) *Daily Chronicle*, July 2, 1981, p. 15.

56. Ramsland, "Willie Bosket."

57. "Outrage to Keep Teen-Aged Killer."

58. For the aftermath of this story, see the postscript.

59. According to John P. Woods, "These crimes are: second degree murder (including felony murder where the juvenile is criminally responsible for the underlying crime), first degree kidnapping, first degree manslaughter, first and second degree arson, first degree burglary, first degree sodomy (where force is used or the victim is incapable of consent but not where the victim is less than eleven), second degree burglary (where the defendant is armed, causes physical injury, uses or threatens use of a dangerous instrument or displays what appears to be a firearm), first degree rape (or by forcible compulsion or where the victim is incapable of consent), first degree robbery and second degree robbery (where the defendant causes physical injury or displays what appears to be a firearm), first degree assault (where a serious physical injury is caused by a deadly weapon or dangerous instrument or where the victim is intentionally maimed) and attempted murder and kidnapping." John P. Woods, "New York's Juvenile Offender Law: An Overview and Analysis," *Fordham Urban Law Journal* 9 (1980): 1, 25.

60. Ibid., p. 25.

61. Office of Juvenile Justice and Delinquency Prevention, "Estimated Number of Homicide Victims of Juvenile Offenders, 1980–2011," *Statistical Briefing Book*, December 16, 2014, http://ojjdp.gov/ojstatbb/offenders/qa03105.asp?qaDate=2011 (accessed June 22, 2017).

62. Patrick Griffin et al., "Trying Juveniles as Adults: An Analysis of State Transfer Laws and Reporting," *Office of Juvenile Justice and Delinquency Prevention, National Report Series Bulletin*, September 2011, https://www.ncjrs.gov/pdffiles1/

ojjdp/232434.pdf (accessed June 22, 2017).

63. "All States Allow Juveniles to Be Tried as Adults in Criminal Court under Certain Circumstances," *Office of Juvenile Justice and Delinquency Prevention, National Report Series Bulletin*, June 2003, https://www.ncjrs.gov/html/ojjdp/195420/page4.html (accessed June 22, 2017).

64. This factual account is based on Erik Eckholm, "Juveniles Facing Lifelong Terms Despite Rulings," *New York Times*, January 19, 2014, https://www.nytimes.com/2014/01/20/us/juveniles-facing-lifelong-terms-despite-rulings.html?mcubz=1 (accessed June 22, 2017); Clara McLaughlin, "Boy 15, Gets 70 Years for Attempted Murder," *Florida Star Online*, May 16, 2010, http://www.thefloridastar.com/boy-15-gets-70-years-for-attempted-murder/ (accessed June 22, 2017).

65. The third charge, aggravated battery, is dropped. McLaughlin, "Boy 15, Gets 70 Years."

66. See generally Eckholm, "Juveniles Facing Lifelong Terms"; Cara H. Drinan, "Misconstruing Graham & Miller," *Washington University Law Review* 91 (2014): 785. Appeals are filed by Gridine's public defender, who argues that "a 70-year sentence imposed upon a 14-year-old is just as cruel and unusual as a sentence of life without parole" (Eckholm, "Juveniles Facing Lifelong Terms"). Gridine's public defender, Gail Anderson, argues before the Florida court in September: "Mr. Gridine will most likely die in prison." (Eckholm, "Juveniles Facing Lifelong Terms"). Despite this argument the court upheld the verdict and sentence, leaving Gridine in prison for a very long time to contemplate the rash actions he took as a fourteen-year-old boy.

67. State v. Green, 348 N.C. 588, 593 (1998).

68. The Supreme Court of North Carolina upheld the sentence of life plus twenty years, stating it was severe but not cruel and unusual. Ibid., p. 612.

69. Naovarath v. State, 105 Nev. 525 (1989).

70. State v. Pittman, 373 S.C. 527 (2007).

CHAPTER 10. CRIMINAL JUSTICE OFFICIALS AS SHADOW VIGILANTES

1. This account and the following is based on United States v. Sheard, 473 F. 2d 139 (D.C. Cir. 1972).

2. Ibid.

3. George C. Thomas III, "Lost in the Fog of Miranda," *Hastings Law Journal* 64 (2013): 1501.

4. Alan Dershowitz, *The Best Defense* (New York: Random House, 1982), p. xxi.

5. Michelle Alexander, "Opinion: Why Police Lie under Oath," *New York Times*, February 2, 2013, http://www.nytimes.com/2013/02/03/opinion/sunday/why-police-officers-lie-under-oath.html?mcubz=1 (accessed June 22, 2017), quoting Peter Keane, San Francisco police commissioner: "Police officer perjury in court to justify illegal dope searches is commonplace. One of the dirty little not-so-secret secrets of the criminal justice system is undercover narcotics officers intentionally lying under oath. It is a perversion of the American justice system that strikes directly at the rule of law. Yet it is the routine way of doing business in courtrooms everywhere in America."

6. Larry Cunningham, "Taking on Testilying," in *Crime & Justice in America: Present Realities and Future Prospects*, 2nd ed., ed. Wilson R. Palacios, Paul F. Cromwell, and Roger G. Dunham (Saddle River, NJ: Prentice-Hall, 2002), p. 26.

7. David Kocieniewski, "NY Pays a High Price for Police Lies," *New York Times*, January 5, 1997, http://www.nytimes.com/1997/01/05/nyregion/new-york-pays-a-high-price-for-police-lies.html?mcubz=1 (accessed June 22, 2017).

8. Orfield quoted in ibid.

9. Jon Loevy, "Truth or Consequences: Police 'Testilying,'" *ABA Litigation* 36 (Spring 2010): 13–14, citing Myron W. Orfield, Jr., "The Exclusionary Rule and Deterrence: An Empirical Study of Chicago Narcotics Officers," *University of Chicago Law Review* 54 (1987): 1016.

10. Myron W. Orfield, Jr., "Deterrence, Perjury, and the Heater Factor: An Exclusionary Rule in the Chicago Criminal Courts," *University of Colorado Law Review* 63 (1992): 75, 83.

11. Milton Mollen, *Commission to Investigate Allegations of Police Corruption and the Anti-corruption Process of the Police Department* (New York: Commission, 1994), p. 36.

12. Ibid., p. 38.

13. Wayne Pethrick and Brent E. Turvey, "Cognitive Ethos of the Forensic Examiner," in *Forensic Criminology*, ed. Wayne Pethrick, Brent E. Turvey, and Claire E. Ferguson (Burlington, MA: Elsevier, 2010), p. 118.

14. Loevy, "Truth or Consequences," p. 29.

15. Case Comment, "Effect of Mapp v. Ohio on Police Search and Seizure Procedures in Narcotics Cases," *Columbia Journal of Law and Social Problems* 4 (1968): 94–95.

16. Nick Malinowski, "Testilying: Cops Are Liars Who Get Away with Perjury," *Vice*, March 2013, http://www.vice.com/read/testilying-cops-are-liars-who-get-away-with-perjury (accessed June 22, 2017).

17. Alan Dershowitz, "A Police Badge Is Not a License to Commit Perjury," *San*

Diego Union-Tribune, April 4, 1991, B11.

18. Orfield, "Deterrence, Perjury," p. 75.

19. This narrative was compiled from the following sources: Gus Burns, "Ramiro Sanchez Gets 6-Plus Years for Rape of Girl with Down Syndrome That Enraged Southwest Detroit," Mlive, March 28, 2014, http://www.mlive.com/news/detroit/index.ssf/2014/03/ramiro_sanchez_gets_6-plus_yea.html (accessed June 22, 2017); Erinn Cawthon, "Detroit Man Beaten after Neighbors Say He Raped Teen, Cite Slow Police Response," CNN, August 14, 2013, http://www.cnn.com/2013/08/14/us/michigan-suspect-beaten/ (accessed June 22, 2017); Jim Schaefer, "Detroit Neighborhood Takes Vigilante Action against Rape Suspect," *Detroit Free Press*, August 11, 2013, http://www.freep.com/article/20130811/NEWS01/308110005/hubbard-farms-rape-vigilante-justice-assault-teenage-girl (accessed June 22, 2017).

20. Schaefer, "Detroit Neighborhood."

21. Ibid.

22. Ibid.

23. Cawthon, "Detroit Man Beaten."

24. One comment on a local forum states, "So it's OK to take the law into your own hands? And the people who beat him up weren't arrested?" Another comment in response states, "Why is that even relevant? There should be No mercy. No compassion for the evil & wicked." Schaefer, "Detroit Neighborhood."

25. This narrative is compiled from State v. Augustine, 125 So.3d 1203 (La. Ct. App. 2013); "DA Frustrated by Revolving Door of Local Criminal Justice System," WWLTV, *Eyewitness Morning News*, January 12, 2011, http://www.wwltv.com/eyewitness-morning-news/DA-Frustrated-by-revolving-door-of-local-criminal-justice-system-113346474.html (accessed June 22, 217).

26. "DA Frustrated."

27. Ibid.

28. Cannizzaro was able to procure such a lengthy sentence because he asked the court to apply the habitual offender law, which increases penalties for individuals with prior felony convictions. In Louisiana, if the prosecutor determines a defendant should be charged under the habitual offender law and a jury finds him or her guilty, the judge's hands are tied, and he or she must impose the strictest sentence possible. Augustine appealed his lengthy sentence, but the appellate court affirmed his 120-year sentence (*State v. Augustine*).

29. Kyle Graham, "Overcharging," *Ohio State Journal of Criminal Law* 11 (2014): 72.

30. Douglas A. Berman, "Overcharging," *Sentencing Law and Policy* (blog),

March 19, 2013, http://sentencing.typepad.com/sentencing_law_and_policy/2013/03/overcharging.html (accessed June 22, 2017) (responding to the abstract posting of Graham, "Overcharging").

31. For example, in the Illinois criminal code, "Chapter 720 includes narrow, specific offenses in addition to a broader prohibition against such conduct generally. For example, although one provision in current Chapter 720 covers theft generally, a number of other provisions in Chapter 720 prohibit the same underlying conduct—theft by taking (or its attempt)—in the context of specific circumstances or forms of property. The same situation exists for assault offenses and property damage offenses. Similarly, in addition to its general perjury offense, current Illinois law contains numerous offenses criminalizing false statements made under oath or affirmation about particular matters, in particular documents, and in particular proceedings." Paul Robinson and Michael Cahill, "Final Report of the Illinois Criminal Code Rewrite and Reform Commission," *Faculty Scholarship*, paper 291 (2003), p. xli, http://scholarship.law.upenn.edu/faculty_scholarship/291 (accessed June 22, 2017). Kirk Dillard, a Republican state senator from Hinsdale and a member of a later commission, acknowledged that lawmakers sometimes push for redundant measures in response to crimes within their districts: "Even though there may have been five or six other ways to charge that individual who did something at a particular legislative district with a crime, the legislator always wants to add a new one for a lot of reasons, including public-relations purposes. . . . We all add to the criminal code, and it turns into a hodge-podge." Mike Ramsey, "Panel Tackles Rewrite of State's Criminal Code," *Copley News Service*, December 13, 2004.

32. Robinson and Cahill, "Final Report," p. xix. "The sheer verbiage of current law is one indication of its failure to consolidate similar offenses. . . . Overall, the Proposed Code's Special Part uses only 14.9 percent—less than 1/6—of the words in the code's special Part, and only 6.7 percent—about 1/15—of the current Special Part plus other, non-criminal code statutory felonies." Paul Robinson, *Final Report of the Kentucky Penal Code Revision Project of the Criminal Justice Council* (Frankfort, KY: Kentucky Criminal Justice Council, 2003), https://papers.ssrn.com/sol3/papers.cfm?abstract_id=1526674 (accessed June 22, 2017). "Nearly three decades of piecemeal modification of the Code have led to the addition of hundreds of new offenses, many of which cover the same conduct as previous offenses." Paul H. Robinson and Michael T. Cahill: "One might expect that over time, as more loopholes or omissions in a code are eliminated, there would be a reduced need to alter or expand that code, but historical trends demonstrate that the opposite is true. . . . The Illinois Code underwent nearly twice as many amendments in its second twenty years of

existence than in its first twenty years." Paul H. Robinson and Michael T. Cahill, "The Accelerating Degradation of American Criminal Codes," *Hastings Law Journal* 56 (2005): 635–36.

33. The commission's report explained that "the drafters have aimed to consolidate offenses. Perhaps inevitably, four decades of piecemeal modification of the 1961 Code have led to the addition of hundreds of new offenses, many of which cover the same conduct as previous offenses or appear in various other chapters of the Illinois Compiled Statutes rather than in the criminal code." Robinson and Cahill, "Final Report," pp. v–vi. Joseph Birkett, the most vocal prosecutor opposing the Criminal Code Rewrite and Reform Commission's work, contended that "many of the special provisions and enhanced penalties are needed." John Patterson, "Are We Too Tough on Crime? Politicians' Fear of Appearing Soft Creates Avalanche of Laws," *Chicago Daily Herald*, April 1, 2001. A Republican member of the Illinois House of Representatives and a member of the Criminal Law Edit, Alignment and Reform (CLEAR) commission (the prosecutor-sponsored successor to the original Criminal Code Rewrite and Reform Commission), James B. Durkin, has acknowledged that "prosecutors are hesitant to change." "Court Reform Commentary," *Chicago Tribune*, June 27, 2000, p. 12. Gino DiVito, a former Illinois appellate judge who cochaired the CLEAR commission, found that the code's illogic stems from laws passed to address a specific crime or a constituent complaint without examining how the new law fits within the overall state code: "The code reform project had barely gotten off the ground when prosecutors expressed their opposition and were unwilling to devote manpower or resources to assist in the project, even though their participation would have assured them a voice within the decision-making group." Robinson and Cahill, "Accelerating Degradation," p. 649.

34. The 1,100-page bill emanating from the CLEAR commission declined to recommend narrowing the number of circumstances that can activate the charge of aggravated battery, among other things. Commission members also declined to eliminate anachronistic offenses such as adultery and fornication, though the last successful prosecution for fornication occurred in 1913, while the charge of adultery was last aired in criminal court in the early 1960s. Mike Ramsey, "Is That CLEAR? Legal Panel Hopes So," *Copley News Service*, December 29, 2006.

35. Graham, "Overcharging," p. 705.

36. Ibid., p. 709.

37. Richard A. Oppel, Jr., "Sentencing Shift Gives New Leverage to Prosecutors," *New York Times*, September 25, 2011.

38. "Sentencing judges, trying to anticipate what the parole commission will do,

undoubtedly are tempted to sentence a defendant on the basis of when they believe the parole commission will release him. . . . In doing so, some judges deliberately impose sentences above the parole guidelines, leaving the parole commission to set the presumptive release date. . . . Other judges impose sentences consistent with or below the guidelines in order to retain control over the release date." Legislative History of the Crime Control Act, S. Rep. No. 225, 98th Cong., 1st Sess. 1983, 1983 WL 25404 (Leg. Hist.), pp. 46–47.

39. Mark H. Luttrell, "The Impact of the Sentencing Reform Act on Prison Management," *Federal Probation: A Journal of Correctional Philosophy and Practice* 55 (1991): 54.

40. It can be a crime to lie to police or refuse to answer questions before a grand jury. See, for example, Brown v. United States 359 U.S. 41 (1959) (finding contempt where a witness refused to answer before a grand jury on grounds of self-incrimination privilege despite being granted immunity); but see Harris v. United States, 382 U.S. 162 (1965) (identifying a similar scenario where criminal contempt was not appropriate); Fed. R. Crim. P. 42 (a, b) (Criminal Contempt); 18 Pa. C.S.A. § 4906 (False Reports to Law Enforcement Authorities). But shadow vigilantes can usually avoid committing such offenses simply by saying nothing to investigators in the first place and never drawing to themselves the kind of attention that might put them before a grand jury.

41. Almost by definition, the shadow vigilante cannot meet the rules for the moral vigilante as laid out in chapter 5: shadow vigilantes typically do not give prior warnings, as rule 6 requires; typically do not report afterward what they have done and why, as rule 9 requires; and also commonly act alone, as rule 8 forbids. However, a group might be formed to coordinate activities in ways that might come closer to meeting chapter 5's rules. An organization might publish guidelines and advice about what shadow vigilante actions people should take and why, and to report what is done and why.

CHAPTER 11. BLOWBACK AND THE DOWNWARD SPIRAL

1. Julie L. Whitman and Robert C. Davis, *Snitches Get Stitches: Youth, Gangs, and Witness Intimidation in Massachusetts* (Washington, DC: National Center for Victims of Crime, 2007), http://archives.lib.state.ma.us/handle/2452/38544 (accessed June 21, 2017).

2. Ice Cube, *Laugh Now, Cry Later*, Lench Mob Records, 2006.

3. David Kocieniewski, "With Witnesses at Risk, Murder Suspects Go Free," *New York Times*, March 1, 2007, http://www.nytimes.com/2007/03/01/nyregion/01witness.html (accessed June 21, 2017).

4. Jamie Masten, "Ain't No Snitches Ridin' wit' Us: How Deception in the Fourth Amendment Triggered the Stop Snitching Movement," *Ohio State Law Journal* 70 (2009): 701, 702–704.

5. Tom Farrey, "Snitching Controversy Goes Well beyond 'Melo,'" *ESPN Magazine*, January 18, 2006, http://www.espn.com/nba/columns/story?columnist=farrey_tom&id=2296590 (accessed June 21, 2017).

6. Masten, "Ain't No Snitches," p. 705.

7. David Kocieniewski, "So Many Crimes, and Reasons to Not Cooperate," *New York Times*, December 30, 2007, http://www.nytimes.com/2007/12/30/nyregion/30witness.html (accessed November 14, 2017).

8. Ibid.

9. Ibid.

10. Ibid.

11. Ibid.

12. Ibid.

13. Kocieniewski, "With Witnesses at Risk."

14. Ibid.

15. David Kocieniewski, "A Little Girl Shot, and a Crowd That Didn't See," *New York Times*, July 9, 2007, http://www.nytimes.com/2007/07/09/nyregion/09taj.html (accessed June 21, 2017).

16. Kocieniewski, "So Many Crimes."

17. David Kocieniewski, "In Prosecution of Gang, a Chilling Adversary: The Code of the Streets," *New York Times*, September 19, 2007, http://www.nytimes.com/2007/09/19/nyregion/19gangs.html (accessed June 21, 2017).

18. Kocieniewski, "Little Girl Shot."

19. David Kocieniewski, "Keeping Witnesses off Stand to Keep Them Safe," *New York Times*, November 19, 2007, http://www.nytimes.com/2007/11/19/nyregion/19witness.html (accessed June 21, 2017).

20. Kocieniewski, "With Witnesses at Risk."

21. Kelly Dedel, "Witness Intimidation, Guide No. 42 (2006)," Center for Problem-Oriented Policing, http://www.popcenter.org/problems/witness_intimidation/ (accessed June 21, 2017).

22. J. David Goodman, "As Shootings Rise in New York, Police Focus on a Small Number of Young Men," *New York Times*, July 21, 2015, https://www.nytimes

.com/2015/07/22/nyregion/as-shootings-rise-in-new-york-police-focus-on-a-small-number-of-young-men.html (accessed June 21, 2017).

23. Kocieniewski, "Keeping Witnesses."

24. Mark Di Ionno, "The Killing Cycle: Inside Story of the Essex County Homicide Squad as It Tries to Break the Murder Chain," *Star-Ledger* (Newark, NJ), August 14, 2011, http://www.nj.com/news/index.ssf/2011/08/essex_county_homicide_squad_in.html (accessed June 21, 2017).

25. "Police: Too Many Murders Are Unresolved Because Witnesses Refuse to Speak," KMOV, October 16, 2014, http://www.kmov.com/story/28469636/police-too-many-murders-are-unresolved-because-witnesses-refuse-to-speak (accessed June 21, 2017).

26. Kocieniewski, "Keeping Witnesses."

27. Rafael Di Tella, Sebastian Edwards, and Ernesto Schargrodsky, *The Economics of Crime: Lessons For and From Latin America* (Chicago: University of Chicago Press, 2010), p. 331.

28. Ibid.

29. Ibid.

30. Justin Fenton, "Baltimore Police Struggle to Close Murders with Few Talking," *Baltimore Sun*, June 7, 2012, http://www.baltimoresun.com/news/maryland/crime/bs-md-ci-jerry-isaac-murder-20120515-story.html (accessed June 21, 2017).

31. Essex County's Murder Map, "Getting Away with Murder," *Star Ledger* (Newark, NJ), http://www.nj.com/news/murder/ (accessed June 21, 2017).

32. Kocieniewski, "With Witnesses at Risk."

33. Ibid.

34. David Kocieniewski, "Few Choices in Shielding of Witnesses," *New York Times*, October 28, 2007, http://www.nytimes.com/2007/10/28/nyregion/28witness.html (accessed June 21, 2017).

35. David Kocieniewski, "Keeping Witnesses."

36. Ibid.

37. Kocieniewski, "With Witnesses at Risk."

38. Todd Murphy, "Ignatow Witness Pleads Guilty to Evidence Tampering," *Courier Journal* (Louisville, KY), December 3, 1991.

39. Kocieniewski, "With Witnesses at Risk." However, in Brooklyn and Prince George's County, Maryland, the state and district attorneys are personally handling all single-witness cases. Even though in Prince George's County the prosecution has lost four cases in the past thirteen months from 2006 to 2007 with single witnesses, he

continues to pursue these cases, stating, "If you have a single witness and you believe their story, I believe you've got to go forward, even if it's a case you might lose. I'm not going to give the gang members, the murderers and the rapists an easy out. And if they know that all they have to do is get your case down to one witness, I think it would encourage them to use even more intimidation."

The total number of murders in Prince George's County has steadily declined from 2005 to 2012 (150 to 49), while the population has grown from 840,000 to 881,000. United States Census Bureau, "QuickFacts: Prince George's County, Maryland," United States Census Bureau, http://www.census.gov/quickfacts/table/PST045215/24033 (accessed June 21, 2017).

40. Kocieniewski, "Keeping Witnesses."

41. Kocieniewski, "Little Girl Shot."

42. Kocieniewski, "With Witnesses at Risk." The same article explains how at least fourteen recent murderers had been identified but not prosecuted due to lack of additional witnesses and evidence.

43. Abby Rogers, "The 25 Most Dangerous Cities in America," *Business Insider*, November 4, 2012, http://www.businessinsider.com/the-25-most-dangerous-cities-in-america-2012-10 (accessed June 21, 2017).

44. For data on Newark, see "Crime Rate in Newark, New Jersey (NJ)," *City Data*, http://www.city-data.com/crime/crime-Newark-New-Jersey.html (accessed June 21, 2017). The average murder rate (per 100,000) was 9.02 for the following thirteen cities (the closest in size to Newark according to the 2013 United States Census population estimates): Anchorage, Stockton, Fort Wayne, St. Paul, Lincoln, Henderson, Jersey City, Buffalo, Greensboro, Cincinnati, Toledo, Pittsburgh, and Plano. The national average murder rate in 2012 was 4.7. "Uniform Crime Reports, 2011–2012," FBI, https://www.fbi.gov/about-us/cjis/ucr/crime-in-the-u.s/2012/crime-in-the-u.s.-2012/offenses-known-to-law-enforcement/cities-and-counties-grouped-by-size-population-group (accessed June 21, 2017). Not all jurisdictions take this approach. In Prince George's County, Maryland, another area with high gang activity, the position is that failure to prosecute encourages witness intimidation. Prosecutors are bringing cases to trial and getting an 80 percent homicide conviction rate. Kocieniewski, "With Witnesses at Risk."

45. Larry McShane, "3 Girls Defy 'Lie or Die' Note, Help Put Shooter Away," *Los Angeles Times*, November 24, 2002, http://articles.latimes.com/2002/nov/24/news/adna-witnesses24 (accessed June 14, 2017).

46. McShane, "3 Girls Defy 'Lie or Die.'"

47. Ibid.

48. Ibid.

49. Buffa, "Jury Jolted by News."

50. McShane, "3 Girls Defy 'Lie or Die.'"

51. For details on the aftermath, see the postscript.

52. This narrative is drawn primarily from the following sources: John Appezzato, "Reputed Bloods Member Arraigned in Newark Slaying," *Star-Ledger* (Newark, NJ), September 3, 2008, http://www.nj.com/news/index.ssf/2008/09/reputed_bloods_member_arraigne.html (accessed June 21, 2017); Damien Cave and John Holl, "Arrest in Newark Alters Story of Year-Old Quadruple Murder," *New York Times*, December 9, 2005, http://www.nytimes.com/2005/12/08/nyregion/arrest-in-newark-alters-story-of-yearold-quadruple-murder.html (accessed June 21, 2017); Alexi Friedman, "Two Men Acquitted in Shooting Death of a 41-Year-Old Man in Newark," *Star-Ledger* (Newark, NJ), March 4, 2010, http://www.nj.com/news/index.ssf/2010/03/newark_man_is_found_innocent_i.html (accessed June 21, 2017); Katherine Santiago, "Newark Man Gets 16 Years in Prison for Killing Witness to Quadruple Shooting," *Star-Ledger* (Newark, NJ), September 17, 2009, http://www.nj.com/news/index.ssf/2009/09/newark_man_sentenced_to_16_yea.html (accessed June 21, 2017).

53. An officer says Melvin "brazenly remained at the scene of the Lamar McMillan homicide and pretended to be a witness to the incident" (Cave and Holl, "Arrest in Newark").

54. For the aftermath, see the postscript.

55. While the jury believed race played no role in their decision to support the officers' actions against Rodney King, much of South Los Angeles vehemently disagreed. Americans across the country were outraged over the verdict. Just a few hours after the world learned of the officers' acquittals, the city, according to *Time* magazine, would be known for "the worst single episode of urban unrest in American history." Madison Grey, "The LA Riots: 15 Years after Rodney King," *Time*, April 2007, http://content.time.com/time/specials/2007/la_riot/article/0,28804,1614117_1615206_1614675,00.html (accessed June 21, 2017). The LAPD did not properly prepare for the verdict and the city's response, as they lost control of the streets in South Los Angeles, Koreatown, Hollywood, Mid-City, Pico-Union, and the Civic Center. Patrick Range McDonald, "Then & Now: Images from the Same Spot as the LA Riots, 20 Years Later," *LA Weekly*, http://www.laweekly.com/microsites/la-riots/ (accessed November 17, 2017). Citizens set more than three thousand fires (damaging over eleven hundred buildings), looted stores across the city, and even physically assaulted other motorists on the road. The riots forced Mayor Tom Bradley to declare a

state of emergency and Governor Pete Wilson to send in the California Army National Guard. The 1992 Los Angeles Riots lasted nearly six days, left more than fifty dead, injured over four thousand, and cost the city about one billion dollars in property damage. Seth Mydans, "The Police Verdict; Los Angeles Policemen Acquitted in Taped Beating," *New York Times*, April 30, 1992, http://www.nytimes.com/books/98/02/08/home/rodney-verdict.html (accessed November 17, 2017).

56. Paul H. Robinson, "Black Lives Movement Can Improve Justice System," *Philadelphia Inquirer*, December 15, 2015, http://www.philly.com/philly/blogs/thinktank/Black-Lives-movement-can-improve-justice-system.html (accessed June 21, 2017).

CHAPTER 12. THE DAMAGES AND DANGERS OF THE COMMUNITY PERCEIVING THE SYSTEM AS BEING INDIFFERENT TO DOING JUSTICE

1. See part II of Paul H. Robinson, *Intuitions of Justice and the Utility of Desert* (New York: Oxford, 2013), pp. 96–208.

2. Paul H. Robinson and Sarah M. Robinson, *Pirates, Prisoners, and Lepers: Lessons from Life Outside the Law* (Omaha, NE: Potomac Books, 2015), p. 61.

3. A follow-up study used a slightly different methodology. Instead of the "within-subjects design" used in the former study, it used a "between-subjects design." That is, instead of asking the same subjects their views before and after being "disillusioned" about the criminal justice system, the study used separate groups. Some were seriously disillusioned, some only mildly disillusioned, and some were not disillusioned at all. Then all subjects were asked the same deference and compliance questions. The study found that the extent of the disillusionment determined the extent to which the subjects would defer to the criminal justice system. Another study did not collect new data but sought to determine whether the same dynamic was present in some of the very large datasets of previously collected survey data. A regression analysis gave these results: the moral credibility measure in the study explains more of the variance in the "willingness to defer" measure than any of the other measures. In fact, it is the only predictor that is statistically significant. Robinson, *Intuitions of Justice*, chap. 9.

4. Paul H. Robinson and John M. Darley, "The Utility of Desert," *Northwestern University Law Review* 91 (1997): 468–69.

5. Mark David Agrast et al., *The World Justice Project: Rule of Law Index 2012–2013* (Washington, DC: World Justice Project, 2012–2013), p. 161, http://www

.worldjusticeproject.org/sites/default/files/WJP_Index_Report_2012.pdf (accessed June 15, 2017). In a global survey of ninety-seven countries, the United States ranked twenty-sixth in the overall criminal justice category, which included questions pertaining to the efficacy and impartiality of a country's criminal justice system.

6. Lydia Saad, "Americans Express Mixed Confidence in Criminal Justice System," Gallup, Washington, DC, July 11, 2011, http://www.gallup.com/poll/148433/americans-express-mixed-confidence-criminal-justice-system.aspx (accessed June 15, 2017). In 1999, the Hearst Corporation authorized a comprehensive national survey, "How the Public Views State Courts," that was coordinated by the National Center for State Courts. The survey found that only 10 percent of the respondents felt the courts in their communities handled cases in an "excellent" manner. Additionally, respondents who reported a higher knowledge about the courts expressed lower confidence in the courts in their community, while 42 to 57 percent of respondents said the slow pace of justice and the complexity of the law contributes "a lot" to the cost of going to court. National Center for State Courts, "How the Public Views State Courts," *University of Nebraska Public Policy Center* no. 25 (1999): 7.

7. "Confidence in Institutions," Gallup, Washington, DC, June 4, 2013, http://www.gallup.com/poll/1597/confidence-institutions.aspx (accessed June 15, 2017).

8. Ibid.

9. *Perceptions of US Justice System* (Chicago, IL: American Bar Association, 1999), http://www.americanbar.org/content/dam/aba/migrated/marketresearch/PublicDocuments/perceptions_of_justice_system_1999_2nd_half.authcheckdam.pdf (accessed June 15, 2017), reprinted in *Albany Law Review* 62 (1999): 1307.

10. Mapp v. Ohio, 367 U.S. 643, in 1961, Escobedo v. Illinois, 378 U.S. 478, in 1964, and Miranda v. Arizona, 384 U.S. 436, in 1966.

11. Allen Rostron, "The Law and Order Theme in Political and Popular Culture," *Oklahoma City University Law Review* 37 (2012): 323, 326.

12. David A. Nichols, *Matter of Justice: Eisenhower and the Beginning of the Civil Rights Revolution* (New York: Simon & Schuster, 2007), pp. 91–101; see also Ronald Kahn and Ken I. Kersch, eds., *The Supreme Court and American Political Development* (Lawrence: University Press of Kansas, 2006), p. 442.

13. Richard A. Leo, "The Impact of Miranda Revisited," *Journal of Criminal Law and Criminology* 86, no. 3 (1996): 621.

14. See George Gallup, "2 to 1 View: Confession Ruling Bad," *Salt Lake Tribune*, July 27, 1966, http://newspaperarchive.com/salt-lake-tribune/1966-07-27/page-7 (accessed June 15, 2017).

15. Tom R. Tyler, "Public Mistrust of the Law: A Political Perspective,"

University of Cincinnati Law Review 66 (1998): 847, 851, table 2. These data are from the US Department of Justice: Michael J. Hindeland et al., eds., *Sourcebook of Criminal Justice Statistics* (Washington, DC: Government Printing Office, 1973), pp. 146–47, tables 2.36, 2.37; Bureau of Justice Statistics: Timothy J. Flanagan et al., eds., *Sourcebook of Criminal Justice Statistics, 1981* (Washington, DC: Government Printing Office, 1982), pp. 204–205, table 2.33; and Kathleen Maguire and Ann L. Pastore, eds., *Sourcebook of Criminal Justice Statistics, 1994* (Washington, DC: Government Printing Office, 1995), pp. 174–75, table 2.43; Rostron, "Law and Order Theme," 326–27.

16. Johnny Firecloud, "10 Best Vigilante Films," *Crave Online*, http://www.craveonline.com/culture/142210-10-best-vigilante-films (accessed June 15, 2017). Note that many of these movies use as triggers for the protagonist's vigilante action some of the failure-of-justice doctrines discussed in chapters 6–9, such as *Law Abiding Citizen* (reliable DNA evidence excluded), *Death Sentence* (improperly short sentence), and *Sudden Impact* (one of Clint Eastwood's *Dirty Harry* movies; evidence excluded for improper search). In a few instances, the storyline plays upon the problems that come from frustrated classic and "shadow" vigilantes (see chapters 13 and 14) who pervert the system, thereby requiring the hero to act, such as *Righteous Kill* (the hero played by De Niro must go classic vigilante to do justice because frustrated shadow vigilante cops have planted evidence, allowing the guilty to hide from justice), *The Star Chamber* (a vigilante judge played by Douglas must be taken down), and *Brotherhood of Justice* (Keanu Reeves as head of a high school vigilante group fighting crime that spins out of control; based on the real case discussed in chapter 4).

CHAPTER 13. WHAT IT TAKES TO STOP THE VIGILANTE ECHO

1. Paul H. Robinson and John M. Darley, "Intuitions of Justice: Implications for Criminal Law and Justice Policy," *Southern California Law Review* 81, no. 1 (2007): 1.

2. Paul H. Robinson and Michael T. Cahill, *Law without Justice: Why Criminal Law Doesn't Give People What They Deserve* (New York: Oxford University Press, 2006), chaps. 9 and 10.

3. Ibid., pp. 222–24.

4. P. J. and J. H. v. The United Kingdom, European Court of Human Rights, Application no. 44787/98, Strasbourg, Germany, September 25, 2001, para. 76; see generally Paul H. Robinson and Sarah M. Robinson, *Pirates, Prisoners, and Lepers:*

Lessons from Life Outside the Law (Omaha, NE: Potomac Books, 2015), pp. 198–203.

CONCLUSION

1. The doctrines that create deviations from deserved punishment and how they might be reformed are examined in Paul H. Robinson and Michael T. Cahill, *Law without Justice: Why Criminal Law Doesn't Give People What They Deserve* (New York: Oxford University Press, 2006).

POSTSCRIPT. WHERE ARE THEY NOW?

1. Darryl Mace, *In Remembrance of Emmett Till: Regional Stories and Media Responses to the Black Freedom Struggle* (Lexington: University Press of Kentucky, 2014), p. 142.

2. "Second Vigilante Committee Organizes in San Francisco," History.com, May 15, 2009, http://www.history.com/this-day-in-history/second-vigilante-committee-organizes-in-san-francisco (accessed November 30, 2017).

3. Adam Gorightly, "A Homosexual Thrill-Kill?" http://feralhouse.com/wp/wp-content/uploads/2014/08/thrill-kill-by-gorightly.pdf (accessed June14, 2017).

4. Jennifer Davies, "Vigilantes: It's Payback Time," *RW Press*, 2014, http://vps101161.vps.ovh.ca/lib/vigilantes-it-s-payback-time-gangs-book-4.html (accessed June 14, 2017).

5. Malini Nair, "Sari Gang to Paint the Stage Pink," *Times of India*, January 17, 2016, http://timesofindia.indiatimes.com/home/sunday-times/Sari-gang-to-paint-the-stage-pink/articleshow/50607712.cms (accessed June 15, 2017).

6. Ken Kalthoff, "Jury Sentences Ex-Husband to 85 Years in Deanna Cook Murder," NBC DFW, May 26, 2015, http://www.nbcdfw.com/news/local/Punishment-Phase-Begins-in-Deanna-Cook-Murder-Trial-305019741.html (accessed June 15, 2017).

7. Ibid.

8. Cook v. City of Dallas, No. 3:12-cv-03788-P (N.D. Tex. filed Oct. 25, 2012).

9. "Man Gets Out of Prison after Killing Bully in '95—Harper Terrorized Spring Valley Neighborhood," ABC KGTV, November 24, 2004, http://www.10news.com/news/man-gets-out-of-prison-after-killing-bully-in-95 (accessed June 15, 2017).

10. Ibid.

11. Gera-Lind Kolarik and Wayne Klatt, *Freed to Kill: The True Story of Larry Eyler* (New York: Avon, 1992).

12. Paul H. Robinson and Michael T. Cahill, *Law without Justice: Why Criminal Law Doesn't Give People What They Deserve* (New York: Oxford University Press, 2006), chap. 6.

13. Emil Guillermo and Frances Kai-Hwa Wang, "Man Charged with Vincent Chin's Death Seeks Lien Removed, Still Owes Millions," NBC News, December 11, 2015, http://www.nbcnews.com/news/asian-america/man-convicted-vincent-chins-death-seeks-lien-removed-still-owes-n478766 (accessed June 15, 2017).

14. John M. Broder, "12 Imprisoned Puerto Ricans Accept Clemency Conditions," *New York Times*, September 8, 1999, http://www.nytimes.com/1999/09/08/us/12-imprisoned-puerto-ricans-accept-clemency-conditions.html (accessed June 15, 2017).

15. Margaret Power, "From Freedom Fighters to Patriots: The Successful Campaign to Release the FALN Political Prisoners, 1980–1999," *CENTRO: Journal of the Center for Puerto Rican Studies* 25, no. 1 (2013): 146.

16. "A Federal Judge Has Ordered the Son of A . . .," United Press International, August 3, 1982, http://www.upi.com/Archives/1982/08/03/A-federal-judge-has-ordered-the-son-of-a/3339397195200/ (accessed June 14, 2017).

17. Carol Wallace and Michael J. Weiss, "The Untouchables: Diplomats in America," *People*, January 17, 1983, http://www.people.com/people/archive/article/0,,20084065,00.html (accessed June 14, 2017).

18. Henry Tatum, "The Legion, the Law, and the Legacy," *Dallas Morning News*, June 12, 1986.

19. Jan Jarvis, "DOOMSDAY," *D Magazine*, July 1985, http://www.dmagazine.com/publications/d-magazine/1985/july/doomsday (accessed June 15, 2017).

20. Tara Edwards, "Suspect in Steve Utash Beating Takes Plea Deal," WXYZ Detroit, June 16, 2014, http://www.wxyz.com/news/first-look-at-steve-utash-since-beating-in-detroit (accessed June 13, 2017).

21. Ibid.

22. Katrease Stafford, "Steve Utash Returns to Work, Thanks Supporters 4 Months after Mob Beating," *Detroit Free Press*, August 6, 2014.

23. Ibid.

24. Marty Griffin, "SCI Pittsburgh Guard Facing Inmate Abuse Charges," CBS Pittsburgh, September 27, 2011, http://pittsburgh.cbslocal.com/2011/09/27/sci-pittsburgh-guard-facing-inmate-abuse-charges/ (accessed June 13, 2017).

25. Ibid.

26. Adam Brandolph, "Former SCI Pittsburgh Prison Guard to Serve Five Years of Probation in Abuse of Sex Offenders," *TribLive*, March 28, 2013, http://triblive.com/news/adminpage/3740580-74/guard-nicoletti-charges#axzz37Y0cqMSp (accessed June 13, 2017).

27. Amy S. Rosenberg and Maida Odom, "Bush: Mantua Example for US," Philly.com, July 25, 1990, http://articles.philly.com/1990-07-25/news/25900197_1_anti-drug-rally-herman-wrice-anti-drug-movement (accessed June 20, 2017).

28. Yvonne Latty, "Mantua Drug Warrior Dies; Herman Wrice Stricken in Fla. before March," *Daily News*, March 11, 2000.

29. *Encyclopedia of American Politics*, s.v. "Arizona Standing in Civil Actions, Proposition 102," 2006, https://ballotpedia.org/Arizona_Standing_in_Civil_Actions,_Proposition_102_(2006) (accessed June 14, 2017).

30. Alia Beard Rau, "Judge Rules against Arizona Rancher in Immigrant Case," *Arizona Republic*, May 31, 2011, http://www.azcentral.com/news/articles/2011/05/31/20110531arizona-rancher-illegal-immigrants-damages-law.html (accessed June 14, 2017).

31. Alex Mindlin, "Patrolling the Streets, and Dissing the Rivals," *New York Times*, June 1, 2008, http://www.nytimes.com/2008/06/01/nyregion/thecity/01patr.html (accessed November 16, 2017).

32. Bill Maher, "Celebrating 20 Years of Free the Animals," *Huffington Post*, April 30, 2012, http://www.huffingtonpost.com/bill-maher/peta-ingrid-newkirk-free-the-animals_b_1464990.html (accessed June 20, 2017).

33. Sue Russell, "When Extreme Animal Rights Activists Attack," *Pacific Standard*, March 16, 2012, www.psmag.com/legal-affairs/when-extreme-animal-rights-activists-attack-40430/ (accessed June 14, 2017).

34. Ibid.

35. "Home Page," Animal Liberation Front, http://www.animalliberationfront.com/index.html (accessed June 14, 2017), see second slide of PowerPoint under "AR Philosophy."

36. Sara Rimer, "Abortion Foes in Boot Camp Mull Doctor's Killing," *New York Times*, March 19, 1993, p. A12.

37. Judy L. Thomas, "Roeder Upset at Operation Rescue," *Wichita Eagle*, July 27, 2009, http://www.kansas.com/2009/07/26/905518/roeder-upset-at-operation-rescue.html (accessed June 14, 2017).

38. Ron Sylvester, "Scott Roeder Gets Hard 50 in Murder of Abortion Provider George Tiller," *Wichita Eagle*, March 31, 2010, http://www.kansas.com/2010/04/01/1249310/roeder-to-be-sentenced-thursday.html#storylink=cpy (accessed June 14, 2017).

39. "George Tiller Was No Hero—and Neither Was Scott Roeder," Operation Rescue, February 2, 2010, http://www.operationrescue.org/archives/george-tiller-was-no-hero-%E2%80%93-and-neither-was-scott-roeder/ (accessed June 14, 2017).

40. Gudrun Schultz, "Christian Groups Protest Wal-Mart Support for Homosexuality, Abortifacient Birth Control," LifeSite News, December 18, 2006, https://www.lifesitenews.com/news/christian-groups-protest-wal-mart-support-for-homosexuality-abortifacient-b (accessed June 14, 2017).

41. Jonathan Silverstein, "Controversial Web Site Claims to 'Out' Would-Be Child Molesters," ABC News, January 10, 2005, http://abcnews.go.com/US/story?id=260587&page=1 (accessed June 14, 2017).

42. Tomas Alex Tizon, "Man Admits to Killing 2 Sex Offenders, Cites Idaho Case," *Los Angeles Times*, September 7, 2005, http://articles.latimes.com/2005/sep/07/nation/na-vigilante7 (accessed June 14, 2017).

43. Tim Eaton, "Prosecutor Kills Himself in Texas Raid over Child Sex," *New York Times*, November 7, 2006, http://www.nytimes.com/2006/11/07/us/07pedophile.html?_r=0 (accessed June 14, 2017).

44. Matea Gold, "NBC Resolves Lawsuit over 'To Catch a Predator' Suicide," *Los Angeles Times*, June 24, 2008, http://latimesblogs.latimes.com/showtracker/2008/06/nbc-resolves-la.html (accessed June 14, 2017).

45. Donald Bradley, "3 Decades on, Who Killed Skidmore Town Bully Still Secret," *Kansas City Star*, August 29, 2010, http://www.mcclatchydc.com/news/crime/article24591469.html (accessed June 14, 2017).

46. Michael Freitag, "Goetz Released after Spending 8 Months in Jail," *New York Times*, September 21, 1989, http://www.nytimes.com/1989/09/21/nyregion/goetz-released-after-spending-8-months-in-jail.html (accessed June 14, 2017).

47. Ibid.

48. Tina Kelley, "Still Seeking Payment from Bernard Goetz," *New York Times*, September 10, 2000, http://www.nytimes.com/2000/09/10/nyregion/following-up-still-seeking-payment-from-bernard-goetz.html?mcubz=1 (accessed June 14, 2017).

49. Jennifer Leahy, "Pasadena Protest over Slain Burglars Heats Up," *Houston Chronicle*, December 3, 2007, http://www.chron.com/neighborhood/pasadena-news/article/Pasadena-protest-over-slain-burglars-heats-up-1809539.php (accessed June 14, 2017).

50. Patrick Michels, "Joe Horn and Five Years with the Texas Castle Doctrine," *Texas Observer*, May 8, 2012, http://www.texasobserver.org/joe-horn-and-castle-doctrine-shootings-in-texas/ (accessed June 14, 2017).

51. "Apr. 29: This Day in History: 1992, Riots Erupt in Los Angeles," History

.com, April 29, 2010, http://www.history.com/this-day-in-history/riots-erupt-in-los-angeles (accessed June 14, 2017).

52. Seth Mydans, "Rodney King Is Awarded $3.8 Million," *New York Times*, April 20, 1994, http://www.nytimes.com/1994/04/20/us/rodney-king-is-awarded-3.8-million.html (accessed June 14, 2017).

53. CNN Wire Staff, "Rodney King dead at 47," CNN, June 18, 2012, http://www.cnn.com/2012/06/17/us/obit-rodney-king/ (accessed June 14, 2017).

54. Michael Burgan, "Richard Allen Davis Trial: 1996—Anger in the Courtroom," JRank Articles, http://law.jrank.org/pages/3701/Richard-Allen-Davis-Trial-1996-Anger-in-Courtroom.html#ixzz3rmLBjFa (accessed June 14, 2017); "Before Being Sentenced to Die, Killer Disrupts a Courtroom," *New York Times*, September 27, 1996, http://www.nytimes.com/1996/09/27/us/before-being-sentenced-to-die-killer-disrupts-a-courtroom.html (accessed November 16, 2017).

55. Burgan, "Richard Allen Davis Trial."

56. Brooke Donald, "Stanford Law's Three Strikes Project Works for Fair Implementation of New Statute," *Stanford Report*, June 6, 2013, http://news.stanford.edu/news/2013/june/three-strikes-project-060613.html (accessed June 14, 2017).

57. John Elgion, "Two Decades in Solitary," *New York Times*, September 22, 2008.

58. Larry McShane, "3 Girls Defy 'Lie or Die' Note, Help Put Shooter Away," *Los Angeles Times*, November 24, 2002, http://articles.latimes.com/2002/nov/24/news/adna-witnesses24 (accessed June 14, 2017).

59. Katherine Santiago, "Newark Man Gets 16 Years in Prison for Killing Witness to Quadruple Shooting," *Star-Ledger* (Newark, NJ), September 17, 2009, http://www.nj.com/news/index.ssf/2009/09/newark_man_sentenced_to_16_yea.html (accessed June 21, 2017).

APPENDIX. ILLUSTRATIVE CASES UNDERMINING THE CRIMINAL JUSTICE SYSTEM'S MORAL CREDIBILITY

1. This narrative is drawn primarily from the following sources: People v. Becktel, 300284, 2011 WL 6268223 (Mich. Ct. App. Dec. 15, 2011); People v. Becktel, 289533, 2010 WL 746438 (Mich. Ct. App. Mar. 4, 2010); Art Aisner, "Saline Man Arraigned in Stabbing of Friend," *Ann Arbor* (MI) *News*, February 28, 2008, http://blog.mlive.com/annarbornews/2008/02/saline_man_arraigned_in_stabbi.html.

2. *Becktel*, 289533, 2010 WL 746438 at 1.

3. This narrative is drawn primarily from the following sources: Matt Harvey, "Charges Dropped against Lewis County Suspects," *Exponent Telegram* (Clarksburg, WV), November 8, 2013, http://www.theet.com/news/court_and_police/charges-dropped-against-lewis-county-suspects/article_32224b16-48f9-11e3-b90c-001a4bcf887a.html; Melissa Toothman, "Murder Charges Dropped in Cold Case," *Inter Mountain* (Clarksburg, WV), November 9, 2013, http://www.theintermountain.com/page/content.detail/id/566104/Murder-charges-dropped-in-cold-case.html?nav=5014; "Marcus Maxine Stalnaker," Charley Project, October 12, 2004, http://www.charleyproject.org/cases/s/stalnaker_marcus.html; "Charges Dropped against Hughes, Freeman, Metz, in West Virginia Murder Case," *Archbold* (OH) *Buckeye*, November 9, 2013, http://www.archboldbuckeye.com/news/2013-11-13/Front_Page/Charges_Dropped_Against_Hughes_Freeman_Metz_In_We s.html (accessed November 30, 2017); "Update: 3 Men Arrested in Connection with 1999 Lewis County Murder," WBOY.com, October 3, 2013, http://www.wboy.com/story/23472117/update-3-men-arrested-in-connection-with-1999-lewis-county-murder (accessed November 30, 2017).

4. Harvey, "Charges Dropped."

5. The narrative is drawn from the following source: United States v. Packwood, 687 F. Supp. 471, 473 (N.D. Cal. 1987) aff'd, 848 F.2d 1009, 1010 (9th Cir. 1988).

6. Ibid., 472.

7. This narrative is drawn from the following source: United States v. Hunt, 656 F.3d 906 (9th Cir. 2011).

8. Ibid., 909.

9. Once the appeal is final, Hunt can no longer face a new trial because of double jeopardy.

10. This narrative is drawn primarily from the following sources: People v. Damiano, 87 N.Y.2d 477 (1996); People v. Birdsall, 215 A.D.2d 878 (1995); People v. Damiano, 209 A.D.2d 873 (1994) aff'd, 87 N.Y.2d 477 (1996); Mike Levine, "Bully Gets a Break; the Victim Didn't," *Times Herald-Record* (Middletown, NY), January 15, 2007, http://www.recordonline.com/apps/pbcs.dll/article?AID=/20070115/NEWS/70115741/-1/NEWS271996%20target=new (accessed November 30, 2017); Paul Schwartzman, "Old Wounds Reopened Kin's Agony over Slay Retrial Ruling," *New York Daily News*, January 28, 1996; "Reward Money Goes to Honor Victim," *New York Times*, May 9, 1993; "Man Convicted in I-87 Rock Death," *Daily Gazette*, October 22, 1992, B9.

11. This narrative is drawn primarily from the following source: United States v. Huey, 76 F.3d 638 (5th Cir. 1996).

12. This narrative is drawn primarily from the following sources: Davis v. State, 90 So.2d 629 (Fla. 1956); Susan Barbosa, "Wheelchair Rapist's Release Expected Today," *Lakeland* (FL) *Ledger*, September 17, 1991, 1B; Susan Barbosa, "Prosecutors Try to Keep Davis in Jail," *Lakeland* (FL) *Ledger*, August 9, 1991, 1B; Bob Greene, "System of Justice Is Helpless, Too," *Chicago Tribune*, May 10, 1989; Gary Stein, "Court System Guilty of Warped Decisions," *Sun Sentinel* (Boward County, FL), May 7, 1989, http://articles.sun-sentinel.com/1989-05-07/news/8901230814_1_muscular-dystrophy-juries-life-sentence (accessed November 30, 2017); Associated Press, "Convicted Rapist Now Will Go Free on Technicality," *Spokane* (WA) *Chronicle*, May 5, 1989, A7; "Wheelchair Rape," *Orlando* (FL) *Sentinel*, May 23, 1989, http://articles.orlandosentinel.com/1989-05-23/news/8905230418_1_physically-helpless-lesser-charges-sentence-for-raping (accessed November 30, 2017).

13. Stein, "Court System Guilty."

14. Ibid.

15. This narrative is drawn primarily from People v. James, 143 Misc.2d 380 (1989); Denny v. Donnelly, 00-CV-04641 (JBW) (E.D.N.Y. July 25, 2003).

16. *James*, 143 Misc.2d at 381.

17. Ibid., 382.

18. The narrative is drawn from the following sources: Commonwealth v. Wideman, 291 A.3d 771 (1972); Commonwealth v. Wideman, 334 A.2d 596 (1971); Commonwealth v. Wideman, 385 A.2d 1332 (1971).

19. This narrative is drawn from the following sources: People v. Skinner, 52 N.Y.2d 24 (1980); People v. Skinner, 71 A.D.2d 814 (1979); Gerhard Falk and Clifford Falk, *Murder: An Analysis of Its Forms, Conditions, and Causes* (Jefferson, NC: McFarland, 1990), p. 15; "Snell Death Goes Back to Court," *Tonawanda* (NY) *News*, January 7, 1982, p. 6.

20. *Skinner*, 52 N.Y.2d at 32.

21. This narrative is drawn from Maine v. Moulton, 474 U.S. 159 (1985); State v. Moulton, 481 A.2d 155 (Me. 1984).

22. *Moulton*, 474 U.S. at 179.

23. The dissent asks the majority what the police should have done instead: "Courts ought to applaud the kind of careful and diligent efforts of the police shown by this record. Indeed, the Court's opinion does not suggest that the police should have—or could have—conducted their investigation in any other way" (ibid., 186). Ultimately, the police gathered information "for legitimate purposes not related to the gathering of evidence concerning the crime for which [the respondent] had been indicted," so the evidence should have been allowed (ibid., 184).

24. This narrative is drawn from United States v. Perdue, 8 F.3d 1455 (10th Cir. 1993); "Local Man Given 15-Year Sentence on Drug Sentence," *Lawrence* (KS) *Journal-World*, April 6, 1992, http://www2.ljworld.com/news/1992/apr/06/local_man_given_15year/ (accessed November 30, 2017); "Federal Grand Jury Indicts Local Man," *Lawrence* (KS) *Journal-World*, October 23, 1991, p. 9A

25. *Perdue*, 8 F.3d at 1459.

26. Ibid., 1459.

27. Ibid., 1465.

28. This narrative is drawn from the following source: People v. Hampton, 200 A.D.2d 466 (1994).

29. Ibid., 467.

30. This narrative is drawn primarily from the following sources: United States v. Bayless, 921 F. Supp. 211 (S.D.N.Y. 1996); United States v. Bayless, 913 F. Supp. 232, 242 opinion vacated on reconsideration, 921 F. Supp. 211 (S.D.N.Y. 1996); Jeffrey Jenkins, *The American Courts: A Procedural Approach* (Burlington, MA: Jones & Bartlett Learning, 2009), pp. 308–12; National Drug Strategy Network: The Criminal Justice Policy Foundation, "New York Federal Judge Reverses Decision in Controversial Drug Case, Clinton, Dole Had Threatened to Ask for Resignation, Impeachment," NDSN.org, April 1996, http://www.ndsn.org/april96/bayless.html (accessed November 30, 2017); Greg Smith, "$4M Drug Suspect Mulls Guilty Plea," *New York Daily News*, April 3, 1996; Greg Smith and Timothy Clifford, "Judge Backs Off Drug Ruling," *New York Daily News*, April 2, 1996.

31. *Bayless*, 921 F. Supp. at 217.

32. This narrative is drawn primarily from State v. Ault, 150 Ariz. 459 (1986).

33. Ibid., 468.

34. This narrative is drawn primarily from the following sources: People v. Moore, 6 N.Y.3d 496 (2006); Corey Kilgannon and Al Baker, "New York's Top Court Reverses Man's Conviction on Gun Charge," *New York Times*, February 22, 2006.

35. *Moore*, 6 N.Y.3d at 497.

36. Ibid.

37. The dissenting judge comments, "When Officers Racioppo and Molinaro observed both that the defendant matched the description the anonymous caller had given of a man with a gun, and that he began to walk away at the sight of the police, the possibility that he did indeed have a gun deserved to be investigated." Ibid., 502. New York police heavily criticized the court's ruling. Police Commissioner Raymond Kelly voiced concerns about safe policing: "Common sense dictates that police should approach cautiously a suspect reported to be armed, and that includes stopping him at

gunpoint from fleeing and arresting him for the illegal gun he reached for." Kilgannon and Baker, "New York's Top Court."

38. This narrative is drawn primarily from the following sources: People v. Torres, 74 N.Y.2d 224 (1989); People v. Torres, 143 A.D.2d 40 (1988); Jonathan Ferziger, "Police Search Limited Unless Lives at Stake: Court Expands Protection of Suspects," *Times Union* (Albany, NY), July 12, 1989, p. B6.

39. *Torres*, 143 A.D.2d at 41.

40. This narrative is primarily drawn from the following sources: Gary Cartwright, "Free to Kill," *Texas Monthly*, August 1992, http://www.texasmonthly.com/story/free-kill; Mike Cochran, Associated Press, "McDuff Likely to Take Grisly Secrets to Grave," *Lubbock* (TX) *Avalanche Journal*, 1996, http://lubbockonline.com/news/112496/mcduff.htm; National Museum of Crime and Punishment, "The Broomstick Killer," Crime Museum, http://www.crimemuseum.org/crime-library/the-broomstick-killer (accessed November 30, 2017).

41. "Broomstick Killer."

42. Ibid.

43. Ibid.

44. Ibid.

45. This narrative is drawn primarily from the following four sources: Bonin v. Calderon, 59 F.3d 815 (9th Cir. 1995); People v. Bonin, 46 Cal.3d 659 (1988); Joan Goulding, "'Freeway Killer' Suspect William Bonin Was a Man with . . .," United Press International, November 4, 1981, http://www.upi.com/Archives/1981/11/04/Freeway-killer-suspect-William-Bonin-was-a-man-with/3420373698000/; Mark Gribben, "William Bonin: The Freeway Killer," Crime Library, http://www.crimelibrary.com/serial_killers/predators/bonin/day_1.html; Juan Ignacio Blanco, "William Bonin: The Freeway Killer," *Murderpedia*, http://murderpedia.org/male.B/b1/bonin-william.htm (accessed November 30, 2017); Andre N. Turner, "William Bonin—Freeway Killer," *True Crime Stories from the Reignmaker* (blog), June 6, 2014, https://reignmaker1911.wordpress.com/2014/06/06/william-bonin-the-freeway-killer/ (accessed November 30, 2017).

46. *Bonin*, 59 F.3d 815.

47. Ibid.

48. Ibid

49. Goulding, "'Freeway Killer' Suspect."

50. The narrative was drawn from the following sources: John Bacon, "Judge Apologizes for Teen Rape Remarks, Not Sentence," *USA Today*, September 6, 2013; Laura Collins, "Exclusive: Cherry Was Raped by Her Teacher at 14 and Shunned

for Reporting It. Then She Shot Herself Dead in Her Mother's Bed. Now Her Mom Reveals Her 'Living Hell' and Fury That Attacker Got Just 30 Days Jail," *Daily Mail* (London), August 28, 2013; Crimesider Staff, "Montana Rape Case Update: State Prosecutors Appeal 30-Day Sentence in Case of Teacher Who Raped Student, 14," CBS News, September 4, 2013, http://www.cbsnews.com/news/montana-rape-case-update-state-prosecutors-appeal-30-day-sentence-in-case-of-teacher-who-raped-student-14/ (accessed November 30, 2017); Crimesider Staff, "Montana Rape Case: Stacey Rambold to Be Released after Serving 30 Days for Rape of 14-Year-Old," CBS News, September 26, 2013, http://www.cbsnews.com/news/montana-rape-case-stacey-rambold-to-be-released-after-serving-30-days-for-rape-of-14-year-old/ (accessed November 30, 2017); "Protesters Call for Billings Judge to Resign over 31-Day Sentence, Remarks about Rape Victim," MTN News, August 29, 2013, http://www.krtv.com/news/protesters-call-for-billings-judge-to-resign-over-31-day-sentence-remarks-about-rape-victim/.

51. Collins, "Exclusive: Cherry Was Raped."

52. Ibid.

53. Crimesider, "Montana Rape Case."

54. Collins, "Exclusive: Cherry Was Raped."

55. Ibid.

56. Eskew v. State, Indiana Court of Appeals, unpublished opinion, June 5, 2008, http://www.in.gov/judiciary/opinions/pdf/06050804ewn.pdf (accessed November 30, 2017); Lori Caldwell, "Old Insult Ends in Man's Death," *Merrillville* (IN) *Post-Tribune*, June 8, 2006; Ruth Anne Krause, "Eskew Defense Says Killer Not Known," *Merrillville* (IN) *Post-Tribune*, June 6, 2007; "Two Jailed after Fatal Shooting at Gary Graduation," wthr.com NBC, June 8, 2006; Ruth Anne Krause, "Gary Teen's Murder Charge Dismissed," *Merrillville* (IN) *Post-Tribune*, June 1, 2007; Ruth Anne Krause, "Isaiah Eskew Convicted of Reckless Homicide," *Merrillville* (IN) *Post-Tribune*, June 9, 2007; Ruth Anne Krause, "Probation in Graduation Shooting," *Merrillville* (IN) *Post-Tribune*, July 28, 2007.

57. This narrative is derived from the following sources: R. L. Nave, "Of Love and Pardons: How They Met," *Jackson* (MI) *Free Press*, February 15, 2012, http://www.jacksonfreepress.com/news/2012/feb/15/of-love-and-pardons-how-they-met (accessed November 30, 2017); "Barbour Frees Convicted Murderer," *Fox Memphis*, January 11, 2012, http://www.myfoxmemphis.com/story/18509660/barbour-frees-convicted-murderer; Holbrook Mohr, Associated Press, "Miss. Gov. Barbour Pardons Convicted Killer," *San Diego Union-Tribune*, January 9, 2012, http://www.sandiegouniontribune.com/sdut-miss-gov-barbour-pardons-convicted-killer

-2012jan09-story.html (accessed November 30, 2017); Charles Hooker, 87 So.3d 401, 402 (Miss. 2012); Campbell Robertson, "Mississippi Governor, Already Criticized on Pardons, Rides a Wave of Them out of Office," *New York Times*, January 11, 2012, p. A11; Martin Savidge and Rich Phillips, "Pardoned Mississippi Killer Says He Wasn't on the Run," CNN, January 14, 2012, http://www.cnn.com/2012/01/13/justice/mississippi-pardons/index.html (accessed November 30, 2017); "Governor Haley Barbour Pardons 2004–2012," *Clarion Ledger* (Jackson, MI), January 12, http://www.clarionledger.com/assets/pdf/D0183728110.PDF; "Barbour Frees Convicted Murderer," *Fox Memphis*, January 11, 2012, http://www.myfoxmemphis.com/story/18509660/barbour-frees-convicted-murderer.

58. "Barbour Frees Convicted Murderer."

59. "Miss. Gov. Barbour Pardons Convicted Killer."

60. The narrative is drawn from the following sources: Cook County Sheriff's Police Department Report, March 17, 1978; Sheriff's Police Department, Supplementary Report, May 18, 1978; interview by Ryan McLennan with Lauren Kustudick in Glenview, IL, November 28, 2000.

61. McLennan, "Interview."

62. Ibid.

63. The narrative is drawn from the following sources: Cane v. State, 560 A.2d 1063 (1989); Associated Press, "Court Overturns Conviction," *Sumter* (SC) *Item*, June 20, 1989; Associated Press, "13 Years Later, Arrest Made in Murder of SC Truck Driver," *Sumter* (SC) *Item*, February 3, 1987, p. 8B; "Search Not Over," *Herald-Journal* (Logan, UT), December 12, 1976.

64. This narrative is drawn primarily from the following sources: Pat Reavy, "Acquitted Man Says He's Guilty," *Deseret News* (Salt Lake City, UT), January 19, 2006, http://www.deseretnews.com/article/635177435/Acquitted-man-says-hes-guilty (accessed November 30, 2017); "Man Confesses to Murder after Being Acquitted," *Larry King Live*, CNN, January 27, 2006, http://www.cnn.com/TRANSCRIPTS/0601/27/lkl.01.html (accessed November 30, 2017).

65. Ibid.

66. Bolden v. Warden, W. Tennessee High Sec. Facility, 194 F.3d 579 (5th Cir. 1999); State v. Bolden, 680 So.2d 6 (La. App. 3 Cir., Apr. 17, 1996); Christopher Rose, "Basketball Slayings: Is Boyfriend Killer, or a Freak Victim?" *New Orleans Times Picayune*, July 9, 1989; "Bolden Faces Perjury Charge in Louisiana," *Memphis Commercial Appeal*, March 10, 1992; "Acquitted Man Booked with Perjury," *New Orleans Times Picayune*, August 29, 1991; "Man Guilty of Perjury Connected with Slaying," *Dallas Morning News*, January 21, 1995; Lawrence Buser, "Families Believe

They, System Were Fooled by Smiling 2-Time Killer," *Memphis Commercial Appeal*, March 9, 1992.

INDEX